In the Course of Duty

"Keith's stirring account of the USS *Batfish* breathes life into the heroic submarine's Pacific saga. Guts and skill abound in epic proportions among the officers and crew of the boat as it prowled the Pacific in search of Japanese targets. Keith's book, written in gripping style, is sure to bring notice to an aspect of the Pacific War that is sometimes overshadowed by the mammoth land and surface battles. This volume would make a splendid addition to anyone's World War II library."

—John Wukovits, author of *Pacific Alamo* and *One Square Mile of Hell*

"A stirring reminder of the hard-fought campaign waged by American submarines sixty years ago. In the era before nuclear power, ICBMs, and deterrence, submariners were genuine warfighters who spared neither their boats nor themselves in pursuit of the ultimate naval mission: sink the enemy."

—Barrett Tillman, author of *Clash of the Carriers*

"The crew of the *Batfish* personifies the courage exhibited by our submariners then and now. This is a must read for anyone who has a concept of duty, honor, and service to one's country."

—Robert Vaughan, author of *Whose Voice the Waters Heard*, helicopter pilot in Korea and Vietnam, U.S. Army (ret.)

"Don Keith has the unique ability to make the reader an intimate part of the action. Anyone who experiences this thrilling story will come away with a whole new appreciation for those men that volunteer for the submarine service."

—Ken Henry, coauthor of *Gallant Lady* and former submarine sailor

"They say you can't go back. Well, that's not true. When I read Don Keith's book on the USS *Batfish*, I was taken back to that time and places when I was there as a crew member." —William J. Isbell, WWII crew member, USS *Batfish* (SS-311)

"*Batfish* is another great Lady. Proud to have served on these Smoke Boats. When you are seventeen, it is hard to realize the rich history, gallantry, and honor of those men who served before me. Don Keith has done the *Batfish* and crew proud."

—Les Brown, USS *Charr* (SS-321), USS *Aspro* (SS-308), USS *Archerfish* (SS-311)

continued . . .

"The *Batfish* story is representative of a 'genetic code,' submariner pride, that transfers from the greatest generation to those that followed. What a great book."

—Gene Whitney, auxiliaryman, USS *Diodon* (SS-349)

"To sink one enemy sub is quite something, but to sink three in a single patrol, while coping with one of your own torpedoes jammed partway out of the launch tube with the potential of arming itself and blowing your own boat to bits with the next big wave—now that's the Super Bowl of submarine warfare for sure. Well told. A fascinating and inspiring true adventure."

—Captain William R. Anderson, veteran of eleven WWII submarine combat patrols and commander of *Nautilus* on the historic 1958 under-ice Arctic crossing.

Final Bearing
cowritten with Commander George Wallace (ret.)

"Not since Ned Beach have readers been treated to such a marvelous blend of authentic submarining and great storytelling. Readers will gladly lose sleep reading this one . . . a magnificent achievement."

—John J. Gobbell, author of *When Duty Whispers Low* and *The Last Lieutenant*

"A ripsnorting submarine adventure as up-to-date as tomorrow's headlines."

—Stephen Coonts

"Riveting. You won't want to put it down. Too close to the truth. Wallace and Keith achieve a winner."

—George Emery, vice admiral, USN (ret.), former commander, submarine force, U.S. Atlantic fleet

"Don Keith and George Wallace take you to the heart of the action as America fights a secret battle in a brilliantly portrayed South American setting. This team spins a great tale."

— W.E.B. Griffin

"Compelling characters, exciting plot, exotic settings, and a fascinating use of military technology combine to make Commander Wallace's and Mr. Keith's book a rousing blockbuster of a story."

—Robert Vaughan

continued . . .

"A full quota of vivid combat scenes . . . and if you are aware of what sailors feel when a beloved ship reaches the end of her career, the book . . . achieves real power. Above average for its salty breed . . . relax and enjoy." —*Booklist*

"Submarine enthusiasts will find satisfaction in the tale of the last patrol of the aging USS *Spadefish*. Do Captain Jonathan Ward and his submarine have what it takes for one more crucial mission? Authors Keith and Wallace take you along to find out while weaving in parallel stories that round out this entertaining book. An engaging read!" —Don Gentry, webmaster, SubmarineSailor.com

"The story is fast-paced, exciting, and one you don't want to put down until the end. A classic modern day story of man and technology in the battle of good versus evil." —*Homeland Defense Journal*

"If you can still feel the roll of a submarine at periscope depth and the anxiety produced by a sudden alarm from the Reactor Plant Control Panel, if you still enjoy action-packed adventure and the surprises a good piece of fiction can bring to your easy chair, you'll love this . . . saga." —*Journal of the Naval Submarine League*

Gallant Lady: A Biography of USS Archerfish
with Ken Henry

"This book has everything going for it . . . great characters, a good plot, and best of all, it's true. A great story!" —Larry Bond

"The next best thing to serving on *Archerfish* is reading this book. It's a great Navy story about a great ship and crew." —Stephen Coonts

"Moving and worthwhile reading." —Norman N. Brown, Associated Press

"A never-to-be-forgotten breathtaking saga . . . we episodically discover why the 'Silent Service' and especially this one submarine totally captivated so many of her postwar crews." —Rod E. Redman

FINAL PATROL

TRUE STORIES OF WORLD WAR II SUBMARINES

DON KEITH

NAL
CALIBER

NAL Caliber
Published by New American Library, a division of
Penguin Group (USA) Inc., 375 Hudson Street,
New York, New York 10014, USA
Penguin Group (Canada), 90 Eglinton Avenue East, Suite 700, Toronto,
Ontario M4P 2Y3, Canada (a division of Pearson Penguin Canada Inc.)
Penguin Books Ltd., 80 Strand, London WC2R 0RL, England
Penguin Ireland, 25 St. Stephen's Green, Dublin 2,
Ireland (a division of Penguin Books Ltd.)
Penguin Group (Australia), 250 Camberwell Road, Camberwell, Victoria 3124,
Australia (a division of Pearson Australia Group Pty. Ltd.)
Penguin Books India Pvt. Ltd., 11 Community Centre, Panchsheel Park,
New Delhi - 110 017, India
Penguin Group (NZ), cnr Airborne and Rosedale Roads, Albany,
Auckland 1310, New Zealand (a division of Pearson New Zealand Ltd.)
Penguin Books (South Africa) (Pty.) Ltd., 24 Sturdee Avenue,
Rosebank, Johannesburg 2196, South Africa

Penguin Books Ltd., Registered Offices:
80 Strand, London WC2R 0RL, England

First published by NAL Caliber, an imprint of New American Library,
a division of Penguin Group (USA) Inc.

First Printing, October 2006
10 9 8 7 6 5 4 3 2 1

Grateful acknowledgment is made for permission to reprint the photo of USS *Pampanito* on page 193. Photo courtesy of Rob Mackie and Steelnavy.com

NAL CALIBER and the "C" logo are trademarks of Penguin Group (USA) Inc.

Library of Congress cataloging-in-publication data:
Keith, Don, 1947–
    Final patrol : true stories of World War II submarines/Don Keith.
        p. cm.
    ISBN 0-451-21951-1
    1. World War, 1939–1945—Naval operations—Submarine.   2. World War, 1939–1945—Naval operations, American.   3. World War, 1939–1945—Regimental histories—United States.   4. Submarine warfare—History— 20th century.   I. Title.
    D783.K45 2006
    940.54'510973—dc22   2006011444

Set in Bulmer MT
Designed by Ginger Legato

Printed in the United States of America

PUBLISHER'S NOTE
While the author has made every effort to provide accurate telephone numbers and Internet addresses at the time of publication, neither the publisher nor the author assumes any responsibility for errors, or for changes that occur after publication. Further, publisher does not have any control over and does not assume any responsibility for author or third-party Web sites or their content.

For veterans of our armed forces,
no matter the time, the war,
the branch of service, or the vehicle
that carried them to battle

CONTENTS

They that go down to the sea in ships,
that do business in great waters,
these see the works of the Lord
and his wonders in the deep.

—Psalms 107:23–24.1

The most advanced nations are the ones
that navigate the most.

—Ralph Waldo Emerson

FINAL PATROL

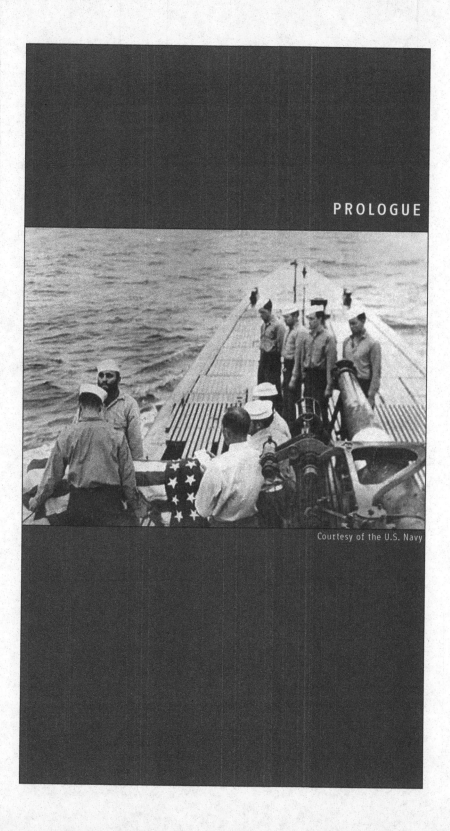

PROLOGUE

Courtesy of the U.S. Navy

I t is the opinion of many historians (and, I might add, most old sub sailors) that submarines and their crews do not receive nearly enough credit for their role in helping to win World War II. Not only do I agree with this assessment, but I find it revealing to consider the reasons for the oversight. Perhaps the very nature of the submarine service makes such a lapse inevitable.

For one thing, it is a relatively small group about whom we speak. Submariners never, at any time during World War II, made up more than 2 percent of the U.S. Navy's total force, yet they and the boats they rode accounted for more than 55 percent of all Japanese shipping sent to the bottom of the Pacific. And their contribution was a major factor in the war ending not quite four years after the United States entered it.

But their success came with a heavy price. Of the approximately 325 submarines that took part in the war, 52 were lost. More than thirty-five hundred submarine sailors died during the war. That represents a death toll of about 20 percent—one in every five of all sub crewmen still remain on what their shipmates reverently term "eternal patrol."

There is another reason why the so-called silent service (silent because its goal is to remain hidden, quiet, while it stalks and attacks enemy vessels) doesn't get the credit it is due, even today. Going all the way back to the War Between the States, submersible vessels were valuable weapons because of their stealth, their ability to sneak up on an enemy, deliver a mortal blow, and then disappear beneath the surface of the sea to fight again another day. They were (and still are) also well suited for reconnaissance work, for patrolling areas while remaining undetected, for maintaining a vigil from beneath the water's surface in areas where more visible means simply could not be used—areas where knowledge of their presence would keep them from effectively doing their jobs.

But the very stealth—the sneakiness, if you will—that makes submarines such powerful weapons also prevents them from finding a more prominent place in the consciousness of the public. Americans will probably never fully understand or appreciate what these ships and their crews do on our behalf. Out of sight, out of mind. But it would be hard to overestimate the power of their deterrence today.

Of course, all branches of the service played their parts in World War II. But the image of an almost invisible vessel sneaking up on the enemy, attacking, and then diving back below the surface to hide simply did not hold the same iconic status as a D-day-type beach landing or as waves of marines ferociously charging up a hill toward their foe. Marines or dive-bombers could be clearly seen in the newsreels as they raised the flag on hard-won land or zoomed in for the kill.

The territory they captured could be represented on maps, too, and lines and arrows could be drawn to show the progress and direction of their assaults. And to an extent, most of us are able to picture ourselves hypothetically doing what those men did, even if we pray we never have to.

That was not the case with submarines. There were no hills or territory to take or blocks of land to color in as captured. Lines marked on a sea chart could and did waver. If an enemy destroyer or battleship was sunk, there could be no flag raised over that spot in the ocean to claim it for the Allied cause. There was only an oil slick, a trail of bubbles, and a temporary field of debris to mark the spot of the victory, until even that was erased by the tide.

Even the targets that submarines were assigned to attack lacked glamour. Often they were freighters or oil tankers. Yet one of the ways the Allies won the war was by having the subs there to choke off supplies, petroleum, and other raw materials. There is nothing about sending a vessel loaded with raw rubber to the bottom of the sea that inspires songs or statues or patriotic poems, but it had to be done if we were to beat an island-based enemy like Japan.

Just like the infantry and marines and dive-bomber pilots, the submariners faced their own particular perils. Depth charges, torpedoes, and aircraft fire were the obvious hazards, but there was one constant peril the ground troops did not have to worry about. That was the natural threat of the sea. The ocean is a harsh, uninviting environment once an interloper is only a few feet beneath its waves. These submersible fighting machines were designed to dive to a depth of no more than three hundred to five hundred feet. Even the stoutest superstructure could give way to the awful pressure of tons of water, however, if something failed or if a crewman made a critical mistake or if the vessel was forced to dive deeper than that in order to escape the enemy. And if the submarine were trapped on the bottom at even a moderate depth, there was little hope for the young men imprisoned in her belly.

War is hell, regardless of which branch of the service is doing the fighting or whichever means of delivery the assault may employ. Brave men participate on all fronts. But a case can be made—beyond just the casualty rate—that submariners and their unique boats faced particularly tough sailing. That is why submariners did then and still do receive more pay than those serving in the surface navy. This has been the case since Theodore Roosevelt took his first ride in a "plunging boat" in Long Island Sound and proclaimed it would be so. Service in submarines has always been voluntary only; no one has ever been drafted into the silent service. And at any time, if a submariner decides he does not want to continue to serve there, he is allowed to transfer off his boat immediately with no black mark on his record for his decision.

Even as we acknowledge these men's sacrifice and bravery, we have a hard time picturing ourselves climbing into one of those steel cylinders, pulling the hatch closed over our heads, deliberately flooding the compartments, and sinking with her into the dark, crushing sea. Or riding along blindly through the cold blackness, "seeing" only with sonar pings and sea charts.

The men who have chosen such duty ride around in vessels that have been called "sewer pipes," "devil boats," "pig boats," and "plunging boats." They do their work in black depths, intentionally keep their heads down and out of sight until they are able to creep up on their targets, fire their weapons, and then skedaddle, running and hiding.

Except for a few Hollywood movies, we have little to go on in picturing the environment in which they worked, how they lived, how they fought, how they did what they did; and those few films, such as *Run Silent, Run Deep*, are limited in how well they are able to serve reality.

Without undergoing a similar experience, it is nearly impossible for us to put ourselves in the place of the World War II sailors, to identify with the submariners who did the work. What manner of man would volunteer to dive beneath the waves to such an uninviting place, knowing full well that the odds were stacked against him? What would compel someone to willingly choose to serve in a force that automatically gets hazardous-duty pay all the time, not just when the nation is at war, because of the unique danger inherent in the job?

The conditions are much better today, but in the 1940s, submarining was a rough life. Only the best were selected to go. Their training was rigorous. They didn't just need to know how to perform a particular task— they were required to qualify at all duty stations on the vessel, just in case they were needed to step in should a man fall. Each sailor was expected to be ready to keep the boat righted, to pull her out of a potentially deadly dive, or to bring her to the surface for a breath of sweet, fresh air. And that was true of every man aboard, whether he was the captain of the boat or the mess cook.

The living conditions on the World War II boats were not much better than in a foxhole or trench. Imagine six to seven dozen men living in cramped spaces, sharing for weeks on end two bathrooms and a dining room not much bigger than a typical suburban house's walk-in closet.

Picture having to sleep on a narrow cot, often hung from the wall among explosive torpedoes, and sharing that same cot in shifts with other crew members.

It shouldn't surprise us, then, that the men who rode the plunging boats constitute one of the strongest brotherhoods going, that even those who served in World War II, over sixty years ago, continue to meet at reunions, to stay in touch with each other. This should also help you understand why they are so determined that the story of what they did does not die with them. Not their own stories, mind you—submariners tend to be very humble types and reluctant to talk of their war experiences—but the stories of their shipmates, and especially those who did not come back.

And that's also why they and others have worked so hard to preserve some of their submarines, to restore and authentically reequip them, and to fix them up so that they, you, and I are all able to visit them. They wanted to help us to see what life was like for them and their brothers—to learn a little bit about their shipmates and their boats as we stand on the bridge, as we walk her decks and climb up and down her ladders, as we peer through the periscope at rush-hour traffic across the harbor.

These submarine sailors are adamant that we breathe in the lingering perfume of diesel fuel, still fragrant in the various compartments throughout their vessels, even sixty years after they swam in the warm Pacific waters. They even want us to know what it smelled like aboard them.

In 1941, the American submarines being built were the most advanced military machines yet developed. And crewing each one of those boats were some of the bravest young men in the history of warfare. Amazingly enough, many of them were still in their teens. The average age of most of the boats' crew members was less than twenty-five years old. The "old man," the skipper, was rarely much over thirty.

Their stories, if we take the time to listen to them, are dramatic, moving, and as fascinating today as they were over half a century ago. They are full of human drama and colorful characters. Many of these adventures have yet to be shared with the general public, however, and we are quickly losing the veterans who lived them, the ones who can tell them the best. That's why it is so important that the boats be saved from the scrap heap or demolition, salvaged and preserved—and opened so we can visit them and learn more about them.

And it is also why the memories recounted by their crew members must be preserved and passed on, so that these men and what they did and how they did it can be properly appreciated.

Among the vessels so preserved is the USS *Bowfin*, dubbed "the Pearl Harbor Avenger." She was put under construction only eight days after the attack on Pearl Harbor, Hawaii, which took place on December 7, 1941. She went on to a brilliant patrol record, including a stint delivering medicine, radio transmitters, ammunition, and money to Philippine guerrillas in a daring, near-suicidal mission. Later, she was depth-charged to the point that the enemy was certain she was dead. They raked a grappling hook down her deck trying to snag her and drag her to the surface but could not grab her.

It was the *Bowfin*'s crew who had to recover from the guilt brought about by one of the war's greatest tragedies. She sank what her crew believed was an enemy troop ship—only to discover later that the vessel carried nine hundred Japanese children who were being evacuated from an island that was about to come under attack from the Allies.

Crew members of the USS *Drum* worked feverishly in water up to their knees after a vicious depth-charge attack. Even with their sub damaged, they loaded and launched torpedoes and finally sank the enemy aircraft carrier they had their sights on. With cold seawater pouring in around them, they cheered as their skipper reported what he was seeing as he watched their damaged target, listing so badly that her decks were clearly visible through his periscope.

Some of the boats carried odd names. There was the *Croaker*, the *Clamagore*, the *Requin*, the *Razorback*. And there was the USS *Becuna*, affectionately called Becky by her crew.

It was aboard the USS *Silversides*, nicknamed "the Lucky Boat" because of her many close scrapes with the enemy, that Pharmacist's Mate Tom Moore successfully removed a shipmate's gangrenous appendix—even though he had never performed any kind of surgery before and had to resort to using knives and dinner forks from the galley for surgical instruments.

Then there was the USS *Cod*, whose skipper, Commander James Dempsey, had sunk the first Japanese destroyer of the war when he was captain of a tiny 1920s-era submarine. And it was the *Cod* that endured a vicious barrage of seventy Japanese depth charges in only fifteen minutes. Twelve hours later, the air inside the boat was so dank that the men couldn't even get a match to strike so they could light their cigarettes; there simply wasn't enough oxygen left. They finally surfaced—into the middle of a tropical thunderstorm. The boat's sound operator was still so deafened from counting the explosions of the depth charges that he couldn't hear the thunder, but he could certainly appreciate the sweet, fresh air that spilled down the open hatch once they were on the surface.

It was the new skipper of the *Batfish* who drew curious stares from his crew when they learned his prior war history. Captain Wayne Merrill had already served as an officer aboard two previous boats in the Pacific. Only a few days after he shipped off each of them, the submarine and its crew were lost. The men assigned to his newly constructed sub wondered if their captain was bulletproof . . . or if maybe his luck was about to run out on this new boat. But the *Batfish* went on to accomplish one of the most amazing feats of the war—sinking three enemy submarines in three days.

The USS *Cavalla* was almost out of fuel and a long way from home, but she stayed on station as ordered to report the location of a massive enemy armada that was forming. Then, when she finally left and headed for port, she coincidentally ran across one of the war's true prizes, the enemy aircraft carrier *Shokaku*. The Japanese carrier was one of the ships that had launched the planes that attacked Pearl Harbor. She was also a veteran of the Battle of the Coral Sea. Later, the *Cavalla*'s skipper, Commander Herman Kossler, happily radioed back to Pearl, "Hit *Shokaku*-class carrier with three out of six torpedoes . . . believe that baby sank!"

One of the other American submarines now open to visitors once steamed right into an enemy-held harbor and torpedoed a cargo ship tied up at the wharf. Then, for good measure, she blasted a busload of enemy soldiers that happened to be sitting nearby.

Another skipper torpedoed a train as it sat on the tracks near a pier. Then he had to risk running aground or being bombed from the air as he backed his submarine out of the tight, shallow confines of the harbor.

The USS *Torsk* was named after a Norwegian fish because, by that time, all the more common fish names had been claimed by other vessels. She and her crew were credited with firing the last torpedo and sinking the last ship of World War II, only hours before the cease-fire was ordered.

Today each of these historic vessels has been preserved and is open to visitors at various memorial sites and museums around the United States. They serve as monuments to all submariners, and especially to those who gave their lives in defense of their country. In all, there are currently sixteen U.S. Navy World War II submarines that can be visited and toured by the public. They are in places like Honolulu and Philadelphia, at Fisherman's Wharf in San Francisco, Cleveland, Galveston, Pittsburgh, the Inner Harbor at Baltimore, and in Hackensack, New Jersey. A couple more are resting on the shores of Lake Michigan. You will even find one in Muskogee, Oklahoma, in the middle of the Cherokee Indian nation, and one in Little Rock, Arkansas, over five hundred miles from the nearest salt water.

Most have been lovingly restored and authentically equipped and are usually maintained in part by volunteers. Each allows visitors to see for themselves the claustrophobic conditions under which these men lived and fought and, in many cases, died. Some of the submarines are listed as National Historic Landmarks. Most are in excellent shape, properly equipped with either original or period fixtures and gear.

Others struggle to keep from rusting away.

All of them are bona fide treasures.

In addition to those sixteen boats, there is one more World War II submarine in this country that has been restored and opened to the public. It is the *U-505*, one of the legendary German U-boats, on display at the Museum of Science and Industry in Chicago. Millions of people have visited the exhibit over the past fifty years.

The story of the *U-505*'s capture, of the bravery of the American boarding party who risked their lives to disarm charges set to scuttle her, and of the fifty-eight German crew members who were taken into custody and held as POWs reads like the treatment for a Hollywood movie. But it is all true, and visitors can relive it for themselves at the beautiful exhibit in Chicago.

Some of the boats in this book had distinguished Cold War service as well; their lives extended several decades, simply because they had a job to do. And in several cases, the story of how the submarines came to the end of their "final patrol," how they came to be where they are today, is just as absorbing as the rest of their biographies.

I will describe how the *Batfish* made her way up the Arkansas River to a mooring spot in a bean field in the middle of the former Dust Bowl, where her final patrol ended.

How the *U-505* came down the St. Lawrence Seaway and through four of the Great Lakes to her berth amidst the skyscrapers of Chicago before her final patrol was complete. And how she eventually was lowered four floors below street level in an amazing feat of engineering.

How the most recent addition to the ranks of preserved boats, the *Razorback*, had the longest final patrol of them all. She was towed from the Mediterranean Sea, all the way across the Atlantic Ocean, and then retraced a part of the *Batfish*'s route to end up in Little Rock, Arkansas, in the shadow of the Bill Clinton Presidential Library.

Several came down the St. Lawrence Seaway. Others took a long river route. At least one ended up being towed only a few miles on her final patrol.

Maybe, after reading about the boats and their crews, you will take the opportunity to visit one or more of them. If you do, perhaps you will better be able to appreciate the experiences those young men had and the sacrifices they made on our behalf.

Maybe, too, when you visit, you will allow your imagination to be freed. Then you can almost hear the raucous sound of the dive klaxon signaling everyone to man battle stations, to get down the hatches in a hurry as the sea quickly swallows up the boat.

Or gaze through the periscope sight and try to picture an enemy battleship out there on the water, sitting right where your forward torpedo tubes are aimed.

Or feel the not so subtle kick of a torpedo as it is launched and spins away toward its unsuspecting target.

Or hear the awful, ominous click of a depth charge as it arms itself just outside the hull of your submerged vessel, ready to explode and take you, your submarine, and your shipmates to the dark, muddy bottom of the sea forever.

In these pages, I will tell true stories about each of these seventeen submarines: how they came to be built and launched, how they worked, how they helped win the war, how they came to the end of their final patrols near enough to dry land that you can cross their brows, go aboard, and take a look around at living history.

But you will see that these are not simply stories of steel cylinders and complicated machinery. They are the stories of flesh-and-blood men. Much of the drama will center around the captains or other officers who commanded these submarines. They were, after all, the most visible. They were often the most colorful characters in each boat's story, too.

But be assured, there were six or seven dozen other men on each vessel who helped the skippers accomplish what they did. Those men were just as much responsible as the wardroom guys were for what they accomplished. And for making us care enough about their boats to go take a look at them.

That's all they ask: that we care enough to listen to their stories, to go to see their boats where their final patrols took them.

Then maybe we will finally and fully appreciate what they did.

INSIDE A WORLD WAR II "DIESEL BOAT"

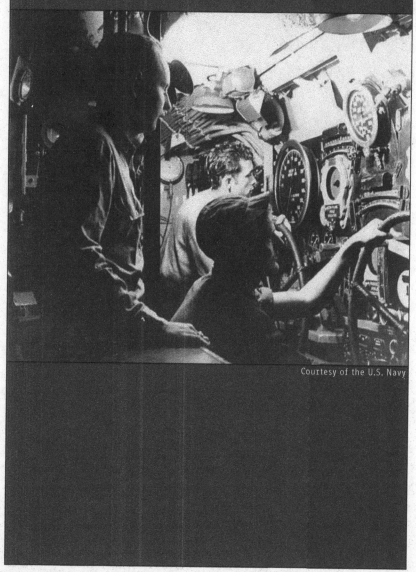

Courtesy of the U.S. Navy

M any people tend to think of submarines as being a twentieth-century invention, but that assumption is incorrect.

There are reports that the ancient warrior Alexander the Great commissioned the building of a submersible vessel, and that he even took a dive in one over three hundred years before the birth of Christ. The famous artist Leonardo da Vinci drew plans for a one-man, double-hulled submersible in the early 1500s. He described it as a "ship to sink other ships." The first record of a diving boat, one that was designed to be navigated underwater, is from 1580 in England. By the early 1700s, designs for more than a dozen submarines had been patented in England.

The first use of a submersible vessel in warfare came during the American Revolutionary War. The *Turtle* was a one-man boat, hand-operated using a screw propeller to push it along beneath the surface. Its pilot, David Bushnell, cranked his vessel up close to the HMS *Eagle* and attempted to attach a cache of gunpowder to the British ship's bottom. It didn't work. The screws Bushnell used couldn't pierce the tough copper sheathing on the *Eagle*'s bottom. Still, the concept was proved.

Robert Fulton, whose name is more closely associated with the steamboat, built a workable submarine (named the *Nautilus*, a moniker that would crop up later in the development of submersibles) in about 1800. That was a good ten years before he developed the steam-powered surface vessel for which he is most famous. Fulton's invention actually resembled the modern-day submarine in many ways. Still, he was unable to convince any government, including his own United States', that the boat had any value when it came to waging war on the seas.

By the time of the Civil War, however, a number of experimental submarines had been developed, their gestation often coming with tragic loss of life. The first recorded successful use of a sub to sink another vessel occurred in 1864 when the *Hunley*, a Confederate boat built from an old steam boiler and carrying an eight-man crew, rammed a spar into the side of the Union ship *Housatonic* in Charleston Harbor. The *Hunley* then backed away, leaving the live charge attached to the ship. Once the submarine was a safe distance away, the explosives were detonated. The *Housatonic* sank on the spot.

While making her getaway, though, the *Hunley* encountered some kind of problem, the exact nature of which remains a mystery. She went down too, drowning all of her crew members. Thus, they became the first submariners to die in battle.

Up to that point in history, submarines were powered by hand or foot cranks—pure manpower—which clearly limited the size and range of the boats. In the late 1800s, several inventors came up with steam-powered vessels. But there was the obvious question of what to do with the smoke and heat from the boilers, which were typically coal-fired. The boats had to stay on the surface so long as they needed to maneuver, then dive and remain in one spot or rely on built-up steam or the old-fashioned crank method if they wanted or needed to move.

One clever solution was to poke a stack above the water long enough to build up steam power, then close the stack in order to dive deeper. A version of that method would actually be used in the twentieth century, after World War II, with the diesel-powered boats of that time.

The electric motor was being used for many other applications by then, so it was inevitable that it would find its way into submarines. The first electric-powered sub was demonstrated in England in 1886. It used two fifty-horsepower motors powered by a hundred-cell storage battery. Because the battery had to be charged so regularly, and because the charge could only be accomplished while the submersible was sitting on the surface, the vessel's range was never more than about eighty miles.

An inventor named J. P. Holland sold the first submarine to the U.S. government and delivered it in 1900. His *Plunger* was a dual-propelled vessel, using steam while on the surface and storage batteries while submerged. He also developed buoyancy tanks and diving planes—devices similar to wings that helped determine the angle of attack as a sub went up and down—so the boats could dive and surface smoothly, quickly, and somewhat reliably. Many of Holland's innovations are still in use today in some form or another, even on modern nuclear submarines.

President Theodore Roosevelt took a ride on the *Plunger* one blustery day on Long Island Sound. He was impressed with the crewmen and in awe of the bravery needed to operate one of these warships. When he was back on dry land, he promptly declared that those who manned submarines would receive hazardous-duty pay from that point forward, whether at war or not. Sub sailors were elated. In fact, prior to Mr. Roosevelt's voyage, submariners received less pay than sailors on surface ships.

By the beginning of World War I, submarines of considerable size and shape had been developed. The periscope, invented by Simon Lake and perfected by Sir Howard Grubb, gave submariners a big advantage. It allowed crew members finally to be able to peek above the surface and watch their quarry while still remaining mostly hidden from view. Using a periscope, a sub could stalk its prey, calculate its movement, and launch weapons, all without ever revealing any more of itself than a skinny pole that stuck out of the water.

The torpedo also became available as a significant nautical weapon. "Torpedo" was no longer defined as simply an explosive charge delivered on a spar. It became a device that was self-powered and could be hurled through the water toward a target from considerable distance.

Submarine propulsion systems also grew more sophisticated. Gasoline and diesel engines had evolved and were becoming reliable sources of momentum for the boats so long as they remained on the surface. The engines could be used not only for propulsion but also to charge new, more advanced banks of storage batteries. Those could then be employed when the vessel was running beneath the surface.

By 1912, all U.S. Navy submarines used diesel engines and batteries. Diesel engines seemed to serve the purpose better than regular gasoline power plants. They required no complicated sparking systems and produced fewer dangerous fumes. The batteries already emitted more than their share of volatile gases, so it was good that diesels were developed that were less dangerous than gasoline engines.

While the United States had two dozen submarines in its fleet at the start of World War I, they were used primarily to patrol harbors and escort ships on short runs. They were seen as defensive weapons at best, and rather ugly, slimy ones at that.

It took the Germans and their U-boats to prove the value of submersible vessels as offensive weapons, perfectly capable of contributing to any navy's war on the high seas. Their toll in the First World War was staggering.

Still, there were mixed opinions among U.S. Navy brass after the war. There was doubt about the wisdom of devoting limited resources to building a big fleet of submarines. Some felt the navy should be concentrating instead on battleships and the new darling of the brass, the aircraft carrier. They were convinced that these would be the most useful warships should our country be forced to go to war again.

Submarines? Too slow. Too small. Too dangerous.

Even so, a number of better submarines were designed and built, primarily at the historic shipyard at Portsmouth, New Hampshire. The first American naval warship was built there in 1690, before it was even a formal government shipyard. President Thomas Jefferson so designated it in 1800. In the 1930s, Portsmouth turned out the first all-welded-hull sub, the USS *Pike* (SS-173). With her much stronger hull, the *Pike* was able to dive to greater depths than ever before. At the same time, the thick steel offered better protection from the depth charge, the primary antisubmarine weapon of the time.

Sonar was also perfected between the wars, and experiments were conducted using the first radar systems. Sonar uses transmitted and reflected underwater sound waves to detect and locate submerged objects or to measure distances. Most people recognize its distinctive "pinging" sound from submarine movies. It was and remains today a major tool used by submariners. The sonarman spends much of his time on duty listening, not only to the pings of his equipment but to the other sounds of the deep. He can tell an amazing amount of detail about another vessel in the vicinity just by listening.

Radar, on the other hand, uses radio signals to detect objects at a distance. That technology would continue to evolve during World War II, and the use of more sophisticated radar on all fronts—including aboard submarines—would be a key element in the Allies' eventual victory.

The U.S. Navy had a relatively small fleet of submarines at the time of the Japanese attack on Pearl Harbor. Still, their impact was felt quickly and mightily. Only one month after the attack on Pearl Harbor, and operating under orders to observe unrestricted warfare, the USS *Pollack* (SS-180) sank a Japanese freighter just outside of Tokyo Bay. That was only the first of many.

By the end of the war, American submarines had sunk over half of the entire Japanese merchant fleet, whether civilian traffic or warships. That success played a major part in how the war turned out. The submarines deprived Japanese industry of fuel and raw materials and did their part to shut down Japan's economy, strangling their war effort.

Most historians note that one of the primary reasons for Japan's imperialistic expansion throughout the Pacific Rim in the years leading up to the war was a quest for natural resources. They had precious few on the Home Islands and believed they would never be a major world power without access to them. American submarines were the primary force that kept the Japanese from taking advantage of the spoils from the lands they had conquered.

Just before World War II, those who felt our country needed a different type of submarine were able to hold sway, and development began on a new kind of submersible warship. Submarine construction jumped from a few boats per year in the mid-1930s to seventy-one vessels on the drawing board for completion in 1941. The prototype for this new breed of submersible vessel was the USS *Gato* (SS-212), a 312-foot-long ship, displacing about two thousand tons. This dynamic, sophisticated plunging boat would be able to drive farther, dive deeper, carry more firepower, accept a larger contingent of sailors, and keep her crew safer and more comfortable than any other war machine ever constructed by man. She may have been ugly to some, but to the admirals who knew its potential, the *Gato*-class submarine was a thing of beauty.

As designed, the *Gato* would be able to cruise 11,400 miles without refueling. She could carry twenty-four deadly torpedoes. Later in the war, the USS *Balao* (SS-285) became the template for a newer, better boat. She was almost identical in design to the *Gato* except for a thicker hull, allowing her and her sisters to dive over a hundred feet deeper and withstand an even more frenzied depth charging.

The most advanced boats used in World War II were the *Tench* class. Only a relative few of those were launched and fewer still saw action before the war came to an end. The atomic bomb brought the war to a close before a significant number of those advanced subs could be deployed.

It may be noted that it was often months between the launch date and the commissioning of a boat. That is because there was a lot to do to get both the vessel and her crew ready for what they would face in the war. The launch typically occurred as soon as the boat was deemed able to safely float. Then it was another considerable period of time before it actually arrived in the Pacific theater and began its first war patrol. There were sea trials to perform, torpedo tests to conduct, and a crew to train and qualify for submarine duty.

The launch was a formal ceremony, usually with a navy band, a group of dignitaries, an assortment of naval officers, and a person—almost always a woman—who was designated the "sponsor" of the boat. Sponsors ranged from the First Lady of the United States to the wives of lowly yard workers. Her job was to christen the vessel by loudly announcing the name as she broke a bottle of champagne across the bow. At that moment, chocks were removed and the sub slid down a gangway into the water, usually with an impressive splash that looked good on the newsreels. A skeleton crew aboard the boat guided her along as tugs nudged her toward a new slip. There work continued until she was fully ready for sea trials.

Once she was ready, another formal ceremony took place—the commissioning—when the sub was officially put into service, her crew lined up along the deck in dress uniforms, saluting as the new skipper took command of his boat. But she was still not yet ready for war. There was much training to do, sea trials to complete, a shakedown period to finish.

Part of that shakedown included a visit to the torpedo test range in Narragansett Bay at Newport, Rhode Island. There the crew practiced lining up on practice targets that were towed behind ships, entering information into the TDC (torpedo data computer), and loading and firing torpedoes. The process not only helped the crew get used to their new vessel and to each other, but it tested the boat's torpedo handling and firing systems. The boat also had to complete a number of dives to various depths and verify her readiness to do those kinds of operations quickly and under adverse conditions.

All along, members of the crew who were not already qualified in submarines were learning, practicing, working toward that goal. During the war, the navy attempted to crew subs with a mix of qualified, experienced sub sailors and those recently graduated from sub school. Officers, too, were sometimes experienced and sometimes new blood. A brand-new skipper was, whenever possible, teamed with an experienced executive officer (XO).

Sub sailors were (and still are) required to graduate from submarine school, where they combined classroom learning with actual onboard training, but they were not finished yet. When they got aboard their first boat, they had to be trained until they could pass a rigorous examination in order to verify that they could take any station on a vessel and perform each job in a satisfactory manner. Once they passed their qualification exam, they were awarded a patch or pin that showed two dolphins, nose to nose. One of a sub sailor's proudest days was when he received his "twin dolphins" and could wear them on his dress uniform. The alternative for those who were not able to pass within a reasonable time was to be assigned to other duty. Incidentally, that procedure is still in place today on nuclear submarines.

Finally, months after the launch of the sub, orders were given and the sub and her new crew were off on patrol.

Though they may look primitive to us today in comparison to modern, nuclear-powered vessels, the fleet-type submarine that was sliding down the launch skids in places like Portsmouth, New Hampshire; Manitowoc, Wisconsin; Groton, Connecticut; and Mare Island, California, was a marvel in its time. And the men who were being trained to crew those boats were destined to be a special breed of submariner.

The first thing most people notice about boats of the *Gato* and *Balao* class when they visit one of the museum boats—at least those that have been taken out of the water—is how much bigger the submarines look than they imagined. The fact is, when afloat, most of the boat is below water, like an iceberg, with only the decks, the top of the conning tower, the bridge, and the shears visible. The shears are the radio and radar antennas, periscope housings, searchlight, flagpoles, and lookout stands. They tower above the bridge and give these vessels their distinctive look.

The next thing that strikes visitors is how cramped and confining the interior compartments of the boats are compared to how massive they look from outside. Diesel tanks and ballast tanks, designed to withstand tremendous water pressure, make up the vessel's bulk. For the range these subs had to be able to travel, they carried a huge amount of diesel fuel in their tanks. And the actions of diving and surfacing require ballast tanks that may be flooded and vented, using thousands of gallons of seawater and compressed air in the process.

Fourteen of the World War II submarines that are open to the public are either *Balao-* or *Gato*-class vessels. Two of them are *Tench*-class boats. Even those are very similar in design to their predecessors, but offered improved internal machinery and a better ballast tank arrangement. And one, of course, is a German U-boat, but that one still followed many of the same principles of design as the American boats.

All were about the length of a football field including one end zone, about twenty-seven feet wide at the broadest point, capable of safely diving to four hundred feet (though most went deeper, whether accidentally or on purpose), and able to steam at twenty knots while they were on the surface and at almost nine knots when submerged.

These boats typically carried six to eight officers and between sixty and seventy enlisted men. When you tour one of these vessels, imagine over six dozen men living and working together in the confines of those tiny compartments. And imagine them doing so for two months while rarely being able to climb the ladders and spend time on the narrow, slick decks. And imagine having to do that without touching land while on patrol in enemy waters, in seas that were often storm-tossed, and while under threat from surface ships, aircraft, floating mines, and other submarines.

Of course, these vessels were designed to be warships. Their jobs were to observe, look for enemy shipping lanes, perform lifeguard duty, deliver men and equipment into hostile places, and do about anything else they were called upon to do. But primarily, they were built to blow things up.

They were especially well equipped for that purpose. In addition to torpedoes, the submarines had various other weapons on their decks, including machine guns and small cannons. The captain usually had the opportunity to choose what type deck guns he wanted on his boat. Despite the assumption by many that subs only did their damage with torpedoes, many enemy vessels were damaged and destroyed using the boats' deck guns. They were used quite often in furious, close-range combat.

These vessels were powered on the surface by four diesel engines, but they did not actually turn the screws (or propellers, much like those on a typical motorboat, though much larger). The engines provided power directly to two electric motors that were, in turn, attached to twin screws that drove them through the water. Those big diesel engines also were used to charge huge banks of storage batteries that were located in two separate compartments in the sub's belly. The batteries provided electricity for the motors so the boat could run quietly and without smoke when she was submerged. They also provided power for all the boat's systems, lights, radios, radar, and the like.

That is why this type of submarine is often referred to as being an "electric boat" in one breath and a "diesel boat" in the next. And why one major builder of these vessels, one that continues to build nuclear-powered subs to this day, is named the Electric Boat Company.

For most people, the most recognizable part of a World War II submarine is her "sail," the structure that sticks up above the deck amidships. The outside portion of the sail contains the bridge, the platform where the captain or OOD (officer of the deck) and another officer usually stood while the boat was operating on the surface.

The shears are the part of the boat that reaches above the bridge, where the perch for young, sharp-eyed lookouts is located. Another platform, often called the cigarette deck, curves around behind the sail. That deck and another small platform just in front of the bridge typically held antiaircraft guns. Some of the submarines on display as museum boats have either original or authentic deck guns installed for your consideration. Others no longer have them.

Those weapons were important. Airplanes were mortal enemies of submarines. A visual or radar sighting of any aircraft usually sent the crew scrambling to get the boat beneath the surface of the sea as quickly as possible. Amazingly, this could usually be accomplished, under ideal conditions and with an experienced crew, in less than forty seconds.

But if the submarine were caught on the surface, those guns were needed for self-defense. Other deck guns were used in attacks against smaller surface ships, picket sampans (Japanese fishing boats used to observe and report Allied shipping and bomber activity), and floating mines. They were also manned when the sub approached lifeboats, rafts, or swimmers in the water—enemy personnel who may have survived an attack. The sub crews never knew when the men in those lifeboats might open fire on them.

A watertight hatch from the submarine's bridge leads down a short ladder to a compartment called the conning tower. This small room is where the OOD controlled the boat when she was submerged. It contains controls for running the ship, including controlling her steering and motor speed. There is intercom equipment and the "annunciator," the device that was used to indicate speed and direction to the maneuvering room, located below and toward the boat's stern.

There are also torpedo controls, the torpedo data computer and firing console, as well as both periscopes (one for attack and one for general observation), and the very important radar and sonar equipment. A watertight hatch leads down from the conning tower into the control room, which is accessed from above by going down a steep, vertical ladder.

The control room is exactly what its name implies. This is where the boat was controlled while submerged. Various equipment typically installed here include the submergence light panel, which is popularly called the Christmas tree because of its display of red and green lights that indicate system status; the bow plane and stern plane controls that allowed the crew to dive and surface smoothly and not too quickly; the inclinometer, which told them how well they were doing in that process; depth gauges, and more. There is other important gear here, too, such as the ship's gyrocompasses, another type of radar, and the radio room.

Below the control room, and accessed by removing deck plates, is a marvelously complicated collection of pumps, compressors, generators, piping, and blowers—the systems for keeping the boat operational and comfortable. This compartment is called the pump room.

Stepping forward through the narrow doorway from the control room, the next area is dubbed the "forward battery." Its name comes from the 126 big lead-acid electric storage cells that rested in the space below the deck plates. Because of their danger and corrosive nature, these batteries have been removed from all the museum boats. More than one submarine has been lost because of explosions either in the battery compartments or from the dangerous gases they released during charging. The storage batteries on subs did exactly what they were supposed to do, provide electricity for the motors and boat systems, but they had to be closely monitored and properly handled or they could turn lethal.

All the boats had indicator meters hanging throughout their compartments so anyone could tell at a glance if the explosive gas from the batteries ever reached a dangerous level. When it did, no matter where they were or what irritated enemy vessels might be on the surface above them, or which airplane could be bearing down on them, the boats had to surface or remain on top, open hatches, and vent the gas to the outside before a stray spark set off a conflagration far worse than any attack by the Japanese.

The area above the batteries contains the officers' quarters and work space for the two steward's mates, which includes a coffee urn, storage drawers, food warmers, and other equipment necessary to serve food to the skipper and other officers. The captain of a submarine was the only officer who had a private cabin. His bedroom is called a stateroom, but it can hardly be compared to a stateroom on a cruise ship. Visitors today can see how small it really is.

The other officers shared rooms in pairs, and they all had use of a single toilet, sink, and shower. Also in this area is the wardroom, where the commissioned officers ate and held meetings around a small table. The yeoman's office is in a tiny room on the starboard (right-hand) side at the after end (toward the rear of the boat) of the compartment. The yeoman was the enlisted man whose duty it was to keep up with the ship's and crew's records.

Moving forward from the officers' quarters, the submarine's "business end" is found in the next compartment, at the front of the boat—the forward torpedo room. This is where a total of sixteen ready-to-load-and-launch torpedoes were stored—six inside the tubes, set to go, and ten in heavy storage racks along the sides and under the deck plates—until ready to be fired from the six tubes at the forward end of the room. Equipment for handling the torpedoes is located here as well. That was some chore, since each torpedo weighed more than a ton and a half.

There is also bunk space here for the torpedomen to sleep when they were off duty. Some of the crew's bunks are hung above and below the stacked torpedoes, others are suspended from the overhead, and the rest are on the starboard side, in the torpedo-loading pit. Regardless of where the men slept in this compartment, huge, heavy, deadly torpedoes surrounded them the whole time.

The possibility of having to evacuate the sub in an undersea emergency was always on the minds of the crew members. Here, in the forward torpedo room, is an escape hatch that the men could open, crawl into, and flood with seawater, allowing them a last-resort way out. There would typically be a supply of Momsen lungs stored there, too. Those were a rudimentary device that could be strapped on in the event the boat had to be evacuated while submerged. They could be used for breathing while rising slowly to the surface. They were not a perfect solution, and the depth at which they could be used was limited, but they were about the only hope sub sailors had if their boat should be damaged or disabled while submerged, whether by enemy fire or equipment malfunction. Sub sailors were lost to both.

Moving toward the rear of the boat from the control room, the next compartment back is called the after battery, also named for a second collection of big storage cells beneath the deck plates of this compartment. The forward end of the compartment, above the deck plates, holds one of the boat's most important areas, the galley. Cooks prepared food for both the officers and enlisted men there, serving the bulk of what they cooked in the crew's mess hall next door and taking the officers' meals forward to serve them in the wardroom. The crew's mess has four fixed tables with stationary benches along each side. In the typical configuration, they could hold two dozen men, a third of the crew, at a time.

Another thing that came out of Theodore Roosevelt's ride in the *Plunger* was the decree that submarines always provide their crews the best food available. Mr. Roosevelt felt that if the men were deprived of daylight, clean air, and open space, they should at least enjoy good meals. Submarine food is legendary in the navy, and many sailors claim to have volunteered for duty for just that reason.

Next in line in the after battery area are the crew quarters, a total of thirty-six stainless-steel-framed bunks stacked in four rows. The crew's duty assignments while at sea were typically four hours on watch and eight hours off watch. That meant that someone was always sleeping unless the crew was ordered to battle stations. Since there were not enough bunks for every member of the crew, some of the beds, known as "hot bunks," were assigned to more than one person to use each day.

A metal door at the after end of the bunk area is the entry into the crew's head, or toilet area. It contains two stalls with toilets, two stall showers, and two washbasins, as well as an automatic laundry machine. More than seventy men were required to share two toilets, two showers, and two sinks. That, in and of itself, may explain the closeness of the submariner brotherhood!

The next area back after the crew quarters holds the forward and after engine rooms. Each engine room contains two diesel main engines that are directly coupled to a high-powered electrical generator. Output

from the engine-driven generators provided power to operate the electrical propulsion motors in the motor room when the boat was on the surface. They also charged the batteries. In the aft engine room, below deck
level, there is a small auxiliary diesel engine that could be used as a low-
power substitute for the main engine if need be. The forward engine
room is almost identical to the aft engine room, except it has a small machine shop in place of the auxiliary engine.

Companies that built railroad locomotives typically manufactured these
diesel engines. They had to be powerful and reliable, for obvious reasons.
A powerless submarine was a sitting duck for enemy ships and airplanes.

Next in line is the maneuvering room and, below it, the motor room.
The two large electric motors in the motor room were what actually sent
the submarine forward or backward, whether she was on the surface or
submerged. Each of those motors drove a screw (or propeller) that is located at the boat's stern. While the submarine was on the surface, the
electric motors got their juice from the diesel-engine-driven electrical
generators. While submerged, their power came from the electric batteries in the forward and after battery compartments.

Huge electrical switches were required to change over from generator
to battery power or to begin charging the batteries. Those switches are
located in the control cubicle, a stainless-steel box that measures eight to
ten feet on a side. The cubicle is shock-mounted to isolate the switches
from the shaking and rattling of depth charges or rough seas. Two men,
called controllermen, handled the switching from the maneuvering panel
that is located behind the cubicle. They adjusted the rheostats and levers
in response to orders from the conning tower or control room.

Theirs was an interesting dance to watch. They followed orders from
the con or bridge by maneuvering the levers, switches, and knobs in a
complicated ballet, creating the correct combination to make the submarine do what the OOD or skipper wanted her to do. Because of the electricity that coursed through the cubicle, this area was also susceptible to
fire, something feared by submariners even more than flood.

The final compartment at the far rear end of the boat is the aft torpedo room. It is very similar to the forward room, only considerably smaller. There are only four torpedo tubes here. Whenever the boat was on patrol at sea, each of the tubes had a torpedo stored in it. Four other torpedoes were stored in the room. This gave the boat a complement of twenty-four torpedoes in the two rooms. Of course, if one torpedo room ran out of "fish," that end of the boat was out of business. There was no way to get the heavy torpedoes from one end of the submarine to the other to reload. Skippers had to always be cognizant of how many fish were left and where they were located.

The after torpedo room also has its own emergency escape hatch with a supply of Momsen lungs.

Life on a submarine could be tedious. Imagine living in such close quarters with other men, not to mention the inevitable tensions of wartime, the pressures of stalking targets for long, nervous hours while attempting to destroy them.

When leaving on patrol, their fuel tanks were filled with heavy diesel fuel, and it was necessary to constantly recalculate the effect of the weight of that fuel as it was burned away. Otherwise diving and surfacing could be especially dangerous. Also, when the boats left port on a patrol, every nook and cranny was filled with provisions for the run. Even the decks were covered with cans of food, and the crew literally had to walk around on their groceries until they were used up.

Even though they were built to run on and under the sea, water was a precious commodity aboard submarines. Seawater could not be used in the storage batteries. Only distilled water was pure enough for that purpose, so the subs carried distilling systems that could convert seawater to something the batteries could tolerate. The old joke among submariners was that if the distilled water was pure enough, it was used in the batteries. If it was not, it was used for drinking and cooking.

There was certainly not enough clean water for regular bathing. A shower aboard a submarine was a rare luxury. It was far more common for the crew to grab a quick bath while running through a rainstorm than to be able to take much more than a spit-bath. When leaving port, the enlisted men's double shower stalls were usually crammed full of potatoes and other supplies. They would not be using them for their intended purpose anytime soon after heading out on patrol.

Another old joke was that nobody noticed body odor aboard the boats. The diesel fumes pretty well took care of that.

Still, the new fleet boats had many advantages over their predecessors. They had better air-conditioning, which was a big factor in the warm climes where much of the war was being fought in the Pacific. Despite how they might seem to visitors today, they were roomier than the boats that came before them. And they were perfectly designed for what they were primarily charged to do: stalk and attack enemy vessels, either on the surface or while submerged. Of course, they also had much greater range and could move faster.

These new classes of submersibles were actually very efficient ships while running on the surface, even faster and more maneuverable than many vessels designed to ride only on the surface. Yet they were capable of virtually disappearing, both visually and aurally, when they submerged. Sometimes aircraft could spot them in the relatively clear Pacific Ocean waters but, for the most part, when they dove to several hundred feet, they were as stealthy as any warship in history. And with the quiet battery power, as long as there were no squeaking bearings or other malfunctions, they ran about as silently as was possible.

As World War II progressed, newer, more sophisticated radar was being developed and installed on the subs, sometimes while the advanced technology was still being perfected. That gave the submarines a strong tool to use in tracking the enemy, and a considerable advantage over the Japanese, whose technology was lagging by this time.

Torpedoes, too, had been problematic in the early days of the war. Skippers maintained that the fish would zoom right up to a target, smash its nose hard into the other vessel's side, and still fail to explode. Other types of torpedoes ran erratically, deeper or more shallow than set to do, and never even had a chance to hit an enemy vessel. But those troubles were eventually fixed and the success of the submarine navy improved markedly as the conflict wore on. The official numbers show it.

Still, even with this advanced warship beneath them, young men risked their lives defending their country every time one of them pulled out of harbor and left on the next war patrol. Thankfully, many more than could ever serve volunteered for submarine duty, and, as we have seen, they did their jobs well.

We can also be thankful for the efforts of those who were determined to preserve these vessels for us to visit, tour, and learn more about. Not only can we walk through them and see for ourselves the conditions under which these men lived and fought, but these museum boats also serve as touchstones for all those men who have served in the submarine navy through the years. These boats are something tangible, something real that they can come back to and relive that chapter in their lives.

There are precious few of them left—boats and World War II sub sailors.

Many of the submarines were lost in the war. Others were scrapped, used for target practice, or ended up in foreign navies. Only a few of the more than three hundred World War II diesel boats remain today, and the job of keeping them in shape for us to see is a difficult and expensive one.

I have read the estimate, too, that we are losing a thousand World War II veterans a day. The World War II Submarine Veterans organization no longer holds a separate convention each year, but has thrown in with the larger United States Submarine Veterans group, which includes members of all ages. There simply aren't enough of the old guys to justify their own get-together any longer.

Their World War II crew reunions, often held at or near one of the museum boats, now attract fewer and fewer attendees. Most of those who are still able to attend such gatherings are men who served in later commissions of the submarines, in the '50s, '60s, and '70s.

But as you learn more about them, as you read the amazing true stories of the boats, of the young men who rode them, and of the people who saved the vessels and who keep them preserved, then you will certainly come to appreciate them.

And I assure you, that appreciation will only grow should you take the opportunity to visit one or more of these gallant old ladies.

USS *COD* (SS-224)

Courtesy of the U.S. Navy

USS *COD* (SS-224)

Class: *Gato*
Launched: March 21, 1943
Named for: the cod, the world's most important food fish
Where: Electric Boat Company, Groton, Connecticut
Sponsor: Mrs. Grace Mahoney, the wife of a shipyard employee
Commissioned: June 21, 1943

Where is she today?
USS *Cod* Submarine Memorial
1089 East 9th Street
Cleveland, Ohio 44114
(216) 566-8770
www.usscod.org

Claim to fame: She was part of the only international submarine-to-submarine rescue in history, and survived a potentially disastrous fire in the torpedo room. She is one of the best-preserved of all the museum boats.

Commander James Dempsey was proud of his new boat. From his perch on her bridge, she was a beautiful sight to behold, even in the darkness of the South China Sea. He could see the sparkling green phosphorescence playing in the wash at her stern, but that was not totally a good thing. The skipper hoped no Japanese lookout somewhere out there in the black night would take notice of the starry wake of the USS *Cod*.

"Keep a sharp eye," he called to the men who stood above him, strapped in the shears, gazing out into the night. Young men, not one among them yet twenty years old. They were specially selected for lookout duty because, it was assumed, youth meant better eyesight. Even with the sophisticated new radar they carried, it was often the human eye that did the best job when the chips were down. Or it was typically one of the kid sub sailors who confirmed what the newfangled radar gear was telling them.

"We don't want to lose sight of that convoy before we get a chance to shoot our popgun at her, boys," Dempsey told them.

"We will, sir."

"We won't lose them!"

The *Cod* was totally shipshape, ready for war, and her crew was as ready as she was. Still, Commander Dempsey knew it was not all about hardware out here in the Pacific theater. It took smarts, hard work, and not a little bit of luck to be successful. And a war-hardened skipper like Jim Dempsey knew this firsthand.

He was a relative old-timer out here, in his thirties, a 1931 graduate of the U.S. Naval Academy at Annapolis. His first command in the war was an old veteran, too, an S-boat, the *S-37* (SS-142), put into service way back in 1923. Though ninety feet shorter than the new *Gato* boats like the *Cod*, limited to only two hundred feet of depth when they dived to hide, and only capable of steaming at about fourteen knots on the surface, Dempsey and his crew had taken her out when the war started and proved the old girl was still capable of striking a blow. His chance came on the last of his three patrols at the helm of the S-boat, only a few months after the attack on Pearl Harbor. Dempsey and his crew on the *S-37* claimed the first Imperial Japanese Navy (IJN) destroyer to be sunk during the war, the *Natushie*, dispatched to the bottom of the Flores Sea in February 1942. He was later on the bridge of the USS *Spearfish* (SS-190), too, on four patrols out of Australian ports in 1942. Though that boat was a *Sargo*-class vessel and closer to the *Cod* in size and design, she simply did not have the capabilities of the new *Balao*-class boats, like the one he now proudly helmed.

Still, his first two patrols as skipper of this new boat had not been as successful as he and the rest of his crew had hoped. On their first patrol, in November of 1943, they were only able to mount a single attack on any kind of enemy target. They sank one ship of unknown type, with an estimated displacement of seventy-one hundred tons. Dempsey had no way of knowing then that even that bagged quarry would not be counted as a kill after the war, as was the case with so many. After World II, the official tally of vessels destroyed was most often based on the spotty records of the IJN and determined by a commission dubbed "JANAC," the Joint Army-Navy Assessment Committee. That group tended to be very conservative in giving credit.

Tonight's our night, the captain said to himself as he peered into the darkness. The big, slow-moving convoy, tankers and transports lined up for miles, was theirs for the taking if they could only maneuver to the proper position without being detected, and then line up to shoot. Through the soles of his shoes, the captain felt the rumble of the big engines vibrating throughout the vessel, steadily driving his boat after their quarry. It was a comforting feeling, sensing the power that was at his disposal, the systems he could now employ in the relentless pursuit of the enemy.

Tonight we justify our groceries, Dempsey thought, his slight smile hidden by the darkness.

Their second run started promisingly enough. They sank a sampan with their deck guns. Not exactly a battleship, but such vessels often acted as spotters, watching and reporting Allied warship positions and the approach of U.S. airplanes on the way to the Japanese Home Islands for another bombing run.

A day later, they torpedoed a Japanese merchant ship and a seven-thousand-ton tanker, sending both ships and their cargo to the bottom in a fury of fire and smoke, where they would be of no use to Emperor Hirohito's war effort, unable to deliver petroleum, rubber, or other natural resources to Japan.

But then, without warning, the entire crew came down with a nasty case of food poisoning. They were hardly able to function, even when they received a message that an important tanker convoy was about to swim right in front of their periscope sights. With their heads in buckets up and down the length of the ship, they simply were not able to do much of anything about such a wonderful queue of targets obligingly passing by.

Dempsey wrote in his patrol report, "The commanding officer accepts full responsibility for this fiasco. The officers and crew, nearly all of whom are still suffering from the effects of the poisoning, did the best they could. Nothing seemed to click. . . ."

Now, from his high roost on the bridge, the captain scanned the eastern horizon, where the sun would soon appear. He rubbed his scratchy growth of beard on his chin and pondered the fact that, with the impending dawn, they were quickly running out of time.

They had been trailing this massive convoy for most of the night now, drawing closer bit by bit, but their best cover, the darkness of night, was about to dessert them, replaced by all-revealing sunlight.

"We better see if we can line up in a hurry if we want to try for a shot before sunrise," Dempsey said to his officer of the deck, standing at his right elbow. Then he gave the command that old submariners still hear in their sleep: "Battle stations!"

That sent a shiver up and down the boat as word came that it was time at last to get serious about those tankers and transports out there. Wallowing tankers and massive transport vessels that they could not even see with their eyes yet, just in the relentless metronome sweep of the radar screen.

Every man raced to his post and quickly got ready to begin firing torpedoes at the enemy vessels they had been chasing all night.

Dempsey's staccato order set in motion the complicated maneuvering all submarines had to do to get into a position to fire their torpedoes at a moving target. Much of that intricate alignment could take place while the submarine remained on the surface, able to travel at just better than twenty knots and to see much clearer what the enemy was doing. Human eyes, radar, and sonar could all be used topside. It was always the aim to avoid diving until absolutely necessary. Once they had to submerge to mount an attack, much of that capability, along with the advantage of surface speed and maneuverability, would be lost, and the ships they were chasing would have a better chance to avoid them.

But as the hint of daylight turned more and more toward full-blown dawn, Dempsey finally ordered the boat to dive, out of sight of anyone who might be on the decks of the vessels they were stalking. Out of view of any radar equipment they or their well-armed escorts may have aboard as well.

"Prepare to dive!" the skipper shouted. Then, punching the button for the klaxon, he yelled, "Dive! Dive! Dive!"

The lookouts were out of the shears and down the hatch to the control room in a blur, even before the first "Dive!" was out of the skipper's lips. The OOD followed instantly behind them, using a strong grip on the side handrails to slow his descent, his feet not even touching the rungs of the ladder that led down into the conning tower.

Then, as the last sound of the dive klaxon echoed up and down the length of his boat, and as the downward angle of the bow confirmed that his order was being obeyed, Captain James Dempsey headed down the hatch himself, the last man off the bridge before it was swallowed up by the sea, just ahead of the first splashes of seawater that rapidly covered the decks. One of the crew pulled the cover closed above him and twisted the lock until the hatch was watertight. Still, a rain of cold water pelted most of the men working in the cramped room. They did not seem to notice the dousing.

"Level and steady, come to periscope depth, maintain heading zero-seven-zero," Dempsey ordered. The men manning the dive planes steadied the *Cod*, keeping her level and just deep enough so the periscope could protrude above the surface of the sea by a scant few feet. High enough to see but low enough to lessen the chance of being seen. The skipper grabbed the handles of the attack periscope and pulled it down from its housing, ignoring the face full of water it brought with it. He wiped his face with his sleeve, snapped down the handles and put his eyes to the eyepieces, circling to look directly toward where the radar said the nearest whalelike tanker should be.

"Bring her to two-seven-zero," he said, loud enough so everyone in the conning tower and in the control room below could hear him. He was swinging their nose farther to the west, to where he now saw the dim outline of a big cargo ship in the predawn mist. But there was another vessel out there, too. It was a smaller blip on the radarscope but one that was far more ominous than the others. An escort vessel. A destroyer. And they were about to steer their submarine to a position somewhere right in between them. "We'll line up for a stern shot at the escort craft and a bow shot at the convoy. Stand by for a bearing, but Lord knows, if we shoot in that direction, we'll have to hit something that floats."

They were going to try to get several of the enemy vessels at the same time, including the nearest destroyer that rode along as protection for the convoy—try, and pray they could pull it off.

Quickly, before the ships could drive out of range, the *Cod* worked her way closer, to within a distance where a spray of torpedoes would be most likely to find targets among the herd of ships. Tension mounted in the conning tower as the captain moved the periscope in an arc, "dancing with the fat lady," intently watching. The boat's executive officer stood opposite him, on the other side of the periscope, calling out bearings he read from the marker on the scope's base. Those numbers were entered into the torpedo data computer, a mechanical device that calculated the information the torpedomen at the rear of the boat needed to set the run parameters for their weapons. They were taking aim, getting ready to fire.

"XO, make a note. That's *Karukaya* nearest us. Think the boss would buy us a beer if we took her down?"

The Japanese destroyer would indeed be a nice target. Besides, that would be one less vessel that would be dropping depth charges on their heads once the attack was over and they were fleeing the scene.

The instant they were lined up to his satisfaction, Dempsey did not hesitate to give the command, even if it would reveal their position to everyone within miles. They would all know that the submarine was there and precisely where.

"After torpedo room, fire one! Fire two! Fire four!"

Everyone aboard the *Cod* felt the pronounced nudges as each of the three big torpedoes whooshed from its tube and began its run toward the enemy destroyer. The call of "Torpedoes away, running true!" confirmed it.

But even as those fish swam quickly away from their tubes and began the run toward their targets, the skipper swung the scope back around to peer the other way, toward the bow of his vessel.

"Forward torpedo room, fire one when ready!"

There was another noticeable kick. Then, one after the other, Dempsey quickly proceeded to order all six torpedoes sent on their way from the nose of the boat. As soon as he had felt each of them being launched, heard the confirmation from the torpedomen, and saw the trails of the weapons pointing away from them on the surface of the sea, he quickly swung back around to look at the *Karukaya*, the destroyer. She was still steaming along, flanking the convoy she was supposed to be protecting, still oblivious to the *Cod*'s presence at their party.

The skipper could hear the man designated as the timer as he counted out loud the seconds that had elapsed since the launch of the first torpedoes, those headed toward the warship. It seemed a long, long time since the kick of their departure.

But then, as Dempsey watched through the crosshatched periscope, there was a sudden and awful explosion along the ship's side, at water level, directly below the destroyer's bridge. The *Cod*'s aim had been perfect. They had hit a moving target from over a mile away exactly where they intended to. And it was clear that she was mortally wounded.

Almost immediately, both smokestacks on the IJN warship collapsed like they were cut off at the knees. Human beings could clearly be seen tumbling and flying, tossed high into the pinkish morning sky by the detonation and the sudden lurch of the ship beneath them. The vessel seemed to sag in the middle, her bow and stern rising, forming a smoking, fiery V, as if some giant hand had delivered a killer karate chop to her midsection.

Then, only seconds later, a second torpedo struck near the main mast, disintegrating most of the rear half of the *Karukaya*. If she was not a goner before, she certainly was now.

That was all Dempsey needed to see. The enemy destroyer was done for.

Leaning on the scope housing for support, he swung it back around 180 degrees, toward the main body of the convoy. He knew his men were already loading more torpedoes into their tubes, fore and aft, but the only weapon he had left for the moment was the one fish that still remained in the stern tube, the one he had deliberately not fired. That was common practice. Don't empty your revolver of bullets in the middle of a gunfight.

You never knew what varmint might still be lurking out there and you might not have time to reload.

The counter had picked up the tally on the second spray of torpedoes. Dempsey was praying under his breath that some of the six fish he had sent on their way from the front of the boat would find something hard enough in their path to make them explode on impact, just as the others had done.

But before he had time to worry, he saw and heard and counted off out loud half a dozen vicious explosions, each of them lined up neatly all along the row of oil tankers. Every one of their torpedoes had found a target!

"Take her to three hundred feet! Bearing two-four-zero. Let's run as fast as we can before they figure out where we went!"

Dempsey knew he had stirred up a hornet's nest. He had seen other escorts out there with depth charges on their decks and torpedoes of their own, and now they had even more incentive to use them.

His firing position would be clearly visible to the Japanese on the surface. They could easily pinpoint the trails of the nine torpedoes and trace them right back to the spot where they were set loose. The *Cod* didn't need to still be there when that inevitability occurred.

So now Jim Dempsey was going to take his boat as deep as he dared and, at the same time, he was going to skedaddle. Or at least he was going to skedaddle at his top submerged speed of eight or nine knots, about a third as fast as the enemy escorts could go.

And he could only do that for about another ten minutes or so without using up all of what remained of his battery power. Then, with dead batteries, they would have very few options.

Who knew how long they might have to stay down? They would need to keep some juice in reserve for maneuvering and keep the boat's systems functioning until they could come up and recharge.

As they raced away, their nose pointing downward and going deeper, there were explosions behind them. Bombs and depth charges shook the boat violently, even though she was by then over a mile away from most of the commotion. A few valves and hydraulic lines up and down the length of the boat sprang minor leaks and a couple of lightbulbs shattered from the rattling concussion of the blasts. Damage-control parties were already assessing.

But even with the thunder of the ordnance, the sonar operators could detect the ominous sounds of vessels breaking up, of hulls crumbling, of water rushing into damaged compartments with a distinctive roar, like some giant beast in its death throes. There was also the snapping and popping of ammunition exploding, likely in the cargo hold of one of the damaged transports. Ammunition meant to cut Allied soldiers to pieces on some far-flung Pacific island.

Some aboard the *Cod* allowed themselves a quick cheer. Even James Dempsey grinned. He knew it would be difficult to claim credit for much more than the destroyer he had actually witnessed going down (they would eventually only be credited with sinking two vessels for a total of eight thousand tons), but he also knew they had struck a significant blow. It would be good to get the pats on the back when they got home.

If they ever got home.

The infuriated blasts of the depth charges had grown closer now as the Japanese anticipated the direction they had likely headed. God help them if the Japanese continued to guess correctly.

The crew members of the submarine had to hold on tight to keep from being thrown to the deck by the nearby explosions. Water trickled down from overhead leaks. Dust sifted from the overhead at every tooth-rattling blast.

Each man listened for the click as the charge armed itself, and then silently counted the seconds until it exploded. Like lightning and thunder preceding a thunderstorm, the time between the click and the blast told how far away the detonation would be. They knew if they couldn't count to one before hell was set loose, it would not be a good thing.

Over the next fifteen minutes, the sonarmen counted more than seventy depth charges dropped on their heads. Only then did the hailstorm finally ease up. But then, every time Captain Dempsey was about to order them to surface, they heard the engines of a patrol boat or a destroyer approaching, hovering, passing overhead, likely listening for any sound that would tip them off to where their attacker hid.

It was maddening. Battery power was flagging. All unnecessary lights had been doused long ago. The air inside the boat had long since grown fetid and thin. It was difficult to breathe and smoking was impossible. The air was so thin a match would not strike and burn long enough to light a cigarette.

Those men not on watch or working on stopping the pesky leaks remained on their bunks. Others only moved when they had to. And when they did, breathing was so difficult they quickly rested again.

What if the sea above them was never clear of enemy craft? Eventually there would be no choice. They would have to surface in the middle of them and take their chances. Gun crews were assembled. They would man the deck guns and try to repel attackers as long as they could. But they would be no match for the destroyers and patrol boats and, likely by now, airplanes.

Maybe they could take some of the enemy with them, though. Maybe.

Finally, after over twelve hours at three hundred feet or better, the skipper ordered them to surface slowly, to make as small a wake as they could. It would be night by now, thankfully, but they would hardly be invisible, especially from radar.

They paused an agonizing few minutes at periscope depth. If the sea was full of enemy warships, they might still stay down a while longer.

Dempsey made a quick 360-degree sweep. A grin slowly spread across his face.

"Bring her on up. It's raining cats and dogs up there."

Sure enough, they were surfacing in the middle of a tropical thunderstorm. Even so, Dempsey signaled for the hatch from the conning tower up to the bridge to be opened. A little rain never hurt anybody.

The crew members ignored the drenching they got as cool, sweet air spilled down the hatch with the rainwater. Everyone cheered.

Then there was a flash, a sudden explosion, followed quickly by another even louder one. Eyes widened. Faces went white.

All except for that of one of the sonarmen, the one who stood closest to the skipper. He didn't seem to have heard a thing.

Then the skipper grinned again. Thunder. Lightning and thunder.

"Scared the fool out of me," Dempsey said to the sonarman.

"Sir?" the youngster asked, his hand cupped to his ear.

"The thunder," Dempsey repeated, louder. "Thought it was our friends again."

"Thunder?" The sonarman shook his head and wiggled a finger inside each of his ears. "I ain't heard nothing since we took that depth charging."

Dempsey smiled and clapped the young sailor on the back.

The *Cod* would not lack for more action during World War II. On April 26, 1945, she was in the midst of her sixth war patrol, now under the command of Captain Dempsey's successor, Commander James A. "Caddy" Adkins. Dempsey, after commanding three different boats on a record ten war patrols, went ashore to be a staff operations officer. Adkins was another old submariner, a 1927 Naval Academy grad. Partly because of his age and partly because of a lackluster patrol in the Atlantic aboard *S-21* (SS-126), he had been taken off submarine duty for a while, but he proved to be an aggressive skipper when he was put in command of the *Cod* for three of her war patrols.

Though he and his submarine were primarily on lifeguard duty, plucking downed fighter and bomber pilots out of the sea, they still managed to claim a target. The day before, they had sunk a minesweeper, *W-41*, and the *Cod* had endured what the captain called in his patrol report "the most severe depth charging of her career." But they came through it fine and would have a wonderful story to tell their fellow submariners when they returned to port.

The crew was in high spirits. Survival was a good thing. Something to be celebrated once they were in port and on shore leave.

Then there came menacing word from the after torpedo room, a report that sent a shiver through the entire length of the *Cod*. One of the electric torpedoes that were stored in a rack and ready to load into a tube was ablaze, the result of a short circuit in its firing mechanism. The compartment was immediately filled with thick, black smoke.

There was every chance the thing could detonate. Nobody wanted to imagine what that might do to the boat's superstructure. What the Japanese had failed to do might happen anyway.

The irony of being destroyed by one of their own torpedoes was not lost on any of the crew members who were aware of the emergency. There was only one thing to do.

The compartment was evacuated. A team of volunteers donned breathing masks and went back inside the room. One of the torpedoes that was already loaded inside a tube would have to be removed. The smoking, blazing torpedo would somehow have to be loaded and jettisoned out to sea before it blew them all up.

There was no choice. They had to find a way to get it done inside a cramped, smoke-filled compartment, knowing all the time that the fiery torpedo could explode.

The men closed the watertight door that led into the crew's quarters next door, sealing themselves inside. That done, they went to work unloading a good torpedo from its tube while they decided how best to get the bad one on a skid and into the empty tube.

There was no debate or hesitation. If the fire grew further out of control or if the torpedo exploded, all men in the isolated compartment would die. But the damage might hopefully be limited to that compartment only for a while. If the boat did not go down immediately, some of the others might have an opportunity to evacuate.

During the fire, two other men bravely went out onto the sub's deck, despite the rolling, pitching sea, and made their way back to open the torpedo room's deck hatch. That would allow some of the smoke to vent to the outside and maybe make the firefighting in the compartment a bit easier. But as they made their way along the slick, teetering deck, the two were hit by a wave and knocked overboard.

One of the sailors, Quartermaster Lawrence Foley, wore a life vest. The other man had volunteered and climbed up the ladder without putting one on.

Meanwhile, below, the crew members in the torpedo room managed to wrestle the good torpedo from its tube and load the burning one in its place. As soon as the tube was flooded, the flames were snuffed out. There was minimal damage. The torpedo could even be repaired and used.

With the crisis in the torpedo room under control, Captain Adkins launched a search for the lost sailors. It took eight hours but they were finally miraculously located, bobbing helplessly in the frothy sea. For the entire time they were overboard, Foley had kept his shipmate's head above water as they fought the towering waves and prayed that their boat would come to rescue them.

SS-224 would have another footnote in the history pages of World War II. She would be a key part of the only international submarine-to-submarine rescue ever conducted. On her seventh and final war patrol, on July 8, 1945, the *Cod* came to the aid of the Dutch submarine *O-19*. She found herself grounded on a shelf of coral near Ladd Reef in the South China Sea. Without a doubt she was a sitting duck for any enemy plane or ship that might pass by, but it appeared there was no way for them to pull her off the reef so she could get back underwater.

Despite the danger of being spotted themselves, the *Cod* and her crew helped the fifty-six Dutch submariners to safety in a discouragingly slow operation. Crew members manned the deck guns, watching for enemy ships or planes.

Then, with every sailor off the doomed Dutch vessel, they used scuttling charges, torpedoes, and their five-inch deck gun to destroy *O-19* so that she wouldn't fall into the hands of the Japanese.

Of course, that meant that the American submarine would be the cramped home to over 150 men for the three days it took to make the run to Subic Bay in the recently liberated Philippines. Still, since the rescue was successful, it was a good trip.

There was one more close call for some members of the *Cod*'s crew. When she resumed her seventh patrol after the *O-19* rescue, she was working off the coast of Vietnam, inspecting junks, sampans, and barges. Those little boats were notorious for pretending to be fishing boats while they were actually carrying supplies to the enemy. During one of the operations, a five-man boarding party left the submarine to inspect one of the tiny vessels.

Without warning, a Japanese aircraft suddenly appeared and began strafing the *Cod*. Their skipper at the time, Lieutenant Commander Edwin M. Westbrook, reluctantly but quickly ordered the submarine to dive. Unfortunately, there was no time to recover the crew members who had boarded the junk. They were left behind in order to try to save the submarine and the rest of the crew.

It would be several hours before the coast was clear for the *Cod* to surface again, and when she did, the sea was filled with junks and sampans, an armada stretching from horizon to horizon. Several other U.S. submarines joined the search, but it did not look hopeful.

But two days later, the USS *Blenny* (SS-324) found and rescued the missing crewmen. It was an especially happy reunion.

One of the men aboard the *Cod* for her seventh patrol was Norman Jensen, a U.S. Navy photographer. He shot color movie footage of both the *O-19* rescue and the return of the lost boarding party. That film was discovered in the National Archives in Washington, D.C., in 1992. The images have been used in several documentary television programs since.

When the *Cod* returned to Perth, Australia, at the end of that patrol, the crew was invited to a "thank you" party by crew members from the *O-19*. And, like submariners everywhere, they couldn't turn down an invitation to a party. It was at the height of the celebration of the Dutch crew's remarkable rescue when a very interesting message arrived. It, too, was something that was well worth celebrating.

The Japanese had agreed to surrender.

That news, of course, kicked the party into another gear.

To this day, the *Cod*'s conning tower fairwater and the official battle flag carry the image of a cocktail glass and the designation "*O-19*" in commemoration of the rescue and the party that celebrated that event— as well as the end of the war.

In all, she sailed almost ninety thousand miles while on patrol and consumed over a million gallons of diesel fuel. She fired 122 torpedoes and recorded thirty-nine hits. The boat earned seven battle stars and was officially credited with almost thirty thousand tons of enemy shipping destroyed.

The *Cod* and her crew were prime examples of the silent service's contribution to the hard-won victory in World War II.

Like many of her sisters, the *Cod* would have a productive if more sedate life after World War II. She was reactivated in 1951 and took part in Cold War NATO exercises. She later was converted for dockside use as a training vessel. That meant her screws were removed, the bunks were taken out of the after battery to make room for classrooms, and the ballast tanks were sealed to make sure she did not accidentally submerge with a boatload of trainees aboard. Of course, the storage battery cells came out, too.

In 1959, the sub was towed from the Philadelphia Navy Yard, where she then rested and was prepared for her next job. She journeyed up the Atlantic Coast and down the St. Lawrence Seaway to Cleveland, Ohio.

There she served as a training boat for the Naval Reserve Center until 1971. By that time, the navy had virtually eliminated all nonnuclear vessels from its fleet.

The *Cod* had outlived her usefulness and was stricken from the register of navy ships. She was likely headed for the junk heap like so many of her sister World War II diesel boats.

A group in Cleveland, however, had another thought. They noted that since coming to town the submarine had always been popular with local schoolchildren. Even as she was being used as a training boat, the kids frequently visited her on school field trips. They also noted that the sub's big diesel engines were built by General Motors' Cleveland diesel plant, a facility located on the city's west side.

The old girl had practically been born a Clevelander! It made perfect sense that she was destined to remain there.

The group formed a corporation called the Cleveland Coordinating Committee to Save *Cod* with the intent of preserving her as a memorial. The plan was to leave her parked on the city's lakefront, accessible to anyone who wanted to see what a real hero of World War II looked like. Veterans' groups agreed and were instrumental in getting her adopted by Clevelanders.

The navy agreed to give the group guardianship of the submarine in January of 1976 under the usual conditions: she must be maintained, made safe for visitors and shipping, and used only to allow the public to appreciate the historic role of the submarine in naval history. The CCC readily agreed.

The *Cod* was officially opened to the public in May 1976 and quickly became a star, major tourist attraction. In 1986 she was designated a National Historic Landmark by the U.S. Department of the Interior.

Today, the *Cod* is considered by many submarine purists to be one of the finest restored submarines on display around the country. Not only does she carry the lowest hull number of any surviving World War II submarine, but she is probably the least-modified. For that reason, visitors must use the same actual vertical hatches and ladders that the crew used during World War II and after. There are no stairways or doors to make it easier for people who come calling, nor has her hull been cut away to give better access, as has been the case with other museum boats. Recently, when the cutaway version of a real torpedo was located and placed in one of the torpedo rooms, it had to be loaded just the way they were taken aboard during the war—through a loading hatch in the deck and down a chute to the torpedo room.

The committee is not content to allow the boat to simply sit there, either. They continue to add to what they have there already. For example, two General Motors diesel engines have recently been obtained, and they will be used for parts to rebuild the *Cod*'s original engines to running condition. Another recent project has also restored the boat's torpedo data computer to its wartime condition.

Also on display near the submarine are a Mark 14 torpedo, like the ones used at the beginning of World War II; a five-bladed, one-ton submarine propeller; and a type 8A submarine search periscope. Visitors are able to get a sub skipper's view of Lake Erie through the scope.

As with several of the other museum boats, the caretakers of the USS *Cod* do not receive any government money. They rely on admissions, donations, gift shop sales, and volunteers to keep the boat in shape and open to the public. And they also appreciate volunteers, including submarine veteran groups, who help maintain the vessel so others can see her the way she was when she was in her finest fighting form, more than sixty years ago.

USS *DRUM* (SS-228)

Courtesy of the U.S. Navy

USS *DRUM* (SS-228)

Class: *Gato*
Launched: May 12, 1941
Named for: a species of fish known for making a distinct drumming noise, primarily the North Atlantic sea bass
Where: Portsmouth Navy Yard, New Hampshire
Sponsor: Mrs. Thomas Holcomb, wife of the commandant of the U.S. Marine Corps
Commissioned: November 1, 1941, just over a month before the attack on Pearl Harbor

Where is she today?

USS *Alabama* Battleship Memorial Park
2703 Battleship Parkway
Mobile, Alabama 36601-0065
(800) GANGWAY/(800-426-4929)
www.ussalabama.com

Claim to fame: The first *Gato*-class submarine built prior to World War II, she completed thirteen war patrols, more than the average for her sister submarines.

S he was a mighty warrior, a new breed of warship, fast, strong, well armed, and perfectly suited for the long-range war patrols she would be called upon to perform in the Pacific. She and the first members of her crew to show up in Portsmouth, New Hampshire, did not necessarily know there would be a war, even though there were already strong suspicions that the United States' entry into the conflict with the Axis powers—Germany, Italy, and Japan—was inevitable. The *Drum* was officially commissioned in November 1941, a mere thirty-seven days before the Japanese attack on Pearl Harbor. The USS *Drum* (SS-228) was the first of the *Gato*-class submarines to slide down the skids at the Portsmouth Naval Shipyard, but she and her sisters, along with the next-generation *Balao* subs that were already on the drawing boards at that time, would prove to make a major difference in the defeat of the Japanese in World War II.

The *Drum* also had something of an all-star commissioning crew. Her new skipper was Robert H. Rice, the son-in-law of Russell Wilson, who was at that time the chief of staff for the Chief of Naval Operations—the big boss. Another one of her officers was Maurice Rindskopf, a young lieutenant just out of Annapolis on the accelerated program. He would go on to serve on eleven war patrols aboard the vessel and become the *Drum*'s commanding officer on her tenth and eleventh war patrols, for which he would receive the Navy Cross and the Silver and Bronze Stars. Rindskopf eventually made rear admiral and became Director of Naval Intelligence.

There was also a young officer named Manning Kimmel aboard the *Drum* during her sea trials and first three war patrols. He would eventually become one of her more tragic figures. Kimmel was born in 1913 to Lieutenant and Mrs. Husband Kimmel. His father was a hard-charging young naval officer, the son of an army major, with an obviously bright military future before him. Even as the senior Kimmel moved up through naval ranks, young Manning decided to follow in his father's footsteps and opted to attend the U.S. Naval Academy in Annapolis, graduating in June 1935. After a stint aboard the battleship *Mississippi* (BB-41), he entered submarine school in Groton, Connecticut, and became an officer aboard the USS *S-38* (SS-143) before heading to Portsmouth to help put the *Drum* into commission.

Manning Kimmel was living his dream, following in his dad's wake, just as he planned. He had two brothers who also chose naval careers. Tom Kimmel commanded four submarines during the war and later skippered a heavy cruiser before retiring from the navy in 1965. The other brother, Ned Kimmel, entered the navy as a reserve ensign and was a lieutenant commander when the war came to a close.

All the time he was learning the ropes as a submarine officer, Manning Kimmel watched with pride—and absorbed the usual ribbing from his shipmates—as his father moved ever higher in the military echelon. In 1937, his dad became a rear admiral and served as head of the Cruiser Division and then as commander of Cruisers Pacific Fleet. Then, in February 1941, just months before his son would help to launch one of the world's most sophisticated new fighting vessels, Admiral Husband Kimmel became the senior admiral in the U.S. Navy as commander in chief of the Pacific Fleet. His headquarters were located in the strategically placed Pearl Harbor Naval Base on Oahu in the Hawaiian Islands. President Roosevelt, in announcing the appointment, praised the new four-star admiral as "one of the greatest naval strategists of our time."

In the early morning hours of Sunday, December 7, 1941, 105 high-level Japanese bombers, 135 dive-bombers, and 81 fighter aircraft attacked the U.S. Fleet as it rested peacefully at Pearl Harbor. The attacking planes came in out of the rising sun, changing the course of world history as they did. Within two hours 18 warships, 188 aircraft, and 2,403 servicemen were lost in the vicious sneak attack.

Back in the States, Manning Kimmel was as shocked at the news as any of his shipmates, but he was happy to learn that his father was unscathed. There was no doubt about war now. The haggling was over. The Japanese had settled it once and for all. His country was about to enter the world war, and there was every indication that he, his crew, and their new submarine would head to the Pacific. He couldn't wait to shake his father's hand when he finally arrived in Pearl Harbor, to let him know that the first of a long line of new warships had arrived to help avenge the losses of that infamous Sunday morning.

But ten days after the attack, Admiral Chester Nimitz was made Commander, Pacific Fleet. Husband Kimmel was relieved of command and was reverted back to a two-star admiral. It was clear that Kimmel, along with his army counterpart, Major General Walter C. Short, were to be made the scapegoats for what happened at Pearl Harbor. The investigations that followed the attack found Kimmel guilty of errors of judgment, and of not coordinating army-navy efforts to defend Hawaii.

In May 1942, Admiral Husband Kimmel, his brilliant naval career most likely done, elected to take early retirement.

Young Lieutenant Manning Kimmel could not believe what he was hearing. He had no idea how the navy he loved so much could be doing this to someone who had served his country so well. Of course, he had no idea of the inner wrangling that was going on in the military in the wake of the surprise attack. Somebody had to take the blame, and it was clearly the two officers closest to the scene. Even today, it is not clear who was actually at fault, but it has become obvious that Kimmel and Short were not totally to blame for what happened. Records have confirmed that there was information available warning of this attack. That information, however, was never provided to either of the two officers, who were subsequently blamed for ignoring it. The United States had decoded Japanese radio message traffic describing the impending attack, yet intelligence at the time still placed the Japanese Fleet, with their aircraft carrier decks covered with aircraft, steaming south from the homeland, not eastward toward Hawaii.

Primarily in response to mountains of research and continual urging from Admiral Kimmel's family (including the grandson of the *Drum*'s Manning Kimmel), Congress passed a resolution in 2000 declaring that Kimmel and Short were not guilty of dereliction of duty at all, that the two officers had performed their duties "competently and professionally." As of this writing, the Defense Department still has not restored the officers' ranks or issued any statement in response to the congressional resolution.

Admiral Husband Kimmel retired from the navy in 1942. He passed away in May 1958. Until he died, Admiral Kimmel maintained that the secret message had deliberately not been delivered to him and Major General Short. Someone in the government was afraid the two might have done something to deflect the attack. And, the speculation continues, if the Pearl Harbor attack had not happened, that might have delayed the entrance of the United States into the world war even longer. There was a strong feeling among many Americans that the United States should have begun the fight against Hitler and Mussolini much earlier. And a declaration of war against Japan—a member of the Tripartite Pact with Germany and Italy—amounted to entry into the war on all fronts. Article Three of that pact reads, "[The three countries] further undertake to assist one another with all political, economic and military means when one of the three contracting powers is attacked by a power at present not involved in the European war or in the Chinese-Japanese conflict." Many still believe those who wanted America involved in the war needed the attack on Pearl Harbor to bring that end about.

Manning Kimmel did not have much opportunity to reflect on what was happening to his dad. Now, with war declared, he and his *Drum* shipmates were busier than ever, getting their boat ready for combat. After training, sea trials, and a series of shakedown cruises and dives, they finally arrived at Pearl Harbor on April Fool's Day 1942, just less than four months after the attack, but Manning's father was no longer in charge there by that time.

The transit through the Atlantic and the Panama Canal had its moments. The *Drum*, along with new sister boats the *Flying Fish* (SS-229) and the *Greenling* (SS-213) were attacked and bombed by friendly aircraft. Luckily there was no damage. Such things happened more often than the navy wanted to admit. Aircraft on patrol for German U-boats would sometimes mistake American subs for enemy boats. At least one submarine, the USS *Dorado* (SS-248), was sunk by friendly fire while making the trip to the Pacific, and that was two years after the *Drum* and her sisters almost met the same disastrous fate.

It is also interesting to note that Manning Kimmel's mother, Admiral Kimmel's wife, was the launching sponsor for the USS *Flying Fish*. That boat's launch had come in July 1941, five months before Pearl Harbor and six months before Mrs. Kimmel's husband's demotion.

There is one more truly tragic note in the Kimmel story. Lieutenant Manning Kimmel served aboard the *Drum* for her first three war patrols. After a short tour of duty with Submarine Squadron Four, which was then based at Pearl Harbor, he returned to the mainland—having been recently promoted to lieutenant commander—to become executive officer on a new construction boat, the USS *Raton* (SS-270). After two war patrols on that submarine, Manning finally got his first command, the USS *Robalo* (SS-273).

It was happily apparent that the fallout from his father's ordeal was having no effect on his son. And the experience he received on the *Drum* and the *Raton* was going to come in handy now that he had his own boat. The *Robalo* was bound for one of the most dangerous parts of the Pacific, and the young officer knew he would need all the smarts he could get—as well as any of the great strategy he may have inherited from his father.

On the *Robalo*'s first patrol under Kimmel (the boat's second war patrol), they attacked several enemy vessels and were credited at the time with sinking one of them. They came under heavy air attack on the way home and had damage to both periscopes, but Kimmel, using the skills he had picked up on his previous boats and relying on the coolheaded-ness of his crew, managed to nurse her safely back to Australia for extensive repairs.

Kimmel and the *Robalo* next departed Fremantle on June 22, 1944, for her third war patrol in the South China Sea. She was scheduled to arrive on station about July 6, but on July 2 a contact report stated the *Robalo* had sighted a trio of interesting targets, a battleship with air cover and two destroyers that were riding along for escort, and they were passing just east of Borneo.

That was Kimmel's last message. When she did not return from patrol, the *Robalo* was reported as "presumed lost with all hands."

It was later learned that the submarine apparently struck a mine as she was maneuvering for an attack on the enemy vessels. She quickly sank. A few of her men were able to get out of the boat and swim ashore. There the Japanese soon captured them, and all of the sailors eventually died in a POW camp. In the end, none of the *Robalo*'s crew survived to the end of the war to tell the full story.

The *Drum* has another interesting footnote to her story. Nowhere in her official history do we see mention of a top secret mission in which she participated before she even began her first official war patrol.

The boat arrived in Pearl Harbor, as noted, on April 1, 1942. Despite the damage inflicted by the Japanese, the naval base there was already back in full service and bustling. The Japanese had made a fatal mistake during the attack. They ignored the ship repair facility at the base, the petroleum storage tanks, and the submarine docks. Instead they concentrated on "Battleship Row." Had the other resources been damaged, it would have been a long time before the sea war could have been waged out of Pearl Harbor. In incredible acts of bravery and skill, several of the battleship crews had managed to get their vessels to a spot where they would not block the harbor. If one of the ships had gone down in the ship channel, that, too, would have put Pearl Harbor out of business for a long time.

Several of the battleships had been repaired and were already back in service by the time the *Drum* arrived. As they approached the sub docks, the men on the bridge of the new arrival could see crews still scurrying to recover as many of the other ships as possible. We were at war—and for the first time in our nation's history, it was in an unrestricted way. On the afternoon following the attack, a stern order came down from the brass back in Washington: for the first time in American history, warships were ordered to fire at any vessels carrying the Japanese flag, be they military or merchant.

Unrestricted warfare was on in the Pacific.

But just before the *Drum* was to pull away for her initial patrol, Captain Rice received urgent orders to stand by, that there was another crucial mission she needed to attempt first. There was great speculation about the nature of their sudden change in orders.

Were they to go stalk one of the aircraft carriers that assisted the December 7 attack? Maybe join a "wolf pack" to attack the Imperial Japanese Navy main fleet? Go mine Tokyo Bay?

No, the *Drum* was deemed a "Transportation and Control" unit, designated to haul "critical stores" to Corregidor, a small island at the entrance to Manila Bay in the Philippines. The Allied forces there were making a last-ditch effort to hold on to the strategic sliver of land in the face of the Japanese invasion of the Philippines.

Lieutenant Manning Kimmel may have been the most disappointed man aboard the boat when he learned their first mission would be little more than delivering cargo. He wanted nothing more than to wreak havoc on Japanese shipping, to help clear the family name. But, as it turned out, that first patrol was to be delayed for a bit. They were to be a cargo vessel for the next few weeks.

The *Drum*'s crew loaded every nook and cranny of the boat with medical supplies and what were later described as "millions of foul-smelling vitamin tablets," and were off to rendezvous with a merchant ship that carried more supplies for the beleaguered island. They only made it as far as Midway. There they learned that Bataan, another crucial island, had fallen and that Corregidor would be given up as well. The *Drum* and her smelly cargo returned to Pearl Harbor, off-loaded the supplies, and quickly got ready for their first "official" war patrol. That began on April 14, 1942.

They sank a seaplane tender, and that turned out to be significant. The tender was the largest vessel sent to the bottom by any means up to that point in the war. Also during May, they torpedoed and sank three cargo ships. Next, on their second patrol, between July and September, they took down a freighter.

As was the case with many of the boats, the *Drum* and her crew were experiencing trouble with the accuracy and dependability of the torpedoes they were firing. They tended to run erratically, and, even if they did hit something solid, the weapons often failed to explode. It would be a year before better torpedoes allowed the submarine fleet to begin to reach its true potential. In the meantime, it was frustrating to expertly maneuver into position, risking life and limb in the process, launch the fish in the direction of the enemy, and then watch them run under or behind the target, or hit it directly amidships and bounce off.

The *Drum* also took part in the hunt for the "Wounded Bear," the massive Japanese carrier *Shokaku*, which had been damaged at the Battle of the Coral Sea. Unfortunately, the navy had overestimated the damage to the carrier and thus underestimated the speed of which she was capable. Rice and his boat arrived on station hours too late to ever have any chance to chase down the highly prized target.

It was on her fourth patrol, now under the command of Captain B. F. McMahon (another *Drum* skipper who eventually made the rank of rear admiral), that the boat bagged what was perhaps her biggest target—and had what was surely her closest call. She was sent to lay mines in the Bungo Suido Strait, the narrow passage that led to Japan's Inland Sea. It was a very heavily traveled pathway for enemy shipping. But on the way, the lookouts and radar operators spotted something else, a particularly tempting prize.

Regardless what the orders might be, any submarine captain was allowed to pause to shoot at a target along the way, totally at his discretion. And Captain McMahon did not have to think twice about this one. There on his radar and through the glass of his periscope was the light aircraft carrier *Ryuho*, along with a couple of escort vessels, and he could clearly see that her decks were crammed full of airplanes—at least twenty light bombers.

The *Ryuho* had begun life as a submarine tender but was converted to a small carrier. While that process was under way, she was damaged, capsized at her mooring at Yokosuka by bombs dropped during the famous Doolittle Raid over the Tokyo area. She had only been back in service for about a month and was now headed to the Inland Sea with her load of planes and pilots, on the way to rendezvous with the fleet. Now the *Drum* had a chance to assure she did not get there.

(The Doolittle Raid in April 1942 was a powerful example of an operation that did relatively little damage—except to the *Ryuho*—but had a tremendous effect on both the enemy and the folks back home. Launched from the carrier USS *Hornet* [CV-8, nicknamed "the Gray Ghost"], Lieutenant Colonel James Doolittle and his B-25 crews were able to penetrate the Home Islands' air defenses and drop bombs on Tokyo. Admiral William "Bull" Halsey, commander of the naval force at the time, described the raid as "one of the most courageous deeds in all military history." They did give a needed boost to Americans back home and those fighting in the Pacific and caused the Japanese to lose face. But most of Doolittle's planes ran out of fuel and had to ditch in and near China. Eight of the crew members ended up in enemy hands, and of those, three were executed and one died of starvation.)

"Man battle stations!" McMahon called out, and every man not already at his duty station was in place immediately, ready to go to work.

"Skipper, you know we are still taking on water, right?" one of his officers quietly reminded him.

McMahon grimaced. It was true.

They had some faulty valves in the forward torpedo room, and the last time he was up there, he saw men wading around ankle-deep in cold seawater. They were still trying to get the leak stopped.

"And you remember that we have mines in two of the forward tubes, right? We only got four torpedoes ready to fire from the bow," someone else mentioned.

"We'll do what we can do," he replied. "Tell the boys in the forward room to tread water if they have to but make sure those four tubes are ready to go."

He and his crew quickly maneuvered their boat to afford them the best shot. Finally, with the carrier in the *Drum*'s crosshairs, the skipper gave the command to launch torpedoes from the rather damp forward room. Through his periscope, McMahon watched the target sailing blissfully along toward the protection of the Inland Sea. A sailor standing nearby counted out loud the elapsed seconds since the first torpedo was unleashed.

Those who stood near the captain plainly saw the two flashes of light from the eyepiece of the scope, even before their skipper announced the obvious.

"One hit! Two hits!"

The roar of the concussion arrived at about the same time, echoing the excited report. Two hits!

"She's listing," McMahon reported. "I can see her flight deck completely. The whole flight deck! Let's swing around and hit her from the stern tubes and finish her off with the—"

There was an ominous pause then as the captain turned the scope a bit to the right. He grunted.

"Uh-oh. It looks like we got company. Splashes, too. They're shooting at us! Take her down . . . two hundred feet, bearing one hundred and eighty degrees, eight knots."

He quickly lowered the scope so the increased underwater speed would not do any damage to the instrument. Besides, there would shortly be little to see.

It was a destroyer, steaming their way at full speed.

But as the *Drum* turned and headed deeper, every man on board could feel the steep angle of descent grow even more pronounced on the decks beneath their feet. Dangerously more pronounced. Every man aboard knew at once that something was seriously wrong.

She was going down much too quickly, out of control. That could be fatal. If the water was deep enough, and they were unable to control the dive, the enormous pressure of the sea would crush the submarine like an egg in a fist.

Or, if the water were relatively shallow, they would hit bottom at a deep angle. If they weren't mortally damaged by the impact, they could possibly sink so deep in the mud that they could never back out of the muck. That would lead to a long, slow death none of them cared to ponder.

"Planesmen, get her under control!" McMahon ordered.

"Captain, the port shaft has stopped turning," the diving officer reported, then swallowed hard. "We don't have but one screw!"

The delicate dance was under way but they were trying to do the waltz on one leg. They needed the power of both screws turning to help control the dive and one of them was not working. The electric motor on that side had failed for some reason. They would have to regain control with the diving planes—the winglike devices that helped determine the angle of the dive or surfacing maneuver—and the right mix of air and water in the ballast tanks.

It was a tough situation. Still, every man did what he was trained to do, watching gauges, turning valves, manning the planes as they tried to "fly" the submarine like an airplane traveling in a particularly cloying atmosphere. And they had to do it with the boat nose-down at a sharp angle, objects sliding and tumbling past them, and gauges spinning dizzyingly all around them.

Slowly, using the planes, the remaining screw, and the constantly changing balance of air and water in the ballast tanks, they stopped the plunge to the sea bottom. But before they could take a breath, the first boom of a nearby depth charge rattled their fillings and popped glass on some of the gauges. In all, two separate waves of vicious depth charging kept them down for several hours.

When they were finally able to surface, they could only stay up for a few minutes before a plane forced them to duck for the cover of the ocean again. Even as the air in the boat grew more and more stale and hard to breathe, as the battery power flagged and the lights grew dimmer, damage crews were working, trying to stop the leaks in the forward compartment, get the other propeller shaft back online, and fix what they could of the damage from the depth charges. But even in those conditions, they were able to patch their boat back together. Eventually they surfaced and could once again breathe in sweet, fresh air.

Their target, the *Ryuho*, was not sunk, but the damage the *Drum* had inflicted on her forced the aircraft carrier to return to Yokosuka for more repairs, taking her out of the game for several months.

The *Drum* continued on with her mining mission and even made two more attacks during the patrol. Captain McMahon's aggressive attack on the *Ryuho* earned him a Silver Star and a strong reputation among sub skippers.

In all, the USS *Drum* accomplished thirteen war patrols. She received twelve battle stars, and was credited officially with sinking fifteen ships, a total of almost eighty-one thousand tons of enemy vessels.

That put the 228 boat in an elite group among World War II submarines—number eight among all of them in total Japanese tonnage sunk.

* * *

Unlike many of her sisters, who ended up being scrapped or used for target practice, the *Drum* would live to continue serving her country. Her Cold War years were spent in a relatively benign part of the world, along the East Coast of the United States.

She was first decommissioned in February of 1946, shortly after she was no longer needed to fight a war. A year later, she was back in service as a Naval Reserve training vessel in Washington, D.C. After she was replaced by another boat in 1967, she was moved to the inactive fleet in Norfolk, Virginia.

Finally, in April of 1969, she was donated to a group in Mobile, Alabama, which had already secured the battleship USS *Alabama* (BB-60) and opened her to the public for tours. They wanted a submarine to complement the battleship and other military displays they had collected on Mobile Bay, near Interstate 10. The *Drum* was towed to Mobile in May 1969 and opened to the public less than two months later, on Independence Day.

The submarine was originally floating in Mobile Bay to the port side of the battleship, but it was determined that the vessel could best be preserved if she was taken from the salt water of the bay and placed on heavy cement supports on dry land. A small canal was dug and she was eventually floated onto the supports, then the water was drained away.

Though her weaponry varied during the war, she now carries one five-inch .25-caliber gun, one 40-millimeter and one 20-millimeter gun.

It is noteworthy that the *Drum* is one of the few museum boats that allow visitors to enter the conning tower. That means people can stand in the very spot where Captain Rice launched the attack on the seaplane tender, and where Captain McMahon ordered the daring attack on the enemy aircraft carrier.

Well, not exactly the same spot.

The truth is, this is not the same conning tower with which the *Drum* was originally birthed and carried for her first seven war patrols. On her eighth run, in late 1943, she came under such an intense depth-charge attack that she had to return to the United States and have her conning tower replaced with a new one. The one you stand inside aboard the boat today only experienced five war patrols!

Today, in addition to the sub and battleship, the park also maintains a hangar filled with military aircraft.

The park did sustain considerable damage from Hurricane Katrina in August 2005. The battleship—on which a number of park employees and their families rode out the deadly storm—was left listing at an obvious angle, the gift shop and ticket area were heavily damaged, and the aircraft pavilion and many of the planes inside were also seriously damaged.

And the submarine? The *Drum*, which took all that pounding in the Pacific and bounced back to fight some more, was not harmed in the least during the vicious hurricane.

The park was reopened to the public in January 2006.

USS *SILVERSIDES* (SS-236)

Courtesy of the U.S. Navy

USS *SILVERSIDES* (SS-236)

Class: *Gato*
Launched: August 26, 1941
Named for: a small fish marked with a silvery stripe down
   its sides
Where: Mare Island Navy Yard, Vallejo, California
Sponsor: Mrs. Elizabeth H. Hogan
Commissioned: December 15, 1941, eight days after the at-
   tack on Pearl Harbor

Where is she today?
   Great Lakes Naval Memorial and Museum
   1346 Bluff Street
   Muskegon, Michigan 49441
   (231) 755-1230
   www.silversides.org

Claim to fame: Nicknamed "the Lucky Boat" because of her
   amazing record of survival, she was also one of the most
   successful submarines of the war. She was the scene of
   what was undoubtedly the most publicized medical procedure of the war.

S he was a West Coast boat, born within sight of San Francisco, named for a flashy little fish with a fashionable racing stripe down its sides. But she had a catchy nickname, one that fit her well.

The moniker "the Lucky Boat" did not come easily. The USS *Silversides* (SS-236) earned it the hard way—by surviving a long series of close calls while building the war's third-best record among all submarines for enemy vessels destroyed, then by sticking around so we could all stop by and take a look at her. The first two subs on the elite list are no longer around for us to see.

One's life ended tragically early. The USS *Tang* (SS-306) was sunk by one of her own malfunctioning torpedoes in October 1944. Miraculously, nine men survived the freak event. Enemy vessels subsequently picked them up. As prisoners of war, they were brutally tortured, often by survivors of ships they had previously sunk, but they made it through the war. Though those men were lucky to have survived, their boat and the rest of her brave crew did not.

The number-two boat in number of vessels sunk was the USS *Tautog* (SS-199). Though she survived the war and served as a training vessel until 1959, she was eventually scrapped.

That leaves the *Silversides* as the most successful surviving submarine of World War II. And, on many counts, she's lucky to still be around.

Her commissioning skipper, Lieutenant Commander Creed Burlingame from Louisville, Kentucky, was a classmate of Bob Rice, the first skipper of the USS *Drum*. Young Mr. Burlingame quickly gained a reputation as a swashbuckling, devil-may-care submarine commander, a captain who preferred cruising on the surface as much as he could manage, driving right into the middle of trouble before blasting away and wreaking havoc all around him and his boat. Central Casting could not have devised a more flashy, daring character than Creed Burlingame.

The first executive officer (second in command) on the *Silversides* was Burlingame's polar opposite, though. Roy Davenport was a teetotaler, which put him in a distinct minority among submariners. He was also a devout Christian Scientist. That made him the constant butt of jokes from his captain, but everyone aboard agreed the juxtaposition at the top of their boat's command structure made them a good team.

On her first patrol, Burlingame took them almost all the way to the Japanese Home Islands on the surface, cruising along at top speed as if they had cargo overdue in Tokyo, before running into the last blustery remnants of a typhoon. That's when the lookouts and radar spied a Japanese trawler.

If the new crew of the *Silversides* had any doubts about the aggressiveness of their skipper, they immediately faded. With a quick, decisive order to man battle stations, Burlingame launched a surface attack, using their deck guns. A trawler would have been hard to hit with torpedoes while submerged. The surface attack was their best strategy, even if it was daring and even more dangerous than submerging. Still, it was an enemy warship and they had been sent out here to sink anything that carried the rising sun flag.

And that is precisely what they did. They managed to quickly send the IJN vessel down in smoke and flames for their off-the-showroom-floor vessel's first confirmed kill. But the win came with a heavy price.

During the skirmish, a young enlisted man named Michael Harbin, who was manning one of the deck guns, was struck by returned gunfire. The sailor died instantly. He was the first submariner in the war to be killed in submarine gun action.

Three days later, Burlingame and his lookouts in the shears spotted a Japanese submarine on the surface. In one of the forward torpedo tubes rested a torpedo with the name "Michael Harbin" scribbled in chalk on its side. That's the fish the skipper ordered launched in the direction of the enemy sub.

Captain Burlingame reported an explosion and claimed a kill, but postwar records failed to confirm the loss of an enemy submarine. The Japanese documentation had no submarine listed at that place and time, though the captain and his crew clearly saw it and watched it disintegrate.

Confirmed kill or not, they had exacted a small amount of revenge for Torpedoman Third Class Mike Harbin.

A few weeks later, the *Silversides* was patrolling off the coast of Japan when she encountered a small convoy of enemy vessels working their way precariously through a large number of sampans, fishermen laying out nets. That was a typical strategy for the Japanese navy, assuming American warships and aircraft would be hesitant to attack when innocent fishermen might be hurt in the cross fire.

They underestimated Creed Burlingame.

He immediately ordered his maneuvering room to proceed at top speed, to do the best they could to miss the small fishing boats, but not to worry if they shoved any of them aside to get to the fat, juicy targets that hid among them. Then, as they lined up for an attack, the skipper took them down so they could draw close enough to get some of the enemy ships within range. The crew prepared to launch torpedoes at one particular freighter the captain decided would be the first to meet its demise.

As they arrived at about sixty feet deep, Burlingame lowered the periscope from its enclosure, snapped down the handles, turned in the direction of the enemy vessel, and took a long look.

"What the . . . ?" he asked no one in particular, the surprise evident in his voice.

"What is it, Captain?"

"It looks like . . . well . . . we have a Japanese flag tied to our periscope!"

"Sir?"

It was true. A small rising sun was somehow tied to their shears, riding along with them as they prepared to attack.

Only then did Burlingame realize that they had gotten entangled in a fishing net. A small glass ball attached to a bamboo pole had buoyed the net. And atop that pole was a Japanese flag.

The captain swung the periscope around and it seemed to be moving freely, not bound by the netting. The flag was not blocking his view either. There was no report of any mechanical problems with the boat. The screws were turning. The dive planes functioned smoothly.

Fishing net or not, the attack was still on.

Their first torpedo hit the freighter amidships and there was a massive, reverberating explosion. Flames and smoke seemed to fill Burlingame's field of vision. More of their torpedoes damaged another freighter and a tanker before a destroyer appeared in the scope sights and headed their way. That new arrival chased them deep, raining down over a dozen depth charges.

Thankfully, the fishing net tangled all around her sail did not inhibit the boat's external systems. She was able to dive to avoid the attack.

After a while, the *Silversides* surfaced, then took a long look around to make sure there were no other warships or enemy airplanes about. Then they emerged on deck to cut away the nets and the enemy flag.

After modest success on her second and third war patrols, the *Silversides* pulled out on her fourth run from Brisbane, on Australia's eastern coast, in mid-December 1942. Her crew had long since adopted their skipper's rather raffish demeanor. As they powered away from the wharf, each man on deck wore nonregulation Aussie "digger" hats. Even their sober XO, Roy Davenport, got into the mood, playing an off-key version of "Waltzing Matilda" on the dented old trombone he always carried with him.

Such a bizarre beginning foretold one of the most storied events in submarine lore. It was appropriate that it occurred on "the Lucky Boat."

About a week into the fourth patrol and after they were well at sea, far from the nearest sizable point of land or civilization, Pharmacist's Mate Tom Moore went to the captain to report a rather serious development. One of the enlisted men was complaining of a serious stomachache.

"You don't guess he's still feeling the effects of Brisbane, do you?" the skipper asked. He knew the answer already. And though they were rolling a bit on moderate seas, he suspected this was not a case of seasickness either.

"No, sir. I've never seen a hangover last a week. And besides, he's running a fever and his belly is hard as a hatch cover."

"Appendicitis?"

"Yes, sir. I'd bet on it."

Burlingame scratched his chin and pondered the options.

"We're a hell of a long way from an operating room, Doc." Pharmacist's mates were typically called Doc, even though they certainly were not doctors. "Do what you can. We'll take the boat down to keep her steady while you do whatever you have to."

Moore was twenty-two years old and trained to treat blisters, bad colds, carbuncles, and typical, minor shipboard wounds. He had no surgical instruments aboard and no serious anesthesia. His surgical experience consisted of stitching up some gashes from bar fights ashore and the usual lesions caused by bumped heads aboard the submarine. He was still the best they had. Nobody else on board who might be willing to assist in an operation had anywhere near that much medical background.

"I will, sir."

The afflicted sailor, George Platter, was in an even worse condition when Moore got back to him. He was wracked with fever, tossing on his bunk. If the appendix ruptured, the sailor would surely die.

The pharmacist's mate quickly corralled some volunteers, procured some eating utensils from the enlisted men's mess, and went to work. They laid the sailor out on the table in the crew's mess. Others gathered up all the lights they could manage and trained them on the makeshift operating table.

The medicinal whiskey every submarine carried was used as anesthesia. There, in a submerged submarine at sea, Tom Moore removed George Platter's gangrenous appendix. All the while, Roy Davenport said prayers and the crew tried to keep the boat as stable as they could manage.

The operation was a success. Platter would survive.

Not until later would the crew learn that this had actually been the third time an appendectomy was performed aboard a submarine. This particular one would catch the attention of the nation, though. The story appeared in major newspapers and would eventually be reenacted in the movie *Destination Tokyo* and featured in an episode of *The Silent Service* television series. It was a great morale builder, both for those fighting the war and for the folks back home. It made a great conversation starter for the crew on the next liberty, too!

As soon as he could, the captain brought the *Silversides* to the surface for fresh air and a battery charge. But almost immediately, the lookouts spotted what they thought to be a Japanese submarine. The boat was sent to battle stations and two torpedoes were launched from the stern tubes. With the fish away, Burlingame hurriedly took the boat back down, out of sight.

Suddenly, the sub was shaken hard by a thunderous explosion and the entire ship bucked as if shaken by some mighty hand. Apparently, one of their own torpedoes detonated only a short distance from the launch tube, maybe as a result of the disturbance of the *Silversides'* own wake. Whatever caused it, the detonation rocked them hard, knocking sailors to the deck and dislodging objects from their resting places. Leaks sprung up and down the length of the sub. Damage teams quickly determined that there were apparently no major problems.

"This [explosion] blew the stern out of the water and us out of our wits," Burlingame would later dryly recount in the patrol report.

To make matters worse, the target turned out to not be a sub at all. It was an angry destroyer, hungry to bag the American submarine that had almost blown herself up. The warship circled overhead for hours, dropping depth charges, watching for an oil slick or debris that would indicate they had done their job. The haggard crew of the *Silversides* remained under far longer than was comfortable.

Finally, at about dawn, it grew quiet on the surface above them. There were no more signs of the irritated destroyer. The captain decided he had to poke his head up and confirm whether their tormentor was gone at last.

But as soon as they came to periscope depth and he poked the scope above the surface, another terrible explosion threw the boat violently sideways, followed almost immediately by two more blasts that were, if anything, even more vicious. Up and down the length of the *Silversides*, men who were lying down to conserve air were thrown from their bunks. That included George Platter, still under the influence of Tom Moore's makeshift anesthesia. Lightbulbs shattered, pipes ruptured, and gauge covers spidered from the intensity of the concussion.

"In a year of being depth charged, we had never had one so close," the skipper would later write. "I thought the conning tower was being wrenched loose. . . ."

"Dive! Dive!" Burlingame shouted, and he felt the boat immediately assume a sharp downward angle beneath his feet.

Much too sharp, the skipper noted.

The bow planes were frozen, likely damaged from the sudden attack, and the *Silversides* plummeted dangerously, heading much too fast toward the distant, cold bottom of the sea.

Before they knew it, they were quickly past test depth, about as deep as they could safely go, yet they were still hurtling toward what submariners term "crush depth." That's the point where the weight of water can squash the thick steel hull of a vessel—even one as well designed and built as the *Silversides*—as if it were made of balsa wood.

Somehow the crew members were able to fight the dive and pull her out, balancing the water and compressed air in her ballast tanks and wrestling with the balky dive planes. But they were too deep for the gauges to accurately measure. The hull that protected them from the pressure of the seawater groaned and creaked as if in agony.

They would all have been gulping in air, taking a deep breath, but there was not enough left in the submarine to do that. As they worked, they sucked in as much of the fetid oxygen as they could, but it was barely enough.

Slowly, being careful not to make a sudden move and send the boat back into another uncontrolled dive, they eased upward—but not too far upward and certainly not too fast. The destroyer they had made mad was still up there, still dropping the occasional load of TNT onto their heads. If they weren't careful, they could overcompensate during their ascent and send the boat suddenly bobbing to the surface like a fishing cork, popping up right there in plain sight of their dogged tormentors.

It was no consolation when the captain shared with his officers that the big blasts that had sent them deep had most likely not been depth charges at all, but bombs, dropped from an airplane. Burlingame told them he had glimpsed the aircraft through the periscope just before its pilot tried to send them all to Davy Jones's locker.

No matter the cause, they had emergency repairs to complete to get the boat ready to surface. When the coast appeared to finally be clear, Burlingame tentatively brought his boat to the top.

The ocean and the sky above them appeared to be empty.

"Anybody have a headache?" the captain asked those around him in the conning tower. They looked back at him, confused. "Headaches? From all that thunder? Seems like we might need some medicinal whiskey if we are experiencing any pain. Right?"

"Yes, sir!" they all agreed, many of them vigorously rubbing their temples.

"Then break it out. Oh, and Merry Christmas!"

Sure enough, Christmas Day had crept up on them while they were doing emergency surgery, dodging explosions, and nearly losing their boat to the clutching fist of the Pacific Ocean.

In his patrol report, Creed Burlingame wrote, "We added [the whiskey] to our powdered eggs and canned milk. With a lot of imagination it tasted almost like eggnog."

Oh, and George Platter made a complete recovery from his emergency surgery. The young sailor was standing regular watch duty aboard "the Lucky Boat" only six days later.

The *Silversides* successfully completed fourteen war patrols and, in the process, sank twenty-three ships. She was awarded the Presidential Unit Citation, the highest award for a navy ship, for each of four patrols, and received twelve combat insignia battle stars for successful war patrols.

She completed a "hat trick," sinking three ships in a single engagement, on four different occasions.

Creed Burlingame was on the bridge for five of her war runs, John S. Coye for six, and John C. Nichols for the final three. Along the way, she not only racked up amazing devastation against the enemy but also survived numerous depth charges, dive-bombings, and even a "hot run" in her own torpedo tube.

A hot run was when a torpedo became lodged in the tube and failed to swim away toward the target as it was supposed to do. The weapon is not supposed to be armed until it is out of the tube, but there is no way for the torpedomen to be sure of that. In some cases, captains had to slam the door closed against the torpedo's nose, trying to drive it back inside the tube, so it could be pressurized again and either refired or removed from the tube.

In the case of the *Silversides*, the captain simply ordered it fired again as he sent the boat "emergency back." He wanted to get away from the device as quickly as possible if they could ever get the thing launched.

It worked. The torpedo was flushed from its tube with no damage to its mother ship. Only to the nerves of her crew.

Creed Burlingame is still recognized as one of the real characters of World War II. His bravado and good humor—not to mention his exploits while on liberty—made him a favorite with his crew members. And, of course, his success against the enemy earned him the respect of his superiors. Much to the chagrin of his straight-and-narrow executive officer, Roy Davenport, Burlingame kept a small Buddha statue that his crew members had given him close at hand as he peered through the periscope. He always rubbed the statue's belly before launching an attack. He said it was for good luck. Most of the crew figured he did it just to gig his XO.

Davenport did not let his skipper bother him. He went on to command two submarines of his own, taking them on a total of six very successful war patrols. He earned five Navy Crosses for those runs, more than any other submarine skipper in the war. Except for those who were awarded the Congressional Medal of Honor, Davenport became the most decorated submariner of World War II.

After his final patrol, Davenport asked to be assigned to shore duty. He was sent back to Annapolis to teach marine engineering.

After the war, the *Silversides* became a training vessel for naval reservists, based on Lake Michigan at Chicago. When her duty there was done, she was struck from the Naval Vessel Register in June of 1969. She had someone waiting to adopt her. The chamber of commerce of South Chicago applied for custody of the boat and docked her at the Navy Pier. There she served as a memorial to veterans and, hopefully, a tourist attraction.

In 1973, the *Silversides* was moved across Lake Michigan to become part of what is now the Great Lakes Naval Memorial and Museum at Muskegon, Michigan. Also at the memorial is the Coast Guard cutter USCGC *McLane* (WSC-146), which has been berthed near the submarine since 1993. She is still undergoing restoration. That vessel's service included chasing down bootleggers on the Great Lakes during the Prohibition era and patrolling the frigid Bering Sea during World War II.

The *Silversides* has been designated a National Historic Landmark.

For years, volunteers cared for the vessel from the waterline up, but now nature has taken her toll. In the past few years, it was determined that she needed her bottom sandblasted and repainted with a protective coating, and that operation would require that she be moved to a dry dock, more than fifty years since the last time she was in a dry dock for maintenance. In 2004 the museum and two different submarine veterans' groups formed a "Save the *Silversides*" fund to raise money to take care of the maintenance that the historic vessel required.

Visitors should be sure to look for the bronze plaque on the *Silversides'* deck, a memorial in remembrance of Torpedoman Third Class Michael Harbin, the young sailor killed on the boat's first patrol.

As with many of the museum boats around the country, the *Silversides* and the Great Lakes Naval Memorial and Museum always welcome volunteers. They may contact the museum by phone or via the link on the Internet site.

USS *CAVALLA* (SS-244)

Courtesy of the U.S. Navy

USS *CAVALLA* (SS-244)

Class: *Gato*, one of seventy-three boats in that class that
   were constructed
Launched: November 14, 1943
Named for: a saltwater fish of the pompano family
Where: Electric Boat Company, Groton, Connecticut
Sponsor: Mrs. Merrill Comstock, the wife of U.S. Navy Rear
   Admiral Merrill Comstock
Commissioned: February 29, 1944

Where is she today?
   Seawolf Park
   Pelican Island
   Galveston, Texas 77552
   (409) 770-3196
   www.cavalla.org

Claim to fame: She sank the *Shokaku*, one of the Japanese
   aircraft carriers that participated in the attack on Pearl
   Harbor and one of the most coveted targets of World
   War II, not only for revenge but for tactical reasons.

The submarine USS *Cavalla* (SS-244) was another boat that tried to lay claim to the title "Luckiest Ship in the Submarine Service." Her record certainly justified the nickname. So did her "birthday."

When her commissioning crew realized she was scheduled to be commissioned in the middle of March 1944, they formed a committee and went to her new skipper with an idea. Lieutenant Commander Herman J. Kossler liked the plan but doubted very seriously that the navy brass would go along with it.

What the crew members wanted to do was move the commissioning date up to February 29, leap day. They felt strongly that sending the new boat out on that particular day would give her good luck. And where she was going, luck was a much-needed commodity, no matter where it came from. Kossler dutifully sent the request along to his superiors, openly stating his reasoning in the paperwork: "My crew thinks it would mean good luck for the boat, and so do I."

To everyone's surprise, the navy went along with the date change, for no better reason than the chance it might bring good fortune. And that is how she became a "leap year ship."

Whether or not luck had anything to do with it, the *Cavalla* immediately had an impact against the enemy when she relayed vital information about a Japanese task force on the move toward a key showdown with the Allies. And her rookie skipper did a good enough job that he remained at the helm of his first command for all six of her war patrols. Although she had close escapes and was damaged severely several times by Japanese attacks, she still survived to be present for a momentous event in world history. The *Cavalla* was among the armada that sailed into Tokyo Bay on August 31, 1945, and she was berthed there not far from the battleship USS *Missouri* (BB-63) for the Japanese surrender ceremony on September 2.

Maybe it was luck that placed the *Cavalla* near the San Bernardino Strait not far from the Philippines in June of 1944, but it required skill and determination to accomplish what Captain Kossler and his crew did on that trip. On her maiden run, she ran headlong into a submerged whale. For a while, the skipper was afraid damage had been done to his new vessel, but everything seemed okay. Not so for the whale. That animal broached in a pool of blood, quite dead. The *Cavalla* was ordered to proceed to a rendezvous point to relieve another submarine, the *Flying Fish* (SS-229). Before she could get on station, though, the *Cavalla* received an abrupt change of orders, a course correction that would make history for the new submarine.

The *Flying Fish* reported some big news back to Pearl Harbor. The Japanese attack force was out of harbor, on the move from Tawi-Tawi between the Philippines and Malaysia, crossing the Celebes Sea and possibly heading toward the Mariana Islands. If so, that meant they were on the way to try to repel "Operation Forager," the American offensive that was already taking place there. It was expected that the enemy would attack the Allied Fleet with its deadly dive-bombers once they got close enough to send off the aircraft. The truth was, the Japanese had decided to launch a devastating attack, called Plan A-Go, and destroy the American Pacific Fleet in one glorious blow.

Admiral Charles Lockwood had a plan, though, and "the Lucky Boat" was a major part of it. He wanted the *Cavalla* to stop and lie in wait for the enemy fleet to come her way. They were not necessarily there to attack but to observe, to report on exactly how big the enemy contingent was, what its components were, and how fast and which way it was headed.

If the enemy could surprise the American fleet it might, indeed, be the turning point in the war that the Japanese so desperately needed. But if the Allies only knew what was coming and when, they could prepare for it.

It was about eleven p.m. when the *Cavalla*'s radar operator let out a gasp and breathlessly reported what he saw on his tiny scope.

"Convoy, bearing two-nine-zero. Looks like a couple of tankers and three escorts."

Captain Kossler grinned. This was not the main component of the IJN fleet, but it still looked like a bunch of promising targets were about to parade right past them. They were almost certainly the forerunners of the big group of warships, sprinting ahead with precious petroleum to fuel the ships and aircraft that would try to knock out the Allies.

Kossler hastily maneuvered on the surface for an attack, making an "end-around" run to get ahead of the ships, bathing the enemy vessels with his radar to keep them within range. But just as he was ready to dive and prepare to shoot, one of the escort destroyers peeled off and headed directly for the *Cavalla*. Either the submarine had been spotted on the surface already or it would be as soon as the destroyer got close enough.

Kossler lost his grin.

"Take her deep. He's probably seen us or detected our radar. Either way, he knows we're here now."

It was almost two hours later before they could surface with any reasonable safety and see if the convoy was still up there. It wasn't. The sea was empty.

All Captain Kossler could do now was report what he had seen to Honolulu, then stand by, as originally ordered, to wait for the rest of the enemy fleet to possibly come his way. Losing such a group of delicious targets had Kossler and his crew deeply depressed.

Here they were, just out on their initial run with a chance to send three tankers loaded with precious fuel to the bottom and deal a big blow to whatever the IJN fleet's plans were. But all they had been able to do was turn tail and hide from the sharp-eyed destroyer. There was little chance of doing any damage at all while they stayed deep and waited for the targets to steam away.

But back at headquarters, Admiral Charles Lockwood had another thought for Kossler and the *Cavalla*.

When they were finally able to surface, the sub's radio operator copied the cryptic message from the big boss and sent it up to the skipper.

"Destruction those tankers important. Trail. Attack. Report."

Lockwood, though a man of few words, suspected the loss of the fuel in those ships could do a lot to disrupt the Japanese attack, wherever it might be planned to take place. Airplanes and ships had to have fuel. Without it, they were nothing more than ballast.

Spirits rose quickly aboard the submarine when the word inevitably spread up and down her 310-foot length. They were going to do more than simply sit there and bob peacefully, waiting on enemy ships that might never show up. They were going to try to go after them. Still, the chase was rough going. Every time they began making progress, enemy aircraft forced them to dive for cover. When submerged, they could only make less than half the speed they could reach while running on the surface.

Finally Kossler received orders to simply trail the convoy as best he could and continue to report its direction and progress. That was still valuable information since it appeared the enemy ships were headed directly for where the American fleet was positioned. There was little speculation about the destination or purpose of the Japanese now.

But then, about ten o'clock that evening, the radar operator once again sang out some good news.

"Captain, I got targets all over the scope!"

Kossler came down the ladder from the bridge in one leap. He looked over the youngster's shoulder. Sure enough, there were blips galore, of varying sizes, pocking the screen.

The night was dark, so the *Cavalla* stayed on the surface, all the better to keep the returns on the radarscope. Now, what to do?

His orders were to tag along and report information on the main fleet. But Kossler and his crew knew they could easily line up for a shot, and with all those potential targets out there, it would be hard to miss something. The convoy did not seem to be in any particular hurry, and most of the vessels were steaming in a straight line, not taking the usual zigzag evasion course to avoid attack by submarines.

The *Cavalla* was still undetected.

"We put our stern to the Japanese fleet and ran with them for about an hour," the skipper later wrote in his patrol report. "They slowly caught up with us. When the fleet was comparatively close to us, we dove and let them pass over us."

As the *Cavalla* hovered there, a safe distance below the surface, the massive enemy fleet rumbling along overhead, they carefully counted each vessel, made the best estimate of its size, and made an educated guess about the type ship it was. A well-trained, sharp-eared sonar operator was able to discern a remarkable amount of detail about a ship simply by the distinctive sounds of its engines, its screws, and other telltale bits of sonic information.

Over two hours after ducking beneath the oncoming fleet, the *Cavalla* finally surfaced and relayed to headquarters by radio the information it had gained from sonar and radar. There was no doubt now. The Japanese had sent out its massive fleet for far more than a nice, leisurely cruise. They obviously had their eyes on the main American battle group, Task Force 58, and they were headed that way to do as much damage as they could manage.

But once again the excited crew of the *Cavalla* was disappointed. In following orders, they had lain in the weeds and watched without firing a shot as a long, long line of perfect targets steamed right on past them. They were beginning to seriously doubt their supposed good luck.

Of course, there was no way for them to know at the time that the information they had already provided would allow Task Force 58 to anticipate the coming attack. Or know that the specific details they had provided would enable the Americans to win one of the most decisive and crucial victories of the war. Although the official name of the sea engagement would be the Battle of the Philippine Sea, it would also come to be called the Marianas Turkey Shoot.

Thanks to the data from the *Cavalla* and her sister submarines, the final destruction of the American fleet did not occur. Instead it was the Allied forces that claimed the stunning victory.

By the morning following their tedious observation of the Japanese fleet on the move, all the submarines in the area received new orders that lifted the spirits of their crews considerably. They were no longer required to hang around, be quiet, and observe. They were now free to do what they did best—hunt and shoot at any enemy vessel they could find.

It was not long before the *Cavalla* ran right smack into something at which they could definitely shoot. Again it was the radar operator who saw the blips appear on his green-tinted scope, even before the sharp-eyed lookouts in the shears above the bridge saw them. And once again, they indicated big targets. Very big.

Captain Kossler quickly ordered the boat down to periscope depth so they would remain unobserved if possible. When he raised the scope above the surface of the ocean, he couldn't believe what he saw.

It was the masts of what was obviously a very large ship, and aircraft buzzed about the vessel like bees around a hive.

He raised the scope again a few minutes later, after they had crept closer still. What he saw would not fit within his viewer.

"The picture was too good to be true," he later wrote in his report. "It was a large carrier and two cruisers ahead on the port bow and a destroyer about a thousand yards on the port beam."

He and his officers quickly consulted their identification manual and compared what they were looking at to the images of known enemy warships that were pictured in the book. There was no doubt. It was a

Shokaku-class aircraft carrier and she seemed too busy at the moment recovering aircraft to pay them any attention. The cruisers were far enough out of the way to not cause them any trouble for the time being, too. But the destroyer, should it determine the *Cavalla* was there, would definitely be able to bestow upon them some kind of headache.

"Boys, I think we say to hell with the destroyer," Kossler told those men working beside him in the cramped conning tower. "Let's get ourselves a carrier and let the chips fall where they may."

There was no hesitation, only smiles and a few excited whoops up and down the length of the boat. After missing out on shooting at the tankers and allowing a whole fleet of sitting-duck targets to steam right over their heads, they were itching to launch some torpedoes at something that flew the enemy flag.

Kossler took one more look through the periscope to make sure he was seeing what he thought he was seeing. They were only twelve hundred yards away, less than a mile. It was a carrier, all right.

There was no mistaking the rising-sun flag on her masts, or the insignia on the tails of the planes on her deck, either. The captain allowed his executive officer and the gunnery officer to take peeks, too. It was rare to get such a perfect setup against such a desirable target.

Now within a thousand yards of the carrier, with the destroyer looming menacingly, and Ensign Zeke Zellmer calmly calling out the coordinates from the ring around the attack periscope's base, Kossler calmly shouted out the command to fire at will the first four torpedoes.

He hastily swung the scope around to peer at where the destroyer was by then. It still had not seemed to notice them, but that would change quickly. The trails of the torpedoes would lead right back to their periscope. If they hit their point-blank target, this whole part of the ocean would know a sub was in the neighborhood.

In the same breath, the commander gave the order to fire two more fish and then to immediately take the submarine down and deep. At the same time, they would drive away from that spot on the Philippine Sea as quickly as the batteries and the electric motors would take them.

As they fled, they heard what sounded like three of their torpedoes exploding as they struck the big carrier. But only moments later, the explosions they heard were much closer, and obviously aimed at them. About half of them were close enough to shake the boat violently. Seemingly close enough to buckle the decks and crack the pressure hull.

But it was not only their nerves that got rattled. The depth charges soon put their sound gear and hull ventilation out of commission. They were now virtually deaf, and it would be very hot and uncomfortable in the interior of the submarine until they could repair the damage or get to the surface to ventilate.

Then, over two hours after the attack, and after the destroyer had apparently decided to leave them alone, the men inside the *Cavalla* heard four numbing explosions in the direction of where the carrier had been hit. They had been listening to sounds of minor blasts and the undeniable noise of creaking metal, crushed by water pressure, ever since the torpedoes hit their big target. The groaning and creaking of a massive vessel sounding its death knell soon followed this latest quartet of detonations. That was a racket all submariners longed for after launching their fish. Water rushing into breached compartments, its awful pressure literally bending beams, renting steel plates, breaking the vessel apart as it pulled the ship down toward the distant bottom of the sea.

As soon as he safely could, Kossler brought the *Cavalla* to the surface and radioed the message back to Honolulu:

"Hit *Shokaku*-class carrier with three out of six torpedoes. Received 105 depth charges during three-hour period. Heard four terrific explosions in the direction of target two and one half hours after attack. Believe that baby sank!"

That last line became a running gag around the Pacific sub command, but nobody was happier to hear the news than Admiral Charles Lockwood and the rest of the headquarters crew. Based on intelligence reports, they strongly suspected the vessel that the *Cavalla* had sent to the bottom was not just a *Shokaku*-class aircraft carrier but the *Shokaku* herself!

The big carrier had been the vengeful target of numerous Allied ships during the war already. Reviled for her role in the attack on Pearl Harbor, she was high atop the list of most desired objectives for not only submarines but for every other warship and airplane in the Pacific. Others had come close. She had been damaged badly enough to be taken out of service twice already, but she was back in the fight, ready to launch her deadly aircraft against the Allies.

That is, until the USS *Cavalla* took care of her once and for all that historic June morning.

Captain Kossler was awarded the Navy Cross and the *Cavalla* and her crew received the Presidential Unit Citation for their accomplishments that day. In the immediate wake of that sinking, however, there was little time to celebrate their triumph. Once they had shaken the destroyer and its depth charges, the primary thing on their minds was fuel. They were already seriously low on diesel when the attack on the *Shokaku* began. Now they could only hope that they could make it to Saipan, the nearest friendly port, where a tanker awaited them.

They did make it. Once on the island, they were only too happy to have everyone in sight buy them beers to celebrate the big blow they had struck against the emperor and his empire.

The *Cavalla* was back on patrol, performing lifeguard duty about ten miles off the Japanese island of Honshu, standing by to pick up downed flyboys, when word came that the war was over. Kossler authorized breaking out the medicinal liquor aboard for every man not on watch, and a toast was made to the victory.

The giddiness did not last long. Shortly after copying the radio message that hostilities had ceased, a Japanese aircraft suddenly appeared in the sky and proceeded to attack the *Cavalla*, seemingly conducting business as usual. The skipper assumed this particular pilot had not received the news yet and ordered a hard-right maneuver to dodge the bomb the plane dropped. At the same time, they executed an emergency dive before they became the first sub sunk *after* the war was over.

The airplane's bomb hit the wave tops and exploded only about fifty yards off the port side of the dodging and ducking submarine, dousing her decks.

Later, when he could safely surface and report the incident, Kossler angrily dashed off a note for the radioman to send back to headquarters, telling them what had happened so others could be warned. Shortly thereafter, Fleet Admiral William Halsey issued a curt message to all naval vessels in the Pacific, telling them that if any Japanese aircraft should launch an attack, then the commanders should feel perfectly justified in shooting them out of the sky.

"But do it in a gentlemanly fashion," the admiral sarcastically suggested in his missive.

Shortly thereafter, the *Cavalla* received orders to join the flotilla of vessels that would enter Tokyo Bay, the first Allied units to go into Home Island waters after the hostilities ended. There was still a good deal of concern about entering former enemy territory. There were rumors that the whole thing was a clever ruse, that suicide boats and planes would attack those vessels entering Tokyo *Wan*, that the harbor was mined, that the Japanese had their own atomic weapon, just not the ability to deliver it to U.S. territory yet, and that they would set it off as soon as the victory party was in the confined waters.

Of course, none of that came to pass. On August 31, 1945, the submarine and eleven of her sisters steamed into the harbor and berthed next to the tender USS *Proteus* (AS-19). From there, they were within sight of the surrender ceremony on the decks of the battleship *Missouri*. Some of the submarines set up speakers on their decks so everyone could listen to the brief ceremony, but the cheers and shouts of their happy crews blotted out most of it.

The war was truly over. The "leap year boat" had done her job and she had done it well.

She contributed mightily to making VJ Day a reality.

The *Cavalla* enjoyed a second life in service to her country. She was one of the few boats reconfigured as an "SSK," and colorfully dubbed a "hunter-killer submarine." In the process, the sail and bow so familiar among the diesel fleet boats were each replaced with an aerodynamic-looking sail that portended the look of nuclear submarines that would come a few years later. She also received an odd, uncharacteristically rounded snout that allowed more room for sophisticated electronic equipment that was eventually installed there.

In 1966, after more than two decades of service, she was unceremoniously retired for good, and then ushered off to the reserve fleet in Orange, Texas. That was typically a graveyard for older vessels that were no longer of any value in their country's defense. There, she was on the verge of being sold to the scrap dealers when her leap year luck intervened once again.

Through the efforts of a dedicated group of submarine veterans, she became a memorial to one of her sister vessels and crew, a sibling that was not nearly so blessed as she was.

That group of Texas vets had long been talking about establishing some kind of fitting submarine memorial for those who had not made it back from the war. They also sought a memorial for one boat in particular. The sub vets named their group the Seawolf Base, deliberately taking the tag from the USS *Seawolf* (SS-197). That vessel had been lost with all hands in a friendly-fire incident in 1944. What better memorial could there be for their shipmates who were still on eternal patrol than a real, live submarine, one that visitors could climb aboard, tour, and inspect as they learned more about the silent service and the heroes who were a part of it all?

The old sub sailors of the Seawolf Base convinced the navy to let them have one of the submarines they knew were about to go to a scrap dealer. They also talked the city of Galveston, Texas, into dredging them a place to park their submarine once they got one. They would put it out near the old immigration station on Pelican Island, a spot the city some-day intended to turn into a park anyway. The city fathers and sub vets mutually decided they would call the place Seawolf Park, and that it would fill the bill as a proper memorial to the more than thirty-five hundred submariners lost in World War II.

At first, the sub USS *Cabrilla* (SS-288), the recipient of six battle stars and a bona fide hero ship because of her assistance to the Philippine guerrilla fighters during the war, was chosen. She was made ready and towed down to Galveston from Houston. She had originally come out of service as a reserve training vessel when she was replaced by—of all boats—a lady named the *Cavalla*. The *Cabrilla* was temporarily moored next to the navy pier in Galveston and was opened temporarily to the public as a museum ship while the better location at Pelican Island was made ready for her permanent home. But it took the city much longer than anticipated to prepare the spot.

The *Cabrilla*, already in bad shape from years of cannibalizing and neglect, quickly rusted away. She was so far gone that the sub vets were unable to do proper maintenance on her, especially below the waterline. They had to keep moving her from one tie-up to another as various berths at the busy moorings were required for other uses instead of for a quickly oxidizing old relic. Visitors never knew where she might be when they stopped by.

As time passed, the staunchest supporter of the sub memorial had to concede that the *Cabrilla* was too far gone to ever be a decent and repre-sentative memorial.

Their lost shipmates deserved better.

Finally, the veterans convinced the navy to allow a trade-in. They swapped the old, rusted-out *Cabrilla* for another boat that they heard was soon to be scrapped. A boat named the *Cavalla* just happened to be available by then, so once again she had the opportunity to replace the *Cabrilla*. Once they heard that a "better" boat was soon to be theirs, the city of Galveston agreed to rush their work at Pelican Island to get the spot ready for her.

In January of 1971, the *Cavalla* was towed down the Houston Ship Channel from Orange and carefully backed into a slip at the island. Slowly, deliberately, the water was drained from around her and bulldozers built up dirt around her hull.

The leap year boat was now permanently in dry dock, ready to begin the next phase of her storied existence.

The USS *Cavalla* has had some tough times since she arrived in Galveston. So has another vessel, the destroyer USS *Stewart* (DE-238), which is also on display at Seawolf Park. When the sponsors asked for designation as a National Historic Landmark, the U.S. government replied, "USS *Cavalla* does not appear to meet the criteria for designation because of her seriously deteriorated condition. The wooden deck has been replaced with concrete, her interior is dirty and vandalized, and her exterior is severely rusted."

But the World War II submariners have refused to allow her to waste away and intend to keep her around long after they are gone, all so others will know what they did and how they did it. In 1998, a new group of vets dedicated themselves to her preservation and began raising money toward that end. Volunteers, including former crew members of both the *Cavalla* and the *Stewart*, have given hundreds of man-hours of dirty, backbreaking work. Among other big projects, her superstructure and deck were replaced in 2001.

Through their continuing efforts, both vessels are in reasonably good shape and offer visitors a realistic look at what they were like while they were still in service to their country. The Galveston Park Board has also been forthcoming with some financial and labor support, so the boat's future looks bright.

Visitors to Galveston should not be surprised if they ask a local resident for directions to the USS *Cavalla* and get a blank stare. Many of them assume the submarine parked out there on Pelican Island is the *Seawolf*, since that is the name of the park.

USS *COBIA* (SS-245)

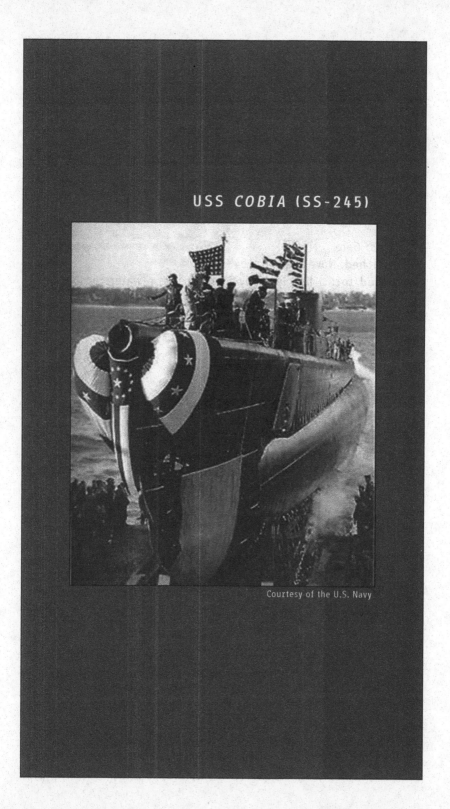

Courtesy of the U.S. Navy

USS *COBIA* (SS-245)

Class: *Gato*
Launched: November 28, 1943
Named for: a fish typically found in warm waters around
the world
Where: Electric Boat Company, Groton, Connecticut
Sponsor: Mrs. C. W. MacGruder, wife of a naval officer
Commissioned: March 29, 1944

Where is she today?
Wisconsin Maritime Museum
75 Maritime Drive
Manitowoc, Wisconsin 54220-6843
(866) 724-2356
www.wisconsinmaritime.org

Claim to fame: She sank a troop transport carrying a Japanese tank regiment with over two dozen tanks aboard,
on the way to Iwo Jima. Though not actually built at
the Manitowoc Shipyards, the *Cobia* is representative of
those that were. None of the twenty-eight fleet submarines built at Manitowoc is still around for us to visit.
The *Cobia* is a worthy stand-in.

I t is not necessarily easy for a few dozen men on a single submarine to realize the importance of their minor chess move on a much bigger board. A relatively small act in the midst of a major conflict like World War II can sometimes turn the tide of history, yet go unappreciated, even by those in the midst of it all.

But when the crew members of the submarine USS *Cobia* saw the famous photo of the marines raising the American flag atop Mount Suribachi on Iwo Jima, they were able to take special pride in the small part they had played in making the indelibly captured moment possible.

If we go back seven months before, we find the *Cobia* steaming away on her very first war patrol, working out of Pearl Harbor. When her skipper opened his orders that day, he found that he, his crew, and the newly minted diesel boat were bound for the Bonin Islands, a spiky chain of rocky but strategically important land in the middle of the Pacific, about eight hundred miles south of Tokyo. Along the way, they encountered a series of enemy freighters and, within five days, sank three of them.

One of those was the *Nissho Maru*, a troop transport with six hundred soldiers and twenty-eight tanks aboard.

The *Cobia* and her crew had no way of knowing who or what was aboard those vessels. They only knew they flew the flag that indicated they were fair game. The crew did exactly what they had been training for and sent a trio of them to the bottom, and then moved on to look for more.

When U.S. troops seized Saipan, the Japanese realized they were in real danger of losing the spinelike chain of islands that dotted that portion of the Pacific Ocean, drawing a slightly bowed line through the sea that pointed right up to the homeland. It appeared the Allies would be able to leapfrog from one island to another, all the way up to Japan. If they were able to do that, then the long-anticipated D-day-like invasion of the Home Islands would be much easier to accomplish.

With such a thing a real possibility, the Japanese generals decided to put all the forces they could muster onto the little pork chop–shaped island of Iwo Jima, throwing up a formidable roadblock. They would dig into the pockmarked volcanic mountains and resist to the last man. In so doing, they would test once and for all the will of the American soldiers. Did the Allies have the resolve to slog through the jungles, climb the mountains in the face of withering artillery, and dig out the Japanese one warrior at a time, even as they took massive losses?

Japanese troops and equipment that were being assembled for the defense of Saipan before it fell were quickly rerouted to Iwo Jima. Among them was the Twenty-sixth Tank Regiment, a battle-hardened group that had been fighting successfully in Manchuria throughout 1943. In April 1944 they were ordered to load up and proceed to Saipan, but when they arrived in Korea they received the news of the fall of Saipan. They were diverted, by way of the homeland, to the next designated hot spot, Iwo Jima.

Most of the troops and twenty-eight of their best tanks were loaded aboard the *Nissho Maru* in Yokohama. They sailed on July 14. Four days later, with the convoy in which they rode only a bit over a day from its destination, they crossed paths with the newly arrived diesel fleet submarine, the USS *Cobia*.

The boat's skipper, Lieutenant Albert Becker, was proud of what his young crew had accomplished already. Two freighters in three days! That was some good shooting, even for a far more veteran crew. Now, here swam another ship, right into the sights of their periscopes.

Becker and his crew made quick work of sending the *Nissho Maru* to the bottom, not knowing at the time that a cargo of deadly new tanks and the men who were to man them were aboard the vessel, nor that their simple, efficient attack that day would make sure the weapons never reached Iwo Jima. Nor that the sinking of this single intercepted ship contributed considerably to the eventual American takeover of the strategic plot of land in the Pacific.

Only two members of the tank regiment were killed in the sinking of the *Nissho Maru*, but it would be a full six months before they and their replacement tanks would make it to their destination. By then, the course of the battle had already turned, the outcome of the war altered.

Later in that same patrol, still her first, the *Cobia* performed the first in a long string of rescues. During the first week of August 1944, Captain Becker and his boys torpedoed a converted yacht. They then plucked out of the water one of the crewmen who had survived the brief attack. That was the boat's first prisoner of war, but it would not be the last to be locked away in the officers' stateroom or the yeoman's office.

On her second run, the *Cobia* seemed to constantly be under attack from above. While destroyers and other vessels were worthy opponents for submersibles, it was the airplane that most struck fear into the hearts of submariners. Even with the new radar that made over-the-horizon detection of aircraft easier, and even with the amazing speed with which a sub could get beneath the waves once alerted to approaching danger, airplanes could often still sneak up on a sub and attack before the boat could dive deep enough to get away. And even if the submarine did get down, it was often easily visible in the clear Pacific waters, fair game for an aircraft's torpedoes, bombs, or guns.

But the *Cobia* did manage to pop her head above the surface long enough to rescue two more Japanese, floating along after their ship was sunk by one of the 245 boat's sister submarines. Just like that, she had two more POWs.

She wasn't finished. Early in 1945, on her third war patrol, the *Cobia* stalked and sank a minelayer named the *Yurishima* off the coast of Malaya. Minelayers were especially coveted targets. Each time they took one of these minelayers permanently out of commission, most sailors assumed they were saving the lives of many of their brothers who would come after them.

After the successful attack and as soon as the view out the periscope showed the coast was clear, Becker sent his boat back to the surface to take photos of its latest victim. But once again she was driven deep by a pesky airplane that suddenly appeared over the smoking, sinking minelayer. It was the next day before the American sub could finally come to the surface for a look around.

The first thing Becker spotted from the bridge of his boat was a life raft with two men in it. Assuming the men were from the boat they had sunk the previous day, they eased closer to rescue them and take them prisoner. The men on deck had their pistols pointed toward the enemy and the deck guns were warily manned, just in case.

But they soon learned the two survivors were not from the *Yurishima* at all. They managed to convey that they had been adrift for forty days! Even if their rescuers were Americans, the two Japanese men seemed more than happy to be picked up.

Not all the *Cobia*'s rescues involved enemy survivors.

Captain Jean Valjean Vandruff was a B-24 bomber pilot with a Hollywood name and a stellar war record. Before the war was over, Vandruff would tally forty-three bombing missions in the South Pacific.

But his luck had turned sour in April 1945. On this particular run, he was riding as copilot on a mission to destroy an oil refinery in Saigon, located in what is now Vietnam. Just before he and the rest of his squadron reached their target, a covey of buzzing Japanese Zeroes attacked them from all angles. Vandruff's plane and the other bomber that flew beside it were able to shoot down five of the attackers and, miraculously, release their full loads of bombs on the targeted refinery.

The problem was that on Vandruff's aircraft three out of the four engines were destroyed in the battle high above the Southeast Asian jungle. Somehow, by jettisoning machine guns, equipment, and anything else they could get rid of in order to help make the plane lighter, they limped almost one hundred miles up the coast, trying to avoid jumping out over occupied territory. The Japanese did not deal kindly with captured airmen.

Finally, just offshore and at fifteen hundred feet above the sea, unable to nurse their wounded bird any farther, Jean Vandruff and the rest of his crew gave up the effort and parachuted out. As the chutes popped open above them and they drifted toward the sea, they watched their plane spiral downward, crashing violently into the waves.

One man's chute failed to open and he was killed. Ten others settled down into the water not far from where their airplane went in. They floated along in a line, too far apart to see each other, their little one-man life rafts bobbing in the sea. A two-engine amphibious navy Catalina appeared shortly and landed on the surface of the sea, taxiing along, intent on working along the line, plucking the bomber crew from the water one flyboy at a time.

But suddenly, after picking up only three of the men, the rescue plane gunned its engines and fled. It appeared they had detected an enemy aircraft or some other imminent threat approaching. The seven other survivors were on their own until it was safe for the Catalina to return.

Unbeknownst to the airplane crew, though, the USS *Cobia* was sliding along beneath them, still on her fourth war patrol but eager to get back into the war after a stopover in Fremantle, Australia, for mid-patrol repairs. She poked her periscope up just in time to see the navy rescue plane speeding away.

"Captain, there's a Catalina up there," the submariner on the scope reported to his skipper. "Wonder what it's doing way out here? And on the water, too."

Becker stepped to the eyepiece and took a look for himself. It was unusual to see relatively short-range aircraft like the Cat this far from any base. The guy had to be looking for something. Or for someone.

"I don't know. Only thing I can think of is he's looking for someone in the drink. Some of our guys."

"Suppose we ought to try to raise him on the radio and see if we can help?"

Becker smiled. "Good idea."

He brought his boat up far enough to use the radio to give the rescue plane a shout. The radioman quickly confirmed that the plane was looking for survivors of a B-24 that had gone down nearby. He had three men from the downed aircraft on board already, and there were almost certainly more floating around out there somewhere.

No one wanted to consider what might have happened if the *Cobia* had come up for a look only fifteen seconds later, after the Catalina was out of sight. Or had not decided to raise the antenna and radio the plane's pilot a few questions about what he was up to. Or if the enemy planes the Cat had detected had decided to come closer and had caught the *Cobia* on the surface.

Meanwhile, Vandruff was already paddling, as were his shipmates, toward where he assumed the shore was, trying to get somewhere to hide for the night. They'd be too easily seen by the enemy in the water.

That's when the pilot spied some kind of odd vessel coming his way. His heart fell. He had survived the attack by the Zeroes, nursed his plane back out to sea, safely parachuted out and survived a water landing, and now was only about five miles from land and a possible hiding place. All that, only to be picked up by an enemy patrol boat and hauled off to a POW camp and certain torture.

Vandruff tried to hide, pulling a blue sheet over the top of himself and his little life raft, hoping to blend into the surface of the sea. At the same time, he cautiously slid his pistol from its holster, ready to fight to his death if need be. He had heard the stories of what the Japanese did to captured pilots. Death would be preferable. And, if he could, he intended to take as many of them with him as he could manage.

But then he saw men on the deck of the vessel, waving and calling to him. It was a submarine. An American submarine. One of those ugly, slimy "pig boats" had never looked so beautiful to the pilot!

Vandruff was quickly brought aboard and taken below for dry clothes and a quick once-over by the pharmacist's mate.

Meanwhile, the other bomber pilot had maneuvered his own raft over to the site where their plane had gone under. Somehow he located a five-man life raft, complete with provisions and a hand-crank radio transmitter. He quickly abandoned and sank his small raft and climbed aboard the much bigger one, ready to row about and look for his buddies.

That's when he saw the low-slung vessel coming his way in the waning daylight. His thoughts were the same as Vandruff's, that he was about to be captured. He flipped the raft over and hid beneath it.

The men on the deck of the *Cobia* spotted the big raft, bottom up, floating amid the debris of the bomber crash.

"We need to sink that thing so there's no evidence left of the plane crash," the ranking man on deck declared. If they did not find the other downed crew members, the junk floating on the water would guide Japanese patrol boats and planes to the area, and they might have better luck. "Which one of you wants the target practice?" he called to the men manning the deck guns below him. They all swung their weapons in the direction of the raft and got ready to fire on command.

But up near the bow, a young sailor held up his hand and shouted a frantic warning.

"Wait! Wait a second!" he called. Then suddenly he slipped off his shoes and dived into the sea. He popped to the surface and began swimming over toward the oily spot where the life raft drifted on the waves.

To everyone's surprise, when the sailor flipped the raft over, there was the pilot.

Again they had been only a moment away from a tragedy.

When they were all safely aboard, Vandruff and his six crewmates raved about the friendliness of the sub sailors and the quality of their food. Seven days later, the *Cobia* made an unscheduled stop and deposited the bomber crew at the naval base at Subic Bay in the Philippines. Each aircraft crewman received a clever, hand-drawn certificate with cartoon renderings of mermaids, a cobia fish, and hummingbirds parachuting into the sea, along with a typed inscription.

The copilot's certificate read: "Know ye of these present that I, Davy Jones, have on this date delivered up one (1) Zeroed Zoomie, Lt. Jean Vandruff, by name, into the custody of the Commanding Officer, U.S.S. Cobia, to dispose of as he may see fit. Signed 'Davy Jones,' Nan-Hai-Branch, Lat. Twelve N., 4/8/45, received in good condition, (Albert L. Becker) C.O.—USS Cobia."

As it happened, the *Cobia*'s crew needed the success of the rescue and the silliness of the send-off for a morale boost after what they had been through just before the incident. The reason for the mid-patrol repairs in Fremantle prior to picking up Vandruff and his guys was a running surface gun battle with a couple of enemy sea trucks. The submarine had been on patrol back in February when she spotted the cargo vessels, traveling without escort, and promptly gave chase.

Captain Becker decided to launch a surface attack since the craft were more than fast enough to escape if he attempted to sneak up on them while his boat was submerged. They would have had no chance to line up and fire torpedoes at such quickly moving ships.

But as they approached them, ready to open fire, one of the vessels unexpectedly fought back. Deck guns on the Japanese sea truck raked the *Cobia* with vicious machine-gun fire, even as the enemy vessels tried to run away from their American attacker.

The first hail of bullets took out the *Cobia*'s radar. The next projectiles struck one of the men on deck as he was desperately diving for cover. Ralph Clark Houston, a 20-millimeter gun loader, was badly wounded. He died the following morning, becoming the *Cobia*'s only casualty of the war.

Becker pressed the attack, even after the crewman went down, chasing the fleeing ships, his deck guns blazing. Both were sunk.

The boat was damaged in the running battle. It would be at least a week before they could make it to the nearest repair facility and get

Houston's body ashore, especially since they would be driving with one eye blinded by the impairment of the radar. They would have to remain especially alert, and they would be even more vulnerable when they were on the surface. That meant they would have to spend more time submerged, hiding from sneaky aircraft or warships.

The captain ordered a rarity for submarines—a formal burial at sea.

The ceremony took place on the *Cobia*'s forward deck, just in front of the bridge. From there, Ralph Houston's flag-draped body was committed to the sea, on eternal patrol.

The rest of the *Cobia* crew almost met a similar fate in a close call that came only one month later. The Japanese minesweeper *Hatsutaka* caught the submarine in relatively shallow water and began a vicious depth-charge attack. The sub went as deep as she dared to try to escape the assault.

They had to be careful. More than one submarine had gotten mired in mud on the bottom and had not been able to get unstuck. While it was possible to use Momsen lungs and the fore and aft torpedo room escape hatches to get out of the sub and to the surface, the crew members of the *Cobia* had no desire to pop up next to a mad bunch of Japanese sailors on the minesweeper.

But before the submarine could sneak out from beneath the warship, a succession of teeth-rattling blasts nearby literally drove the boat into the mud, about 120 feet below the surface. As near as the crew could tell, the belly of the *Cobia* was bogged down more than twenty feet deep in the clutching bottom of the Gulf of Siam.

They were in a fix and they knew it.

If they did too much maneuvering to try to get the submarine unstuck, the noise and the muddy water they would send to the surface would show the minesweeper precisely where they were sitting. And if they simply sat there quietly, hoping the nightmare would end, and the depth charges continued to rain down on them, they could easily get themselves blown to smithereens if the Japanese got lucky.

Even if the attack ended, if the enemy ship did not move on, the *Cobia* would eventually run out of air. Then she would have to try to pull out of the muck, regardless of the danger that might result.

If they could not get unstuck, they would have no choice but to abandon the *Cobia* and try to get up top—one man at a time. The Japanese could then simply snag each sailor as he popped to the surface.

Fortunately the enemy vessel, assuming their target had sneaked away, soon gave up its assault and went on about its business. As soon as they could no longer hear the warship swinging back and forth overhead, looking for any signs of them so they could home in with their barrels of TNT, the *Cobia*'s skipper began using the screws and electric motors, rocking the boat until he was finally able to get her free.

Though heavily damaged, they cautiously eased away from the shallows, back toward deeper water, where they could hide for a while and lick their wounds.

The *Cobia* and her crew earned four battle stars for her service in World War II, and they were ultimately credited with sinking almost seventeen thousand tons of enemy shipping. After the war, the submarine had long tenure as a training vessel in New London, Connecticut, near her birthplace. She finally served out her years of duty at the Milwaukee Naval Reserve Center on Lake Michigan in Wisconsin, far from salt water.

In 1970, she was towed to Manitowoc, Wisconsin, about eighty miles north of Milwaukee. The people at what is now known as the Wisconsin Maritime Museum wanted a submarine similar to those that had been built in the nearby shipyard during the war. They thought it would be a good idea to have a representative boat to stand as a memorial to those twenty-eight Manitowoc vessels, twenty-five of which saw action in the Pacific, as well as to serve as an international memorial to submariners wherever in the world they may have served.

There was one showstopper. None of the Wisconsin-built boats remained. They had all done their duty well but had long since been given to foreign navies or scrapped when their berthing and upkeep became more of an expense than the taxpayers should have to endure for a vessel that was no longer of use to her country.

The *Cobia*, which was then berthed only a short distance south, appeared to be a good stand-in. She was virtually identical to her Manitowoc-built sisters. If there were no true daughter of Lake Michigan to bring home, then those involved with the museum figured this heroic boat would make a perfectly acceptable symbol. She would do nicely as a memorial to the tremendous achievement of the people of the area who contributed to the victory in World War II by building these powerful war machines.

Besides her class, the *Cobia* had another link with the Manitowoc-built boats. The minesweeper *Hatsutaka*, which had almost done the sub in, had successfully sunk an American submarine only a week before trapping the *Cobia* in the mud on the bottom of the Gulf of Siam. The submarine was the USS *Lagarto* (SS-371). On the night of May 3 and 4, 1945, the *Lagarto* was patrolling in the Gulf of Siam. One of her sister boats was supposed to connect with her early on the morning of the fourth but never heard from her. After more than sixty years, the *Lagarto* is still "overdue" from patrol and her crew of eighty-six men is presumed lost. Japanese war records confirmed that the *Hatsutaka* sank the submarine.

The *Lagarto* was built at Manitowoc, Wisconsin.

There is one more improbable connection in this story, though, and it has a ring of revenge to it. Only a week after the *Hatsutaka* almost made the *Cobia* its second American submarine victim in seven days, the Japanese minesweeper was dispatched to the muddy bottom herself. She was sunk by the USS *Hawkbill* (SS-366).

The *Hawkbill* was a Manitowoc boat.

So that is how a Connecticut-built boat came to be in a museum dedicated to Lake Michigan–built vessels.

In 1986, the *Cobia* was declared a National Historic Landmark and placed on the National Register of Historic Places.

Now restored as closely as possible to her original 1945 condition, the *Cobia* is one of the museum's top attractions and draws a large number of tourists and visitors to the museum each year. In its continuing effort to equip the boat as she was during the war, the museum publishes on its Web site a long "wish list" of period items they would like to locate and either install or put on exhibition. The list includes everything from common tools and equipment like flashlights, pots and pans, and a period ice-cream maker to machine guns and a fuel pump for the engine room.

Employees and volunteers have rebuilt two of the boat's main diesel engines and restored the radio shack to its 1945 appearance. The boat's SJ-1 radar has also been reinstalled, and the museum claims it to be the oldest operational radar system in the world. Like some of the other museum boats, the *Cobia* remains an active training vessel for navy reservists, and their work and drills help to maintain the equipment visitors will find when they go aboard her.

In addition to the submarine, the site offers a museum of shipping and shipbuilding in the area, including a cross section of a schooner, along with a model ship gallery and exhibits of boats that were built nearby.

USS *CROAKER* (SS-246)

Courtesy of the U.S. Navy

USS *CROAKER* (SS-246)

Class: *Gato*
Launched: December 19, 1943
Named for: various fishes that make croaking noises
Where: Electric Boat Company, Groton, Connecticut
Sponsor: Mrs. William H. P. Blandy, wife of chief of the Bureau of Ordnance; commander, Group 1, Amphibious Force, Pacific Fleet; and commander, Cruisers and Destroyers, Pacific Fleet
Commissioned: April 21, 1944

Where is she today?
Buffalo and Erie County Naval and Military Park
One Naval Park Cove
Buffalo, New York 14202
(716) 854-3200
www.buffalonavalpark.org

Claim to fame: After six successful war patrols, she was refitted for Cold War duty as one of the first "hunter-killer" submarines.

The relationship between a new submarine's crew and their commanding officer is something of a shotgun marriage. During World War II, the navy tried to keep a balance of newly graduated sub school sailors salted in among those who already had combat experience or who had, at least, qualified for submarine duty.

But as the war drew into its third and fourth years, and as the number of fleet submarines sliding sideways down the skids at Portsmouth, Groton, Manitowoc, and other shipbuilding locations increased, it became more and more difficult to find crew members with that kind of experience to place on the bridges of those new-construction boats. That was especially true of the other officers, too, including those with the unique skill set to eventually become submarine captains. While more and more officers were gaining valuable knowledge aboard submarines in the Pacific, boats were being built so fast it was often difficult to get experienced sailors to crew them.

The United States Naval Academy at Annapolis had already gone to an accelerated program, graduating officers as quickly as possible, especially if the young men showed an interest in submarines. A special school was set up to train prospective skippers, bringing them into classrooms where the textbooks were actual duplicated copies of patrol reports from real runs that had happened only a few weeks before, half a world away from New London, Connecticut.

In no time, those young officers were in wardrooms of subs all over the Pacific, getting the very best on-the-job training, learning as much as they could from the men who had been out there already. Promising academy students were ushered into submarine officer programs offering

119

intense training. Usually they, too, used charts and patrol reports only a few weeks old to study the tactics being used in a real war of which they would soon be a part.

Naturally, when crew members—officers and enlisted men alike— learned what ship they would be riding, their biggest question was about their new skipper. What kind of a guy would he turn out to be? A sailor's skipper or one who was simply angling to become an admiral, no matter what it took? Was he experienced? Passive or aggressive? Would he be too intense and drive them all directly to their demise, or would he be one of those guys who hung back, stayed out of trouble, and tried to hide somewhere until the war was over?

To a lesser extent, the same questions were asked about the executive officer, the XO, who was always second in command, and usually working on getting his own boat someday. Or, on the enlisted men's side, of the chief of the boat, the COB, who was typically the most senior—and the most powerful—of the nonofficers.

This is where the luck of the draw came in. Few of the men who rode the diesel boats had much say in who got the short straw, who ended up with the best CO, XO, and COB.

Those who showed up to commission the USS *Croaker* in the spring of 1944 were happy to note that their captain was an old hand, John Elwood Lee. There was plenty of information available on him in addition to the usual scuttlebutt. Though only recently promoted to the rank of commander, Lee had considerable war and prewar experience. A 1930 grad of the Naval Academy, Lee's first command was the *S-12* (SS-117), a vessel about one hundred feet shorter than the *Gato*-class boats and not nearly as sophisticated.

The *S-12* was built in 1920 in Portsmouth, New Hampshire, and recommissioned in 1940 when the threat of war was heavy in the air. Lee took her on four patrols in the Caribbean and Atlantic in 1942, trying to protect shipping from the increasing numbers of German U-boats that were preying on most any target they could shoot at. The *S-12* saw no action to speak of, though, and Lee soon learned there was almost as much threat from friendly fire—trigger-happy pilots who mistook American submarines for U-boats—as there was from the Germans.

But his next boat took him right into the heart of the war. He was assigned the USS *Grayling* (SS-209), a *Gar*-class Portsmouth boat, launched in September 1940. Lee took her out of Pearl Harbor for her fourth war patrol in October 1942. It was the first of four successful runs on the boat.

Then, in July 1943, when Lee took the *Grayling* into Fremantle to end her seventh patrol, he learned he was to return to Groton for new construction—the brand-new *Gato*-class USS *Croaker*.

That was typical. A sub commander would normally make up to a half dozen runs and, if he seemed to know what he was doing and impressed the right people, he was either promoted to a higher command position ashore, reassigned to another boat, or sent back to the States to commission one of the new subs as it was being built.

After sinking a claimed eight enemy vessels on his four patrols, Lee turned the keys to the *Grayling* over to a relative newcomer, Robert Marion Brinker. Brinker was a young skipper, a member of the academy class of 1934, and a real up-and-comer. While Lee made his way back to New Hampshire to take over the *Croaker*, the *Grayling*'s new captain took his boat to the Philippines. His mission was to deliver supplies to the guerrillas that were fighting a vicious war against the Japanese occupation force there.

After leading a couple of attacks on enemy vessels and sinking at least one, something happened. The *Grayling*, her new skipper, and the crew seemingly disappeared. She was never heard from again.

It is unclear what tragedy befell the boat, but she was presumed lost with her crew of seventy-six men, on or about September 9, somewhere either in the Lingayen Gulf or along the approaches to Manila. There are some reports in Japanese war records that the passenger-transport vessel *Hokuan Maru* rammed a submerged submarine about that time. It is presumed that it was the *Grayling*.

The official and succinct description of her status still reads: "Overdue from patrol, December 24, 1943." That was the day, Christmas Eve, that she was supposed to return from her eighth patrol. That was the only one of her runs that was not declared "successful."

Meanwhile, John Lee was back in Connecticut, overseeing the construction and sea trials of his new boat, the *Croaker*, when he heard the news of his former boat and many of the crew members with whom he had served aboard the *Grayling*. There was nothing he could do but mourn their loss and prepare to seek some measure of revenge once he successfully got his new submarine and crew through sea trials, training, and on to the war.

As with his previous command, his tenure aboard this vessel would be successful. On her first patrol, out of Pearl Harbor, the *Croaker* and her crew sank a light cruiser, a minesweeper, and two freighters, earning the Navy Unit Commendation for their efforts. On at least one occasion, Lee made color motion pictures through the periscope as he watched an enemy cruiser take the worst of the *Croaker*'s torpedo attack, the explosion as the fish hit their target, then the ship burning and smoking as it went down. Those movies survived and are often used in documentary features about the war and the submarines' role in its successful prosecution.

The boat's distinguished record would be extended under her second skipper, Lieutenant Commander William Bismarck Thomas, a Kansan who also had previous Atlantic submarine experience. He was skipper of the *R-15* (SS-92), keeping watch for U-boats in the Caribbean and near the entrance to the Panama Canal, much as John Elwood Lee had done.

Both the *Croaker* and her final wartime skipper would go on to have interesting postwar histories.

After the peace treaty with Japan was finalized, William Bismarck Thomas was assigned to help launch a naval school in the old Del Monte Hotel in Monterey, California. There he became interested in amateur theatrics, and he wrote, directed, and starred in a number of stage productions. In the audience one night was the Hollywood comedic star Harold Lloyd. He was impressed enough with the ex–sub skipper's performance that he went backstage to meet him after the show. Lloyd convinced Thomas to come down to Hollywood to take a screen test. Executives at Paramount Studios were interested in the naval officer as well, and they promptly offered him a movie contract.

Thomas considered the offer but decided to stay with the safety and security of his naval career. After a distinguished tenure, including command of a couple of surface ships, he retired in 1966 and promptly became a high school math teacher. Hollywood's loss was a definite gain for the U.S. Navy and high school math students in the San Diego, California, area.

Thomas passed away in February 2004, and his ashes were scattered in the Pacific Ocean by the U.S. Navy, just as the former sub skipper had requested.

His last sub, the *Croaker*, steamed back through the Panama Canal after the war was over, headed to her birthplace in Connecticut. There she eventually served as a school ship, based in New London, only a few miles from where she was built. Later she was taken up the coast, around Cape Cod, to Portsmouth, New Hampshire, for what proved to be an interesting makeover.

Not only did she get a new hull number (SSK-246) and intriguing designation ("hunter-killer submarine"), but a completely different look as well. Gone was the distinctive sail that was so familiar on her *Gato* and *Balao* sisters. Some said the new sail looked more like a stack of garbage cans or that she most resembled some weak copy of Jules Verne's famous submarine, the *Nautilus*.

The *Croaker* got a nose job, too, to conceal powerful, new long-range sonar equipment. And she became a "guppy," too, after being fitted with a snorkel so she could run her diesel engines, even while submerged. Her six bow torpedo tubes were removed to make room for the sophisticated new gear, and many of her other systems were given special silencing treatment. The navy had secret plans for this old warship, but she needed considerable cosmetic surgery to prepare for the new and mysterious job she was about to undertake.

Over the next dozen years, the *Croaker* traveled the world in her new role, sailing to England for NATO exercises, through the Mediterranean and the Suez Canal, and to exotic ports like Karachi, Pakistan. Much of what she was called upon to do was kept top secret for years but involved plenty of Cold War exercises and truly frightening what-if scenarios.

By 1968, the navy had decided that the future of submarining lay in the nuclear boats and that the old, tried-and-true fleet boats had limited viability. They simply lacked the range and stealth of the nukes, which could be gone from port as long as need be, and which could stay submerged until the food aboard the submarine ran out. Otherwise there were few limitations on the new generation of subs.

The *Croaker* entered semiretirement as a training vessel in New London.

There she served for three more years, until it appeared she would end up in the scrap yard, just as so many of her sisters had done. That's when a group of sub vets rescued her and fixed her up so we could visit her, learn more about her, and appreciate what she and her crew did for us.

After six successful war patrols in World War II and almost twenty-six years of additional service during the Cold War, the *Croaker* deserved a better fate than some of the other historic submarines. Many of them were cut up for scrap. Others were donated to foreign navies. More than a few were used as target practice in ASW (antisubmarine warfare) drills. It was the Submarine Memorial Association in Groton, Connecticut, that stepped in and saved the *Croaker*.

There, in a city so closely associated with submersible vessels, they took custody of the boat, did what they could to restore her, and opened her to the public in memory of those fifty-two subs that did not return from the war, as she had been fortunate enough to do. The veterans did what they could to make her safe to visit and to equip her with enough actual period equipment to properly show off her war trim. It was a tough go keeping the aging vessel shipshape enough to allow people of all ages and physical conditions to come aboard and look around. And it was a constant battle against the elements, vandals, and the inevitable action of oxidation on steel.

The old girl's future was once again in doubt.

In 1988, the city of Buffalo, New York, stepped in. They offered to move the historic submarine to what is now called the Buffalo and Erie County Naval and Military Park. Opened in 1979, the park was intended to pay homage to the navy in particular, but to all branches of service in general. It was also designed to draw the public's attention to the Erie Canal Harbor, a multimillion-dollar project to develop a section of the city's waterfront as a tourism destination. The addition of a real World War II submarine fit right into the boosters' plans, so the *Croaker* took one more voyage before she could rest for good.

Today, the park is also home to the guided missile cruiser USS *Little Rock* (CLG-4) and the destroyer USS *The Sullivans* (DD-537) as well as the *Croaker*. It is interesting to note that *The Sullivans* is named after the five Sullivan brothers from Waterloo, Iowa, who all served together aboard the light cruiser USS *Juneau* (CL-52) during World War II. The navy had a firm policy against having more than one member of a family fighting in the same place, but the Sullivans insisted they wanted such an arrangement. The brothers were eventually allowed to serve together aboard the *Juneau*. Their smiling faces appeared in newsreels and in magazines all over the country and became symbols of the dedication and sacrifice families were making to help win this war.

Tragically, the worst happened. All five brothers were killed near Guadalcanal when their ship was first struck by a torpedo from a destroyer, then cut in two by a Japanese submarine's torpedo. The navy named one of its new destroyers *The Sullivans* to commemorate their loss.

Today, the *Croaker* and the other museum vessels are maintained by the City of Buffalo and Erie County with the help of volunteers from the Buffalo Base of the United States Submarine Veterans.

Besides the ships, other exhibits include Marine Corps memorabilia dating from World War I, donated items from prisoners of war, a display on contributions of African-Americans and women to our country's military history, military aircraft, and memorials to those who fought in both world wars, Korea, or Vietnam.

USS *BOWFIN* (SS-287)

USS *BOWFIN* (SS-287)

Class: *Balao*
Launched: December 7, 1942, on the first anniversary of the attack on Pearl Harbor
Named for: the hard-fighting, aggressive, voracious breed of fish found in fresh water from the Great Lakes and southward, a species dating back to the Jurassic period. It can use its swim bladder as a primitive lung and thrives in water with low oxygen content, surviving for days at a time in little or no water.
Where: Portsmouth Naval Shipyard, New Hampshire
Sponsor: Mrs. Jane Gawne, wife of U.S. Navy Captain James Orville Gawne
Commissioned: May 1, 1943

Where is she today?
USS *Bowfin* Submarine Museum and Park
11 Arizona Memorial Drive
Honolulu, Hawaii 96818
(808) 423-1341
www.bowfin.org

Claim to fame: Christened on the anniversary of the Pearl Harbor attack, she was dubbed "the Pearl Harbor Avenger," but despite her stellar record and insatiable appetite for destroying enemy vessels, she may go down in history as much for her inadvertent part in one of the saddest occurrences of the war. Appropriately enough, "the Pearl Harbor Avenger" returned to and now awaits visitors in Pearl Harbor, Hawaii.

Every fighting vessel is christened with high hopes for her future success. Prayers are said, speeches are made, bands play patriotic songs, and, as the sponsor crashes the champagne bottle across the bow and the chocks are released to allow the boat to slide down into the water, everyone is assured that this may well be the boat that changes the course of history.

As we know, fifty-two boats just like the *Bowfin* never returned triumphantly to home port, flying their battle flags, a broom strapped to their masts to signify a successful patrol, and bragging of their accomplishments. That is why everyone involved with launching a new vessel—from builders to sponsors to the naval brass—was looking for good omens with each submarine they sent steaming away from their yards.

The *Bowfin* seemed to carry the ultimate good omen—her birthday.

Only eight days after the Japanese attack on Pearl Harbor in 1941, the order came down from BUSHIPS (the navy's Bureau of Ships) to immediately begin construction on a new class of submarine, the *Balao*, whose blueprints were already complete. Though these boats did not look that much different from their *Gato* predecessors, they offered one major advantage: their hulls were thicker, allowing them to safely descend over a hundred feet deeper to escape enemy bombs, torpedoes, and depth charges.

The first of these boats to be built were at the Portsmouth Navy Yard, on the Piscataqua River, which served as the border between New Hampshire and Maine. The third *Balao* boat to have her keel laid was the *Bowfin*. Her launch ceremony was deliberately scheduled on December 7, 1942.

The new warship was immediately dubbed "the Pearl Harbor Avenger."

Her first skipper, Commander Joe Willingham, Naval Academy class of 1926, was not daunted by the hefty hopes being placed on his brand-new boat. He had already seen his share of action as captain of the USS *Tautog* (SS-199), aboard which he and his crew claimed credit for sinking eight enemy vessels. That included six on their second patrol. Among those was the German submarine *I-28*, sent to the bottom with her eighty-eight hands. It was extremely difficult for one submarine to sink another, but Willingham did it twice on the *Tautog*. He earned two Navy Crosses for his good work before he ever set foot on the new *Bowfin*.

The skipper had also had his share of close calls. Only a couple of days before sinking the enemy submarine, he and the *Tautog* launched an attack on one of the Japanese ships that was returning from the Battle of the Coral Sea. In the assault, his torpedomen fired two torpedoes.

One of them hit the target vessel and exploded. The other did a truly dangerous trick.

For some reason, the fish inexplicably circled and headed right back toward the *Tautog*. Willingham ordered his boat deep to attempt to avoid the errant torpedo. They managed to do so, but only by a whisker.

The *Bowfin*'s commissioning party was held on April 24, 1943, at the Pannaway Club in New London. As usual, there was much drinking, dancing, and tall tale telling. By the end of the celebration, most of her crew was convinced they would win the war by themselves, if they could only finish fitting out the boat, training new crew members, and running sea trials on their magnificent new submarine. A week later, on May Day, the official commissioning ceremony was finally held on her deck. The crew lined up in formation in their dress uniforms while navy higher-ups had their say behind a podium, and then they formally put the *Bowfin* into service. On July 1, she departed New England for the Pacific.

The impatient crew had no clue what a colorful tour they and their new boat would have. They would eventually receive credit for sinking sixteen enemy vessels, accounting for close to seventy thousand tons. On one patrol alone, in November 1943, they claimed to have sunk a dozen vessels, but, true to form, they only received formal credit for five. Still, Rear Admiral Ralph Waldo Christie, commander of the U.S. Submarine Force, Southwest Pacific, became the *Bowfin's* biggest fan, praising the crew for their efforts on that run.

"They fought the war from the beginning to the end of the patrol," he gushed during the award ceremony.

By then the submarine was under the command of Lieutenant Commander Walter Griffith. Captain Willingham had done so well on the *Bowfin's* first patrol that he was promoted to squadron commander.

The boat was awarded the Presidential Unit Citation for that patrol and Griffith received the Navy Cross. There were rumblings of an even higher award for the *Bowfin's* second skipper. Admiral Christie, in collusion with General Douglas MacArthur, had been awarding army medals for exceptional valor to navy personnel, simply because he was so proud of the job they were doing against incredible odds. Walt Griffith may well have been in line for the Medal of Honor for his cool leadership aboard the *Bowfin*, but Christie's boss nixed the whole cross-branch award thing.

Griffith was a studious-looking, slightly built redhead with a most pleasant demeanor. One of his fellow officers described their commander as "a mild, kindly, even poetic type." Looks can deceive. Griffith had quickly developed a reputation as being fearless while at the helm of a warship. We may never know how close he came to receiving our country's highest award for bravery for his actions during the *Bowfin's* second patrol, but there is no doubt he was an exceptional sub commander, deserving of all the accolades he did receive.

One November evening while patrolling off French Indochina (now Vietnam), they decided to go topside for a bit. They were expecting to emerge into a moonless, cloudy night, for fresh air and a battery charge. Griffith brought his boat to just below the surface, to periscope depth. When they got there and the captain took a look through the scope, he found more than simple darkness. They were in the midst of a blinding tropical deluge. No matter, the batteries needed more juice, so the skipper ordered that the crew prepare for the charge to begin as soon as he gave the order to bring the boat to the surface.

Then, as he peered intently through the periscope into the stormy darkness, the skipper suddenly gasped when he realized they had popped up smack in the middle of something else—a full-blown Japanese convoy.

"All back emergency! All back full! Hard right rudder!" he shouted, and then he braced as the boat yawed dizzily in response to the crew's carrying out his frantic commands.

They were on a collision course with a big tanker!

Somehow they got the boat into reverse, ducked back beneath the surface, and carefully backed out of the mess in which they found themselves. As soon as everyone got back his breath, they circled and lined up for a brazen attack, firing nine torpedoes total, sending them off in all directions, their magnetic exploders armed and ready. Black darkness, pounding rain, and blustery wind—it did not matter. Before it was over, the *Bowfin* dispatched two ships to the bottom for certain and probably did in one more for which they would never receive credit.

That wasn't all the excitement for that run, though.

A few days later, along with its sister submarine the USS *Billfish* (SS-286), the *Bowfin* attacked a convoy, using another rainstorm as cover for a surface assault. They sank one ship and were lining up to fire on a second when a five-inch shell from one of the enemy vessels hit the *Bowfin* hard, damaging the main air induction piping on her right side, pouring torrents of cold seawater into the engine room. Captain Griffith saw no use in abandoning the attack, whether they were wounded or not, so he and the *Bowfin*'s crew proceeded to send another ship to the bottom.

They were firing at yet another vessel when their last two torpedoes exploded early. That seemed to be some kind of a sign. The *Bowfin* finally pulled away and did emergency repairs before steering toward Fremantle in Australia and a more permanent fix for all the things that had gotten broken in their bold attack.

Admiral Christie was so impressed with the *Bowfin* and her crew that he chose her for a history-making ride. He had already penned in his diary how he felt about Commander Griffith and his boat's exploits in November 1943. He called the run "a classic of all submarine patrols." The admiral treated the crew to a spectacular dinner when they returned to port, and, when his cocker spaniel had puppies, he even named one of them Bowfin.

The admiral had long vowed that he would ride along aboard one of his submarines while she was on patrol. After all that the great boat had done, the *Bowfin* was his obvious choice. The submarine had been out on the first leg of a "double-barrel" patrol when she put in to Darwin, Australia, to replenish her torpedoes and pick up a load of mines to plant near Borneo. Without even asking permission from his superiors this time (he had been denied approval twice already—his bosses were afraid of what might happen if someone of his rank were captured by the Japanese), Admiral Christie flew to Darwin and went aboard the *Bowfin* to ride along on the second half of the run.

He did not have to wait long to see some action.

On their second night out of Darwin, Griffith and his crew picked up a large blip on their radar. It was a merchant ship, likely delivering supplies to the Japanese garrison at Timor. With the admiral at his elbow on the bridge, Captain Griffith, while remaining on the surface in full view, swung his submarine around and shot off two torpedoes. Both hit the enemy vessel and sank her in less than two minutes. Unbelievably, even with an admiral observing the whole thing firsthand, the *Bowfin* was never credited with sinking the merchant ship that evening.

Shortly after that, the sub received a message that an enemy seaplane tender was apparently operating in the area. That was certainly a worthy target! And it was not long before Griffith and his crew spotted the ship, complete with an armada of escorts and impressive air cover.

Griffith did not hesitate for a moment. He began stalking, diving eight times to avoid aircraft. Still, no matter how hard he tried, he could not get the boat into a good firing position. That is, until the next evening. At times during the long, nerve-racking trailing operation, the rear admiral acted as officer of the deck while the boat's regular contingent of officers grabbed a few hours of rest.

Finally, just before midnight and under the cover of almost total darkness, with his boat running along on the surface to keep the targets within reasonable sight, Griffith fired torpedoes at the tender. There was some kind of miscalculation. All of them missed. They did, however, stir up a hornet's nest. The escorts, now aware there was a submarine out there shooting at them, began dropping depth charges even though the *Bowfin* was still riding on the surface the whole time.

From his spot on the bridge, Admiral Christie grew uneasy.

"We were very close to him," he later wrote of the target. "Within machine gun range. I thought we would dive but Griffith chose to hold the initiative."

The admiral was seeing firsthand why the redheaded young officer had already become a sub skipper superstar.

But Christie was certain the target vessel and her escorts could see the *Bowfin* and would begin raking them with gunfire any second. Meanwhile, Griffith swung his boat around, putting his stern toward the Japanese ship, and fired two more torpedoes at almost point-blank range. It took only a moment before a stunning explosion lit up the tropical night.

"I could see the luminous wake [of the departing torpedoes] and WHAM! An enormous detonation, which shook us up as though our own ship had been hit."

Christie felt the boat rock beneath them, shaken by the concussion, and he saw the night sky full of smoke and debris. Then suddenly they were bathed in bright light from a searchlight somewhere on their victim's deck. Before they had time to react to the light, they clearly heard the ominous pinging of bullets striking the steel hull of their submarine.

The *Bowfin* was already racing away, trying desperately to get out of range of the ship's guns. But Griffith, with one more torpedo loaded in the aft tubes, gave the order to fire. There was no way to hear, amid the din of roaring engines and the squawking of the dive klaxon, if it hit anything.

To the relief of the crew and their high-ranking hitchhiker, there were no depth charges that night. And to the disappointment of all, they later learned the enemy ship they blasted did not sink after all. Heavily damaged, she was beached in the shallow waters nearby, and then later towed to Singapore for repairs. Still, a valuable asset to the enemy was out of service for a considerable time.

Admiral Christie also got to see the boat deposit her mines where they were supposed to be. He watched as the *Bowfin* sank a couple of sampans while the sub was on the way to the admiral's rendezvous with a plane at Exmouth Gulf. Christie was the first force commander and admiral to ever ride along on a submarine patrol, as well as the second-oldest officer, in his late fifties, to ever take such a ride. Nothing he witnessed on his short run with Walt Griffith and the crew of the *Bowfin* changed his opinion of the boat, her crew, or its exceptional skipper.

And he still had no desire to name his cocker spaniel pup anything else but Bowfin.

After guiding the *Bowfin* on her fourth patrol, Walt Griffith was dispatched back to Portsmouth, New Hampshire, to oversee construction and take command of a new submarine, the USS *Bullhead* (SS-332). He would command her on her first two successful war patrols before being reassigned to a higher post. Griffith went to work for Vice Admiral Charles Lockwood at ComSubPac headquarters in Honolulu.

As we have seen, the lore of the submarine service in World War II is filled with narrow escapes and close calls. That was the case with Walt Griffith as well.

The boat Griffith put into commission after the *Bowfin*, the one he ushered to the Pacific and took on her first two successful war patrols, ultimately suffered a tragic fate. After Griffith turned over command to her new skipper and she sailed away on her third patrol, the *Bullhead* went missing off Bali. It is believed that an enemy airplane surprised her, her radar possibly blocked by the high mountains on the island of Bali, and that she was sunk with all hands—eighty-four men—in August of 1945.

The USS *Bullhead* was the last of the fifty-two U.S. submarines lost in World War II.

The *Bowfin*'s new skipper after Walt Griffith was Commander John Corbus, a 1930 grad of the Naval Academy and another experienced submarine sailor. Corbus got the command almost by default. He had been removed from the bridge of his first boat after a couple of less-than-stellar patrols, but Admiral Christie felt the young officer still had promise and deserved a second chance. When the officer who was supposed to take over the *Bowfin* after Griffith came down with a bad case of gout, the much-decorated boat went to John Corbus instead. He was on the bridge for her fifth and sixth war patrols, both of which were deemed successful, giving a boost to her skipper's flagging naval career even as he and they did their part to win the war.

Obviously eager to show his bosses that the results aboard his previous boat were not typical of what he could do on the bridge of a submarine, Corbus was aggressive from the very beginning of his tenure on the *Bowfin*. On her fifth war patrol, he and the *Aspro* (SS-309) sank a Japanese army cargo ship north of Palau. Then, on the next run, he took his new sub right into a harbor in chase of a three-ship convoy. There, he proceeded to destroy two of the ships, the dock, a crane, and a bus full of Japanese soldiers. He still felt bad that he did not get the third ship he had tailed into the harbor before he was forced to slip back out of its narrow confines and shallow waters.

A dozen days later, in an attack described as "brilliant" in later accounts,

Corbus and the *Bowfin* sank what they reported as being a convoy of three ships and two destroyer escorts, all in a frenzied, full-bore night attack. One of those vessels was identified as another army cargo ship, the *Tsushima Maru*. Ultimately, that was the only vessel of the five for which the *Bowfin* received official credit for sinking, even though he and his crew clearly saw the others afire, listing, apparently on their way down.

But there was no problem receiving credit for the *Tsushima Maru*. There would be survivors who would vividly attest to her destruction.

Kiyoshi Uehara was ten years old, in the Japanese equivalent of the fourth grade, when he got word of the evacuation. He and his classmates were to be transported from Japanese-held Okinawa to the Home Islands because the Americans were inching closer and closer to that outpost.

He was frightened. His mother was dead and his father was in Osaka. He lived in Okinawa with his grandmother and older brother, and neither of them seemed willing to temper his fear of leaving home, going to some strange place.

"It is all right," his teacher assured him and the others in his class. "It will be a wonderful trip. You will go to the Home Islands and you will see snow."

That was a wondrous thought. Kiyoshi felt better when he heard that. It would be a great adventure. Besides, his friends in class seemed excited about the trip as well. And maybe, on this trip, he would be able to see his father again for the first time in so long.

Soon the children were watching cartoons and movies on the yellowed screen that hung at the front of the classroom—movies that showed them all the glory of growing up while pledging loyalty to the emperor, and then valiantly fighting and dying for the preservation of the empire.

Before they left home, the children were issued brand-new uniforms, better to withstand the cold weather they would encounter once they arrived in Japan. His older brother bought Kiyoshi a new pair of brown leather shoes. Then, on the day of their departure, he carried a ragged bag that contained the rest of his clothes as he marched along with his friends, singing and laughing to mask their nervousness, their sadness at leaving their families behind.

At the dock, they saw for the first time the ship that waited to take them to their home for the next few months—a safe place to be until the American threat had been repulsed. Kiyoshi could not believe the size of the vessel that towered over the other boats in the harbor. She was so big she could not even get close to the wharf.

Kiyoshi and the other children had to climb aboard fishing boats and were floated a few at a time out to the huge transport. Along the way, he saw some of his teachers, several members of families he knew, and other students from his school. They were all laughing, excited about sailing away on such a big boat.

Kiyoshi and his classmates were shown to one of the lower cabins, where tiny beds seemed to fill every inch of the stuffy quarters. They were given small boxes that contained food for the trip. Life vests were given to each of them, along with quick instructions on how to strap them on if there should be an emergency. The young boy looked at the contraption for a long time. It was the first time he had thought of the possibility of the ship sinking, of their not making it across the sea to Japan. But how could such a massive vessel sink?

His thoughts were interrupted by bells ringing, whistles blowing.

Then they were off.

On the second night of their voyage, Kiyoshi and a friend finally gave up trying to sleep in the stifling little room they shared with all the other student passengers belowdecks. The games they played did not help either, and some of the other children fussed at them for keeping them awake. They took their blankets, food boxes, and life vests and went to the ship's main deck to try to find a cooling breeze.

Though not nearly as bad as it was in the cabins below, it was sweltering topside as well. Still, with the gentle rolling of the ship and a humid, fitful breeze in their faces to help make the air bearable, he and his friend were soon able to find sleep.

A thunderous, dull *whoomp!* woke them with a start. The deck of the big ship improbably shuddered beneath them. It was surreal. How could such a big ship tremble so?

At first, Kiyoshi thought it was a dream, but the shrill, panicked shouts around him brought him out of the fog of sleep at once. Something had happened to their ship. Something awful.

"Get ready for jumping!" a sailor screamed at them as he ran past, and then he sprinted on down the deck, rousing others who had come topside to sleep in the cooler air. "Hurry! The ship will sink! Get ready to jump!"

But Kiyoshi did not wait for any order to jump into the sea. If the ship was going to sink, it would do so without him still aboard.

Besides, he could already see blazes and was choking from all the acrid smoke. And there were screams. Screams of panicked, hurting people coming from somewhere beneath them, from the lower decks of the ship. Kiyoshi wondered for a brief moment how they would all be able to get up the ladders to the deck to get off the ship. Wondered about his friends and classmates and teachers.

But he sensed he did not have time to wonder for long. Using the flickering light from the flames that climbed up the side of the ship behind him, the youngster strapped on his life vest, just as he had been instructed to do, held hands with his friend and another student, stepped through the railing, and jumped from the already listing ship.

The fall was not nearly as far as he expected. It seemed that they were in the sea almost immediately.

And once they landed in the surprisingly cold water, they swam as hard as they could. Instinctively they knew that it would be best for them to get as far from the sinking vessel as they could. Somehow they knew there was a danger that they would be sucked down with her.

As they swam away from the flames, the smoke, the screams and shouts, they sang songs, the ones taught to them by the teachers when they were back at school in their hometown. Many of the teachers who taught them those songs were aboard the ship with them. They were songs of glory, of dying to serve the emperor if called upon to do so in order to make a stronger empire.

Their voices sounded eerie and hollow to them. There was no echo on the rolling sea waves. The words and tune were seemingly gobbled up and swallowed by the black night. They sang anyway. They dared not look back as explosions continued behind them, the brightness flickering like close-by lightning strikes, the blasts rolling across the water, stunning their ears.

Surely someone would soon pick them up. Several naval vessels were escorting them. They had seen them from the decks, wallowing along all around them.

But no one came.

Then, almost lost in the smoke and darkness, a small bamboo raft came floating near. Kiyoshi and his friend climbed aboard, joining two other survivors who had made it off their ship.

It was a terrible ordeal. A typhoon was nearby so the water was rough, bouncing them sickeningly from wave trough to high in the air on a peak. Yet it did not rain. There was no water to drink.

After several days on the raft, Kiyoshi hallucinated, believing he could stand, walk off the raft, and go find a cool, bubbling spring. There he could finally drink his fill. One of the other people on the raft slapped him hard and convinced him he must stay put, that there was no cool spring. Later, they drank their own urine to survive. They managed to catch a small fish and the four of them shared the meager morsel.

Still no one came.

When the sun was up, they could see the sharks, slowly circling the raft. One of the boys used a sharp stick he had salvaged from the sea to poke at them. Thankfully, they went away.

It was six days of drifting before they spied a beach in the distance. All four of them paddled that way as furiously as they could, trying to overcome the current that threatened to carry them past the spit of land. But they made it. They were on land for the first time in over a week.

Later, a fishing boat came by and saw them jumping up and down on the sand, yelling for attention.

They were saved.

Kiyoshi suffered a high fever and was in a coma for a while. When he finally awoke, he was given rice and fish, but with it came a stern warning.

He was to tell no one what had happened. No one.

When he was well enough, he was sent back home, back to his brother and grandmother. But first, before he was even allowed to see them, he had to pay a visit to the police station. There, once again, he was ordered to remain silent about the sinking of his ship—not even telling his grandmother or older brother.

It was imperative that no one should ever learn what happened to the young passengers of the *Tsushima Maru*.

When, in 1944, it was clear to them that the tide of the war had turned against them, the Japanese began to prepare for the long-anticipated invasion. The first step was to evacuate schoolchildren and their teachers out of major cities and key territories around the Pacific and place them in rural camps. Their motives were not totally humanitarian. They wanted to assure a supply of soldiers for the future of the empire once the invasion had been repulsed and the war had been won.

Over half a million children were successfully moved to those camps.

Eight hundred and twenty-six children were aboard the *Tsushima Maru* on the night of August 22, 1944. She was unmarked, not flying any flag or indicator that she was anything but a troop transport. She was unlighted, too. Even Japanese cargo vessels typically had lights. The escort vessels around her—a destroyer and a gunboat, each undeniably a warship—seemed to confirm that whatever cargo or personnel the ship carried, she was certainly a military target.

That's what Captain John Corbus and the *Bowfin* crew assumed as well. There was no reason for anyone on the American submarine to believe otherwise.

Seven hundred and sixty-seven children died in the sinking. Only fifty-nine survived.

Those passengers of the *Tsushima Maru* who lived were forbidden to speak of the disaster under threats of severe punishment, both to them and their families. The Japanese simply could not afford for news of the tragedy to reach an already demoralized populace.

It was twenty years after the war before the truth of the *Bowfin*'s target was ultimately known. Even now, more than sixty years later, little has been written outside Japan about the incident. Ironically, in Japan, where the tragedy was to be kept absolutely quiet, there have been several books published on the event, as well as documentary broadcasts. There has even been an animated feature movie produced dealing with the subject.

Memorial ceremonies are regularly held at sea near where the ship sank, and there are monuments for those lost at several cities from which the victims came.

None of the books, movies, or monuments blames America, John Corbus, or the *Bowfin* for the tragedy that occurred that night. They consider it to be but another example of the horrors of war.

The *Bowfin* came directly to the East Coast after the war ended and began an on-again, off-again career as a reserve fleet boat, a pier-side trainer, and an auxiliary research submarine. She was decommissioned for the final time in December 1971 and her name was struck from the Naval Vessel Registry. Her service was done and she, like many of her sisters, was likely headed for the scrap heap—literally.

But in 1978, the Pacific Fleet Memorial Association was chartered, and a year later made the *Bowfin* one of its first purchases. Admiral Bernard Clarey, a former commander of the Pacific Fleet, was instrumental in obtaining custody of the submarine for the memorial group. Admiral Clarey was a young lieutenant at the time of the attack on Pearl Harbor and was in Hawaii that fateful Sunday morning. He had just returned from patrol aboard the USS *Dolphin* (SS-169) and was enjoying breakfast with his wife and fifteen-month-old son when the attack began. He served aboard submarines throughout the war.

In 1980, the *Bowfin* was made ready for an ocean transit and then towed across the Pacific to be docked adjacent to the USS *Arizona* Memorial Visitor Center. The *Arizona*, of course, is the best-known victim of the attack on Pearl Harbor and still rests at the bottom of the harbor, an underwater tomb for many of her crew who perished that day. Her memorial is one of the most visited naval history sites on the planet.

A year after arriving at her new home near the battleship, the *Bowfin* was opened to the public as a museum ship.

The "Pearl Harbor Avenger" had returned to her unofficial hometown.

In 1986, the submarine was designated a National Historic Landmark by the U.S. Department of the Interior. The ten-thousand-square-foot museum has a large collection of submarine-related exhibits, including weapons systems, submarine models, battle flags, photographs, and more. That includes a Poseidon C-3 missile, the only one of its kind on display anywhere. The museum also holds a collection of more than fifty episodes of the television series *The Silent Service*, a program that told the true stories of the exploits of submarines in World War II. These and other submarine videos are screened in the facility's mini-theater.

Visitors may rent a cassette player that gives a narrated audio description while they tour the submarine.

On the grounds is a special memorial to the fifty-two submarines and the more than thirty-five hundred submariners who were lost in World War II.

The USS *Arizona* Memorial nearby is maintained by the U.S. Park Service and paid for by taxpayers. On the other hand, the *Bowfin* and her museum is run by a nonprofit group, so, unlike at the *Arizona* Memorial, visitors are charged an admission.

The boat is located right next to the Arizona Visitors' Center, a couple of miles off Highway H1. In addition to the USS *Arizona* Memorial, the battleship USS *Missouri*, aboard which the surrender by the Japanese took place, is also nearby.

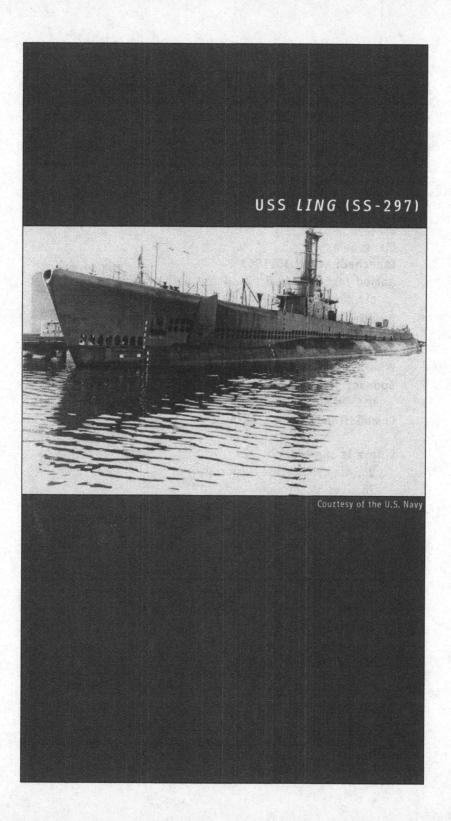

USS *LING* (SS-297)

Courtesy of the U.S. Navy

USS *LING* (SS-297)

Class: *Balao*
Launched: August 15, 1943
Named for: the ling fish, which is better known as the cobia. Near the end of the war, those responsible for naming vessels had almost run out of fish names and had resorted to using less accepted or regional names for fish that had already been used.
Where: Cramp Shipbuilding Company, Philadelphia
Sponsor: Mrs. E. J. Foy, wife of the captain of the battleship USS *Oklahoma* (BB-37)
Commissioned: June 8, 1945

Where is she today?
USS *Ling* Submarine Memorial
78 River Street
Hackensack, New Jersey 07601-7110
(201) 342-3268
www.njnm.com

Claim to fame: Though her keel was laid down in November 1942, the *Ling* did not sail for the Panama Canal and the Pacific until February 1946, after the war. Her brief activity in the Atlantic before the surrender of the Axis powers made her the last of the *Balao*-class submarines to operate in World War II.

I f you check the list of World War II Pacific Ocean submarines that helped beat Japan, you will not find a mention anywhere of the USS *Ling*. The submarine war in the Atlantic Ocean, at least from the U.S. perspective, was almost nonexistent and did not feature a hero boat of that name either.

The simple truth is that she was late to the party, through no fault of hers or her commissioning crew's.

The *Ling* was slated to be built by the William Cramp and Sons Ship and Engine Building Company in Philadelphia, Pennsylvania. The Cramp yard was legendary in the shipbuilding field and was acknowledged to be the preeminent iron shipbuilder in the United States, if not the world, during the nineteenth century.

Established in 1825 by William Cramp, the yards turned out literally hundreds of vessels for private industry, governments, and navies all around the globe. It became a target for takeover after a successful run during World War I. The company was sold to American Ship and Commerce Corporation just after the First World War, but the new owners ran into hard times and were forced to close the facility in 1927, ironically at the height of an American manufacturing boom just prior to the Great Depression.

In 1940, with war looming once again, the U.S. government, eager to put any war industry capacity back online if possible, advanced the owners of the Cramp shipbuilding yards $22 million to reactivate the facility. The government also promptly began awarding them contracts for new construction of various vessels, forcing them to get back up to speed as quickly as possible.

Some of those contracts to Cramp and Sons were for the new *Balao*-class submarines. There is speculation that Cramp was reactivated because one of its owners was W. Averell Harriman, the financier, politician, and ambassador. He was closely allied with President Franklin Roosevelt, served in several New Deal roles, and represented the president as his special envoy to Europe just before World War II. Clearly, the reactivation of the yards in Philadelphia was quite profitable to Harriman.

Regardless of the reasons, from the beginning of the company's return to active shipbuilding there were reports of shoddy workmanship, and completion of some ships was delayed for months and even years. Some of the vessels that began construction in Philadelphia had to be moved to other shipyards for final work to be finished.

That is what happened to a new *Balao* boat named the *Ling*. When she was formally launched in August 1943, the navy realized she needed more work to get her shipshape. They moved the submarine to the Boston Navy Yard for completion and testing.

Her first skipper was Commander George Garvie Malumphy, a man with two previous submarine commands already on his résumé. His previous boat before taking the helm of the *Ling* was the *Skipjack* (SS-184), on which he and his crew had undergone a particularly harrowing experience.

During an attack on a convoy using the *Skipjack*'s stern torpedo tubes, one of the tube valves failed to close when the fish was flushed out. The aft torpedo room quickly took on fourteen tons of seawater. Fourteen tons!

The submarine was forced to surface and make emergency repairs amid all the enemy shipping at which they had just been shooting. Otherwise there was a real danger of the flooding dragging them down so far and so fast that they would not be able to recover.

It took some fine seamanship by Malumphy and his crew to keep the boat afloat and get her fixed. They not only accomplished that tough assignment but also managed to chase down the convoy and sink one of the ships in it, a sea tender they had been shooting at before the near-fatal malfunction occurred.

That was the mind-set that George Garvie Malumphy brought to this new ship he was commanding.

As soon as the *Ling* was deemed seaworthy and her crew was trained, she was ordered to head to the Panama Canal, but by then, the war had already ended. She never made it to the Pacific Ocean. She spent a month in Panama and then made a U-turn and dutifully steamed right back to New London, Connecticut, where she had been based since her completion and had undergone sea trials.

The *Ling* did operate in the Atlantic in early 1945, getting ready to go to war, and she was formally commissioned in June 1945. Even though the war in Europe ended in May 1945, Japan surrendered in September 1945, after the *Ling* was placed into service. Her preparations for going to battle and her operations in defense of our Atlantic Coast during that time period are officially considered to be wartime service. She was most certainly a World War II submarine, even if her service was brief and not in the Pacific.

Upon her return to New London, she became part of the Atlantic Reserve Fleet, and then, in 1960, she went down to Brooklyn Navy Yard to serve as a training vessel. She was struck from the naval register in 1971.

Only six months later, she found someone else who wanted her.

Frank Savino was vice president of marketing at the *Record*, a newspaper in Bergen, New Jersey. He was approached by a local group of submarine veterans who had created the Submarine Memorial Association. They had come up with the idea of obtaining a vessel from the navy to moor near the newspaper's headquarters, prime real estate located on the banks of the Hackensack River, about a dozen miles northwest of Manhattan. It would be good publicity for the paper as well as honoring veterans, they argued, and the paper had the perfect place to locate such a memorial.

Savino was sold. He enlisted the aid of his boss, Donald Borg, the paper's owner and publisher. Borg thought it was a fine idea, too, and agreed not only to help obtain a suitable vessel but to make available the use of some of his newspaper's riverbank land for a memorial and park. He agreed to do so for the princely sum of one dollar per year.

The group soon learned about the recent retirement of the USS *Ling*, a perfectly good submarine that was berthed not that far away, in Brooklyn. They petitioned the navy to allow them to bring the sub up the Hackensack River to serve as a memorial ". . . to perpetuate the memory of our shipmates who gave their lives in the pursuit of their duties while serving their country." With the commitment from the *Record* for the location, and with the support of other groups and companies, the deal was quickly struck.

In January 1973, the *Ling* was hooked to a tugboat and towed upriver. A group of the submarine vets went to work on her as soon as she was parked at her new site. She was already in reasonably good shape because she had so recently been removed from service. Still, the group scrubbed, polished, and painted, getting her ready for public tours.

Over the years, much authentic gear has been reinstalled on the boat. Instructors and students from the Naval Submarine School in Groton, Connecticut, have "adopted" the boat and still make periodic trips to fight the worst enemies of the old boats—corrosion, rust, and dirt.

There is still much to do to keep her presentable. Vessels left in water tend to deteriorate quickly if they are not properly protected. The World War II sub vets who first brought the boat to Hackensack suffer from dwindling numbers, and those who are left are hardly able to do much physical labor on the boat. New volunteers are needed.

While visitors continue to come in relatively big numbers, there is not enough money being generated to keep the boat in good shape. There is even a report at the time of this writing that the diesel tanks still contain fuel, left there for better than thirty years.

There was something else left aboard the *Ling*, too. Her five safes— including one in the executive officer's quarters, one in the yeoman's office, and one in the captain's stateroom—were locked for the last time in

1946. The combinations for all the safes have long since been lost and no one could tell for certain what might be contained inside them.

In recent years, X-ray equipment confirmed that there was something in each of the twenty-by-twenty steel-reinforced boxes—including documents and metallic objects. Over the years, several locksmiths have attempted to open the safes without using drills or explosives. The memorial group did not want to damage anything aboard the submarine, not even to solve the mystery of what might be in her safes.

There is historical interest. The boat's orders for her lone trip could well have been in there. The other objects could have been personal effects of the crew members. But there was still a certain mysterious air about the whole thing, and it continued to bug all those associated with the vessel.

Finally a professional safecracker was brought in to see what he could do. In January 2006, locksmith Jeff Sitar kneeled down in the XO's stateroom, working in cramped quarters, a pair of sensitive headphones strapped to his head, listening as he gently turned the combination lock on the old safe. As he worked, dignitaries, onlookers, reporters, and cameras from the NBC television network crowded in around him in the tiny compartment.

It took him only four minutes to get that safe open.

Sitar continued the quest over the next five hours, sometimes relying on sensitive amplification equipment, sometimes only on the safecracker's touch. One by one, he was able to open each of the *Ling*'s safes, revealing after almost sixty years their mysterious contents.

It turns out there was little in them that was all that exciting—except maybe to military historians and World War II submarine buffs. They found a dozen pennies, a couple of sets of keys, equipment manuals, blueprints of the sub, a list of all her equipment, and other paperwork—the typical stuff that a submarine crew would have kept handy and safe during that period of time. There were also a couple of cans of 180-proof grain alcohol in the yeoman's safe. That would have been used for cleaning small parts. There was also a collection of patrol logs, and a full set of qualification tests, the exams that were employed to confirm that crew members were proficient enough at all duty stations to receive their dolphin pins.

The last couple of items would have been classified as top secret in their day, but nothing really earthshaking came out of the safes. Still, the buildup to their opening gave the old boat some much-needed attention as well as national publicity on a major television network.

Other exhibits have been added to the park over the years, including a Vietnam War–era patrol boat like the one featured in the movie *Apocalypse Now*. There is also a Japanese-manned suicide torpedo, a German two-man "Seahund" mini-submarine, and more.

USS *LIONFISH* (SS-298)

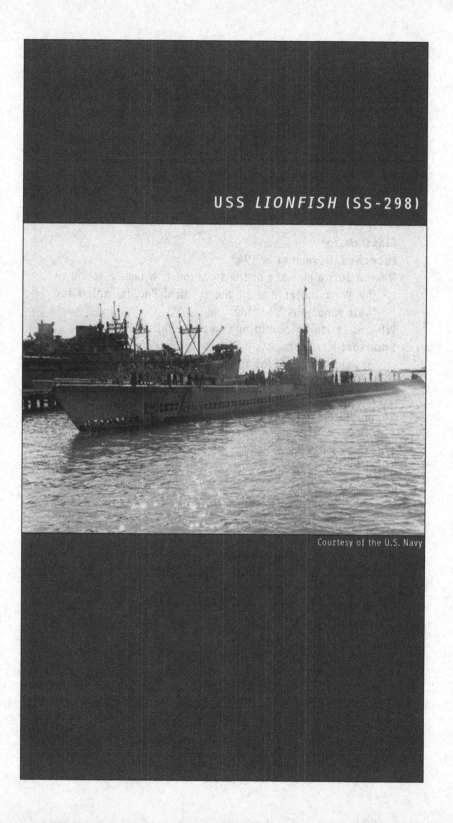

Courtesy of the U.S. Navy

USS *LIONFISH*

Class: *Balao*
Launched: November 7, 1943
Named for: a member of the scorpion-fish family, found in the West Indies and in the tropical Pacific, noted for their venomous fin spines
Where: Cramp Shipbuilding Company, Philadelphia
Sponsor: Mrs. Harold C. Train, wife of the gentleman who was chief of staff for the naval battle group commander at Pearl Harbor on December 7, 1941, and later a rear admiral and commander of the Fifteenth Naval District
Commissioned: November 1, 1944

Where is she today?
Battleship Cove
5 Water Street
Fall River, Massachusetts 02722-0111
(508) 678-1100
www.battleshipcove.org

Claim to fame: Like many of her sisters, her usefulness extended beyond her two war patrols, including NATO exercises, helping train the navy in antisubmarine warfare.

Like her sister boat, the *Ling*, the USS *Lionfish* was relatively late getting into the Pacific war. Also like her sister, she encountered construction delays at the Cramp yard in Philadelphia and was moved to another facility for completion. In her case, it was to Portsmouth, New Hampshire. Still, when she was commissioned in November 1944, her crew had no idea that the war would be over in less than a year. They were convinced that they, too, had a real chance of affecting the war's outcome, just as other submarines were doing daily half a world away.

With early torpedo problems solved and with cutting-edge new radar and other equipment, the submarines were having spectacular success against a desperate enemy in the Pacific. That was especially true of the submarines' primary job, cutting the supply lines for raw materials and petroleum, keeping the lifeblood of the enemy's war effort from reaching the places where it was most needed.

Of course, there were still far too many of the American boats going on eternal patrol, but that was inevitable, considering the ferocity of this conflict. At the time of her commissioning in November 1944, the *Lionfish*'s crew was eager to get through the canal and into the war to do their part. They worked hard, getting themselves and their submarine ready for combat.

The *Lionfish*'s commissioning commanding officer was Edward Spruance. For once, nobody aboard the new boat needed to ask who their new skipper was or where he came from. The Spruance name was already legendary. Lieutenant Commander Spruance's father was Admiral Raymond Spruance, one of the heroes of the Battle of Midway, an early turning point in the war, back in June 1942. The younger Spruance was torpedo officer on the submarine USS *Tambor* (SS-198), patrolling near Oahu the morning of the attack on Pearl Harbor. He and the rest of his shipmates were unaware of the attack until the night of December 7, when they surfaced off Hawaii and, to their horror, saw the fires still burning at their base. Spruance was still an officer on the *Tambor* when she participated in the Battle of Midway, the same fracas in which his father played such a major part. There is no evidence that his famous dad had any role in the younger officer getting a submarine command. He was, by all accounts, a competent submarine officer, and there was certainly a need for all those the navy could find at that point in the war. Nepotism was apparently not a factor.

Whether it was the skipper's fault or not, the *Lionfish* did not have an especially distinguished one-and-only war patrol under the command of young Spruance. She did some nifty maneuvering to avoid torpedoes fired from an enemy submarine near Bungo Suido. She sent a Japanese schooner down in flames a few days later, but, for all the usual reasons, never received official credit for the sinking. She picked up some downed B-29 pilots (some of the more than five hundred pilots rescued by submarines during the war) and took them to safety at Saipan. Not bad. Not outstanding. The patrol was declared "successful."

On her second run, Commander Bricker Ganyard assumed the helm, but pickings were slim for targets by this time. They crew did launch one attack on a surfaced Japanese submarine, and though they saw smoke and heard clear breaking-up noises, they were not given credit for destroying the highly desirable target. As it turned out, no one would be willing to take their word for it. As happened so often, spotty postwar records, most of them kept by the Japanese, simply did not back up what many of the sub skippers were certain they had accomplished.

The *Lionfish* and her crew served out the balance of the war performing lifeguard duty, supporting the massive bombing attacks on the Japanese Home Islands. That is what they were doing when the ultimate bomb

runs—the ones that took the atomic bomb to Hiroshima and Nagasaki—
brought the war with the Japanese to an abrupt end.

After being decommissioned at Mare Island, near San Francisco, the USS *Lionfish* had five years of rest before being called back
into duty. She was recommissioned in January 1951 and made the long
return trip back through the Panama Canal to the East Coast. From
there, she took part in a number of training exercises, helping other naval
vessels hone their antisubmarine warfare (ASW) skills. Many of the World
War II submarines performed well training the next generation of sub
sailors, emulating enemy vessels, using the stealth with which they were
born to educate sonar operators and others in the fine art of detecting
submersibles.

She also took part in a series of NATO exercises, showing up in the
Caribbean, the Mediterranean, and various places in the Atlantic Ocean.
Much of that Cold War service still remains classified.

The *Lionfish* finally served out her useful years as a training vessel,
moored in Providence, Rhode Island.

In 1973, she became part of an ambitious naval display colorfully
dubbed Battleship Cove and located at Fall River, Massachusetts, about
fifty miles south of Boston. There she rests today, on the Taunton River
near the Charles Braga Bridge, only a short distance from busy Interstate
195, the highway spur that runs from Providence to New Bedford and on
to Cape Cod. The location is only about an hour's drive by car from the
U.S. Navy Submarine School in Groton, Connecticut, and the display of
historic naval vessels spans over sixty years of maritime history.

Alongside the *Lionfish* are the battleship USS *Massachusetts* (BB-59),
nicknamed "Big Mamie," the recipient of eleven battle stars for her service in the Pacific in World War II, and the destroyer USS *Joseph P.
Kennedy* (DD-850), named for the son of Ambassador Joseph Kennedy

and the older brother of future president John Kennedy. Joseph Jr. was an aviator who was killed in the war. The destroyer was in service without interruption from December 1945 until July 1973, including duty during the Korean War, the Cuban missile crisis, and the blockade of Cuba.

Other exhibits at Battleship Cove include a Russian-made missile corvette, the *Hiddensee*, and two PT (patrol torpedo) boats, similar to the one on which President Kennedy served during the war. Helicopters, an airplane, a landing craft, and other hardware are also on display. The attraction claims to have the largest collection of military exhibits in the world, based on sheer numbers.

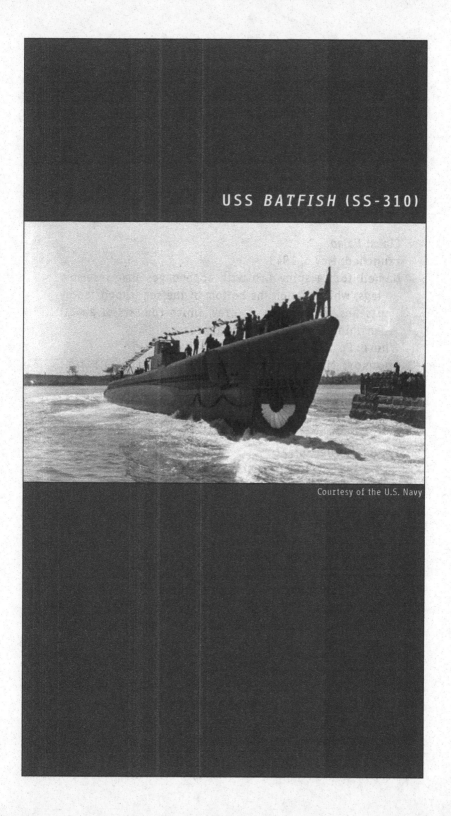

USS *BATFISH* (SS-310)

Courtesy of the U.S. Navy

USS *BATFISH* (SS-310)

Class: *Balao*
Launched: May 5, 1943
Named for: a spiny fish with appendages that resemble
legs, which sits on the bottom of the sea, supported by
its fins, waiting for its prey, which consists of almost
anything that comes within its reach
Where: Portsmouth Navy Yard, New Hampshire
Sponsor: Mrs. Nellie Fortier, the mother of six sons
who were all, at the time of the launching, fighting
in the war
Commissioned: August 21, 1943

Where is she today?
Muskogee War Memorial Park
3500 Batfish Road
Muskogee, Oklahoma 74402
(918) 682-6294
www.ussbatfish.com
www.batfish.org

Claim to fame: She was dubbed the "sub-killer submarine
of World War II" for her amazing feat of sinking three
enemy submarines in just over three days, an almost impossible feat.

The incessant radar signal that was pounding away on 158 megacycles was undeniable. Whatever kind of vessel was out there in the indelible darkness, it was dangerously close by the submarine USS *Batfish*. Too close for comfort.

Eleven thousand yards away from them was the best estimate, tracking on a rock-steady course of 310 degrees. The electric thrill of it all ran up and down the length of the submarine. The chase was on!

It was a perfect night for stalking, with nothing out there between them and their quarry but velvet blackness. The sky was cloudy. No moon. Even the phosphorescence that usually played in the sea wash at the boat's stern seemed to have gone away, given up trying to fight the darkness.

Every minute or so, as the officer of the deck (OOD) looked on, the radar operator in the conning tower below the bridge called a series of numbers up the hatch, citing the range and course of this new contact. The vessel they were trailing was not varying its speed or direction of travel a bit. And so far, it seemed unaware that the *Batfish* was out there in the night, too.

Two men stood on the bridge of the submarine, just above the open hatch, staring intently into the darkness. It was February 9, 1945, just after ten p.m. local time. The *Batfish*, a U.S. Navy fleet submarine, was now in the midst of her sixth patrol in a relative backwater of the South China Sea.

The pair of officers who stood on the *Batfish*'s bridge used the railing to steady themselves against the slight roll of the waves as they searched the night for any sign of this unidentified vessel. The lookouts above them peered off in each direction of the compass, looking for the new contact, but also peering into the blackness for other vessels that might be slipping up on them.

Captain John K. "Jake" Fyfe stared fiercely, trying to make out something up there ahead of their bow. There was nothing to see. Nothing but tropical night. Only the intercepted radar signal tipped them off that there was somebody else out there.

The skipper could hear the voices of the lookouts in the shears above him, talking about the rumors that the enemy submarines they had been sent to intercept might carry enemy generals, their mistresses, collaborators, and, scuttlebutt had it, a fortune in gold in her lower decks.

Fyfe grinned. He liked the men with whom he rode on the *Batfish*. Like most of his fellow submariners, they were such a close brotherhood. Though he could see and feel and smell the fear on them sometimes, he had never heard a whimper or a cry or even so much as a whispered prayer, no matter the ferocity of a depth charging or the viciousness of an aerial attack.

Intelligence claimed that the Japanese had sent four submarines—almost half the boats they had left in the entire sixth fleet—down to the Philippines. They were supposed to be on a high-risk mission to evacuate the last of the Japanese brass left in the Philippines, and to pick up pilots, aircrews, and technicians who were stranded there, trying to get them out before General MacArthur made his promised return.

Whatever they were hauling on those subs, the Japanese were in one hell of a hurry. There was some thought they might be distracted, easier to sneak up on. It was a chore for anybody, but especially another submarine, to bag one of those slippery Japanese plunging boats. Subs were perfectly designed to shoot at surface ships, vessels that had only the horizontal options when it came time to get away from a torpedo. Submarines had the vertical option—dive or surface—and that made it a complicated game.

"You think this might be one of the boats we're looking for, Skipper?" the man standing on the bridge next to Fyfe asked. He was Lieutenant

Clark Sprinkle, the executive officer of the boat. He knew that the captain had a sixth sense about these things. Sometimes it appeared that he could smell a destroyer before it showed up on the SJ radar.

"I'd bet on it," Fyfe replied with certainty.

Sprinkle grinned. He liked his skipper's sense of humor almost as much as he did the man's aggressiveness. Fyfe believed in attacking first, before the enemy had any idea he and his submarine were there, and then collecting the details and doing the postmortem later, when things cooled off.

The radar signal remained strong, potent. It was still nearby. It had to be a submarine.

Almost an hour after first contact, Fyfe got the call up the hatch that he had been eager to hear since the first report of the mysterious radar signal.

"Captain, SJ contact. Bearing two-four-zero true. Range, eleven thousand yards."

The target had finally shown up on the *Batfish*'s radar. Fyfe repeated the bearing loud enough for the men in the shears above him to hear, and then asked, "You boys see anything?"

"No, Skipper."

"No sir. Not yet. We will."

Fyfe and his crew made certain that they kept the boat to the east of the contact, the darker quadrant, ready to dive in an instant if need be. Or, if possible, make a surface attack.

"Sound reports quiet screws, four thousand yards," came the next report.

Fyfe dropped his glasses and looked at Sprinkle, a grin on his face.

"XO, if I were you, I wouldn't take my bet. Looks like we got an Imperial Japanese Navy submarine."

No one had to mention how difficult it would be for one sub to bag another. They were simply too stealthy, too sneaky, but the *Batfish* and her crew had no thought but to try.

"Battle stations—surface," Fyfe sang out.

Every man on watch was quickly at his position, if he wasn't there already. Those who were not officially on watch ran to whatever their assigned stations were, ready to get to work. They were poised to launch torpedoes at one of their own, at fellow submariners. And the sailors in the enemy boat could very well be lining up to attempt the very same thing, to launch torpedoes at the *Batfish* after luring them closer with their blatant, enticing radar signal.

The best guess from the *Batfish*'s radar and sound gear had the target's speed at twelve knots. The speed and course information had been fed into the TDC (torpedo data computer). Torpedoes were loaded and ready in all tubes fore and aft. Everyone was on station.

"Let's stay up top," Captain Jake Fyfe ordered from the bridge. He preferred a surface attack.

"Aye, Captain."

One thing worried Fyfe. He knew that there were at least five American submarines operating in the area in addition to the *Batfish*. There was a chance that this target could be one of their sister boats. If he wasn't careful, his torpedoes could send one of their sisters to the bottom. He had to take the risk of making a call just so he could be sure.

"Prepare a message for our boats," Fyfe ordered. "Let's make sure we are shooting at somebody we don't like."

The radioman composed the message and the skipper gave the okay to transmit it. Within minutes, replies came in from all five of the other boats that were operating in their wolf pack. To a man, they reported, "Not me."

That settled it.

Fyfe gave the command to maneuver into position to fire a complement of four torpedoes from the forward tubes. Range to the target was dwindling. They were getting close.

There was still no visible sign of anything out there in the darkness. They had to trust radar and sound to tell him where the enemy was and where he was headed.

"Right full rudder," Fyfe barked. "All ahead flank."

The *Batfish* was moving in for the kill. This was what this vessel had been designed and built to do. This was what each of these men had signed on for and trained to do.

At eleven thirty p.m., with the target at a range of 1,850 yards, Captain Jake Fyfe ordered, "Fire one!"

Everyone on board could feel the kick of thrust as the first torpedo was flushed out of the tube. Twelve seconds later, the skipper sent the second torpedo away, then two more. One successful hit was all it should take to send a target such as this to the bottom, but they wanted to make sure.

The sailor designated to be the counter stared at his stopwatch, listening for the explosion when the warhead on the first torpedo struck and detonated. But all he heard was the ticking of the watch and the breathing of the men around him in the conning tower.

Jake Fyfe didn't need a stopwatch. All four of his torpedoes had missed.

Eight minutes later, they heard four distant explosions when the fish finally found ground on distant Fuga Island, detonating harmlessly on the beach.

The submariners aboard the enemy vessel could have heard the explosions, too, if they were listening at all. They would surely begin evasive maneuvers now. Or start shooting back with their own torpedoes or deck guns.

But the radar operator reported, "No change in course or speed."

Captain Fyfe dropped down the hatch from the bridge to the conning tower and stepped to where the attack officer stood over the plotting board, still staring and scratching his head.

"We had her speed wrong," the attack officer said without looking up at his captain. "She's doing fourteen knots, not twelve. We missed astern."

Fyfe considered the complicated geometry of what they needed to do next to make another attack on the enemy boat. It never crossed his mind to pull back and regroup.

"Let's go take another shot at him before he gets all the way to Formosa."

They pulled out to five thousand yards, running all-out, trying to make an end run. Meanwhile, the torpedomen in the bow room reloaded their tubes. By midnight, they were in place, within fifteen hundred yards of the radar blip they had been pursuing for over two hours.

"I see her," one of the lookouts in the shears called out. "Two points to the starboard of the bow."

"I see her, too," Clark Sprinkle said quietly.

There was no longer any doubt. It was the unmistakable profile of a Japanese submarine, possibly an I-class. Jake Fyfe pressed the bridge intercom button.

"We have visual on a Japanese submarine . . . range one thousand yards. Prepare to fire."

In the forward torpedo room, each man stood poised, sweating, as much from the tension as from the heat in the compartment. In the conn, the firing officer calmly and deliberately fed data from Captain Fyfe and the radar operator into the TDC and relayed the results from the machine to the torpedomen up front.

"Clear the bridge!" Fyfe barked, sending the lookouts below.

There was a risk in that. Once they went below, their night vision would be ruined for a while, but the skipper wanted to be able to dive instantly should this attack go sour, or in case someone else out there in the darkness decided to crash their little party.

He ordered the torpedoes to be made ready. Fyfe could feel the gentle motion of his vessel as the doors on tubes one, two, and three opened and flooded with seawater.

"Ready to fire," Sprinkle finally reported from below.

"Bridge to conn. Fire when ready," Fyfe ordered.

"Fire one!" came the response from the conn.

The captain waited, but oddly, there was no recoil in response to the command. Something was wrong. A Mark 18 torpedo weighed close to three thousand pounds—a ton and a half—and had the kick of a mule when it left its tube. But this time, there was nothing.

"Hot run in tube one! Number one failed to fire, Captain! She's stuck in the tube. About six inches of her nose is outside."

Torpedoes were not armed to explode immediately upon being fired from their tubes. To allow the weapon to put distance between itself and the boat that fired it, a wire umbilical was snapped at launch, allowing the arming vane in its nose to begin spinning as it made its way toward the target. It usually armed itself over three thousand feet out, ready then to explode on contact with an enemy vessel.

It was certainly possible that the umbilical had been snapped already and the arming vane could be spinning away on the nose of the torpedo that was stuck in the *Batfish*'s number-one torpedo tube. The torpedomen in the forward compartment knew what they were up against. They had the nose of a live and potent weapon stuck out of tube one and not budging. The torpedo would almost certainly do mortal damage to the submarine should it explode in the tube.

"Fire one again—manually!" Captain Fyfe yelled into the intercom. "And fire number two when ready!"

They had the perfect setup on the enemy target. Even if they were about to be sent to kingdom come by one of their own torpedoes, they could still take the other guy down.

This time everyone on the boat plainly felt the welcome nudge as the fish whooshed away clear. Up on the bridge, Jake Fyfe kept his glasses on the target and tried not to think about the ticking time bomb still in tube one. If the Japanese happened to turn around and look, the *Batfish* was clearly in sight. Fyfe would have a hard time evading, what with a hot fish in one tube and two other forward doors open to the sea.

Meanwhile, in the forward torpedo room, the torpedomen had evacuated the rest of the crewmen out of the compartment and closed the waterproof door behind them. With only the two men in the room now and working quickly, they hit tube one's FIRE button three, four, five times.

Nothing happened except for a flood of bubbles. The torpedo was still there, its nose sticking just out of the end of the tube.

"Fire three!" Captain Fyfe barked from the bridge. A satisfying kick verified that this one was safely away as well.

In the conn, the assistant attack officer was staring at his stopwatch, marking time since the firing of the weapon from tube two, waiting for the boom that told him they had struck their target. Up on the bridge, Jake Fyfe was keeping his own count, an eye in the direction of the target, praying for a detonation. But he couldn't keep from worrying about the hot run in tube one.

"What do you recommend we do?" he finally called down to the men in the forward torpedo room.

"Captain, I don't think we can build up enough pressure to get it out without closing the door. And she's sticking out beyond the mouth of the tube."

"Can you tell if she's armed?"

"Well, sir, we don't think she got out far enough to arm, but we can't be sure."

"Then try to close the door," Captain Fyfe said.

That might be all it took to set the thing off, but there was no choice. They had to do something.

Without even thinking about the possible consequences any longer, the senior torpedoman jabbed the button to close the door to tube number one. It clanged hard against the nose of the stuck torpedo but the stubborn torpedo still didn't budge.

He waited a moment and then punched the button again. This time, the door clanged hard against the torpedo, somehow nudging all the way closed, sliding the hot-run weapon backward, deeper into the tube.

The two men held their breath as they forced compressed air into the tube. They had to be careful not to raise the pressure too high or the tube might rupture. That was not a good thing either. The compartment would certainly flood and the two sub sailors would drown. It would also be difficult to submerge with the front room filled with water and a tube ruptured.

Once again, as both men held their breath, the torpedoman opened the tube door to the sea.

"Here goes," he said and hit the firing switch once again.

Whooosh!

Up on the bridge, Jake Fyfe felt the most wonderful, subtle jolt. An instant later, he heard the confirmation: "Number one fired manually!"

Incredibly, the whole episode had lasted less than a minute.

Jake Fyfe swallowed hard and then sucked in another deep breath. They still had two other torpedoes away, hopefully bearing down on the IJN submarine.

Then, a thousand yards away across the calm sea, a hellish bright sun of concussion illuminated the dark night. A column of fire climbed hundreds of feet into the black sky. Jake Fyfe felt the shock wave of the blast on his face and chest and he was temporarily blinded by the brightness of it.

The men around the radar console below watched as the single blip they had been watching on their screen suddenly disintegrated into many tiny pinpoints of light, then disappeared altogether.

"Permission to come on the bridge?" Clark Sprinkle inquired from below.

"Permission granted."

The XO climbed up quickly and stared at the continuing explosions and smoke that had once been an Imperial Japanese Navy submarine.

Fyfe smiled broadly. He was proud of his men. Proud of how they had responded to the attack and how well they had carried out their jobs despite the near disaster of the stuck torpedo.

"Radio, tell the rest of the wolf pack we bagged a red one," Fyfe said.

A minute later, word came up the hatch, "*Scabbardfish* sends her congratulations and says, 'Welcome to the club.'"

The USS *Scabbardfish* (SS-397), under the command of Frederick A. "Pop" Gunn, sank an enemy submarine just off the main Japanese island of Honshu on November 28, 1944, a bit over three months before.

The other boats quickly radioed their congratulations as well, but Fyfe knew the fun was over for the moment. There was work yet to be done.

"Clear the bridge. Take her down and let's reload. There's supposed to be more of them swimming around out here. Let's be ready for them."

With that, the brief celebration was over. With her bridge and decks cleared of crewmen, her hatches shut and dogged, the *Batfish* slid smoothly beneath the surface of the dark sea. As she did, she slipped through the oil and flotsam, the remains of what had recently been an enemy submarine and her crew.

Over the next three days, the *Batfish* and her crew stalked and sank two more Japanese submarines. It was an amazing feat, not equaled by any other boat in the war. While sinking three submarines in three days was remarkable, it was especially noteworthy that it was accomplished by another sub. Submarines are designed to shoot at targets on the surface and can have a tough time trying to dispatch vessels like enemy submarines.

Captain Fyfe acknowledged that there was some sadness in taking the lives of fellow submariners, even if they were enemy warriors. The submarine fraternity is a wonderfully close-knit brotherhood.

Shortly after sinking the third enemy sub, Fyfe made a brief announcement on the *Batfish*'s intercom system, his words ringing throughout the quiet compartments of the boat.

"Within three days, we sank three enemy submarines. There were no survivors. Those men aboard the Japanese subs who died as a result of our actions were combatant enemies. They knowingly risked their lives in war, just as we do. We attacked and sank them in the course of our duty. Within our good fortune that we did not lose our boat or our lives, there is of course some sadness that these submariners have died, and by our hand. But the only way that could have been otherwise in this war, would have been for us to die by theirs. Thank you for your excellence, and congratulations on your success."

For her amazing accomplishment, the *Batfish* received the Presidential Unit Citation. She completed a total of seven wartime patrols, all deemed successful, and claimed credit for destroying thirteen enemy vessels. Along the way, she earned nine battle stars, one Navy Cross, four Silver Stars, and ten Bronze Stars in addition to the Presidential Unit Citation.

In the course of her duty, she had struck a series of mighty blows against the enemy.

In the 1960s, a group of Oklahoma submarine veterans decided they wanted a sub as a memorial to their shipmates who did not return from World War II. It was a long shot at best, but those who doubted such an odd thing could be done—putting a submarine in the unlikeliest of places—did not understand the passion of the plan's pilots.

Using some fortuitous political connections, they convinced the state legislature to create a body that would ultimately be dubbed the Oklahoma Maritime Advisory Board. The irony of a maritime board in a state best known for being a part of the Dust Bowl was apparently lost on the legislative body. Since the bill had the right people supporting it, however, the lawmakers quickly passed it and the veterans—who constituted most of the members of the board once it was established—were in business.

Of course, if anyone had bothered to read the fine print, he would have seen that the law creating the panel only specifically authorized its members to take custody of the USS *Piranha* (SS-389), the original boat on which the veterans had settled. The legislation purposefully and clearly failed to authorize the board to enter into contracts or spend a penny of the taxpayers' money for anything—not even pencils and paper, much less a World War II diesel boat and all that would be necessary to bring her to Oklahoma.

The board promptly went right out into the world, signing contracts and spending money, but for another submarine, not for the *Piranha*.

When members of the oddly named maritime board went down to New Orleans to arrange for the delivery of the boat they thought they wanted, they spied another vessel that happened to be moored nearby. That submarine was the *Batfish*, and she not only had a more impressive war record, but she was also in better physical shape. The *Piranha* had been raided, stripped, and much of her World War II equipment cannibalized for use on the remaining few active diesel training boats. Even the *Piranha*'s conning tower had been removed and hauled off to a museum in Texas, leaving her little more than a headless hulk.

No worries. Like any good sub captains, the board made a midcourse correction to assure the best possible outcome. Protocol and procedure went out the window in the name of expediency. The vets promptly signed up with the navy for delivery of the 310 boat, the *Batfish*, instead. Without hesitation, they also began entertaining bids to prepare her for the long journey to Muskogee.

When those bids arrived, the board met, approved the selections, and signed the contracts, all without asking permission from anyone. They were confident that they would have an actual, historic submarine open to Oklahomans in short order, and they were intent on doing it without any unnecessary red tape or input from anyone back in Oklahoma City.

But bringing the boat upriver turned out to not be that easy. Some of the problems they faced were political. Others were based simply on the fact that the Arkansas River was not deep or wide enough, and that it made several critical bends that a 311-foot boat would have trouble making. The Army Corps of Engineers were busily working on the problem, not specifically for the *Batfish* effort but because they had been authorized to make the Arkansas navigable all the way to the outskirts of Tulsa. That was one of the ways the sub vets group sold their idea in the first place to both the Oklahoma legislature and the U.S. Navy. What better way to show off the advantages of this marvelous new transportation route than to bring a saltwater critter like a submarine all the way to the middle of the Dust Bowl?

Of course, none of them counted on a near catastrophe when a big oil tanker sped by the docked submarine in New Orleans only a day or two before she was to begin the trip upriver. The massive wake kicked up by the tanker sank one of the barges that was to help float the sub. Several others were damaged. So was the *Batfish*, but fortunately not seriously. And it was a miracle that no one was killed or that the *Batfish* did not end up on the muddy Mississippi River bottom alongside the barge.

But if anyone thought the project would be abandoned, he underestimated the determination of the World War II submarine vets.

After several years of delays—in the spring of 1972, about ten years after the idea was first floated among the submarine veterans—they were finally able to begin the *Batfish*'s historic journey up the Mississippi River. She pulled away from the Port of New Orleans, propelled by a couple of tugboats, one in front towing, the other behind the submarine, shoving her with its snout. The ingenious method they had devised—a phalanx of barges three to a side and a series of big straps that formed a sling beneath the submarine's belly—worked even better than anticipated. They made good time, their progress followed by local media along the way as well as by news representatives from back in Oklahoma.

Then, through some complicated navigation, they made a left turn and floated her on up the much more narrow and shallow Arkansas River, still pointing toward her new home. There, in a spot donated by the city of Muskogee, Oklahoma, they intended to have her rest, to open her for visitation "by the schoolchildren of Oklahoma," as their charter stated.

But simply getting there was only the beginning of her long final patrol. Politics, money, squabbling, floods—they all played a role in the delay in getting the old boat into the final resting spot that had been prepared for her. There were points at which the navy threatened to re-claim the boat and send her off to the scrap yard after all. At other times, the Corps of Engineers threatened to declare her a navigation hazard, a threat to their newly navigable waterway, and to tow her away. A prom-ised bond issue to raise money for moving her out of the river into her slip at the proposed park never materialized. Vendors, who had done their jobs but had not been paid a penny, filed lawsuits. The State of Oklahoma backpedaled from the whole mess, claiming they never au-thorized any of this, and that, on top of it all, the veterans had brought the wrong submarine upriver. What was this *Batfish* vessel, and where was the *Piranha*, the boat specifically named in the authorizing legislation?

The darkest time may have been the winter of 1973. That's when heavy rains swelled the river out of its banks and the submarine almost capsized.

But those stubborn submarine vets never gave up. The minutes of the Maritime Advisory Board meetings are filled with optimistic plans and scant few discussions of all the dire predictions about their boat. Eventu-ally, their perseverance paid off.

Volunteers used a bulldozer to help pull the *Batfish* into a muddy channel that had been scooped out of a former bean field next to the river. With the help of the Corps of Engineers, who closed a floodgate downstream, the level of the Arkansas River was raised so the boat could more easily be nudged into the temporary channel. With that, she began the final three-hundred-yard portion of her journey.

In a park dedicated to veterans of all wars and services, she rests to-day in a moat of dirt, captured forever by a mound of Dust Bowl soil. Held in place a long, long way from the nearest sea. Half a world away from the site of her three-subs-sunk-in-three-days triumph. At the high-est elevation above sea level any submarine had ever been taken.

The complete story of how a submarine came to rest in a former bean field in the middle of the Dust Bowl and Cherokee Indian territory is far more complicated than that, of course. But the bottom line is that the vets, in true submariner fashion, refused to give up on their dream.

The *Batfish* was unofficially opened to the public on July 4, 1972, half a decade later than originally planned. Despite some rocky times since, the boat is still a part of Muskogee, Oklahoma's, War Memorial Park, and a fixture alongside the Muskogee Turnpike. More than a few motorists have been startled to glance across the field and see what appears to be a submarine sitting out there in the grass, over a thousand miles from the closest body of salt water. But there she is, where the Verdigris River meets the Arkansas, and she is open much of the year for everyone to see.

The War Memorial Park operates a museum with many *Batfish* and World War II items inside. Out its back door is a series of bronze stands, bearing the names of the fifty-two submarines lost in the war. Their plaques also include the names of each crewman who was lost aboard those sacred boats. The display is similar to the one at the submarine memorial near the USS *Bowfin* at Pearl Harbor, Hawaii.

Other military items are also on display on the grounds, including several types of armament. Those include actual 20-millimeter, 40-millimeter, three-inch and five-inch guns and a real (though disarmed, obviously) torpedo like the ones the World War II submarines carried and fired. And 20-millimeter and 40-millimeter deck guns have now been mounted on the *Batfish* to make her appear more as she did during the war.

Volunteers are always being sought to help in the upkeep of the submarine. Even though she is surrounded by dirt and not water, there is still plenty of work to do to keep the sub in good shape. Regular annual workdays are scheduled.

There is now an effort to get new wood to replace the *Batfish*'s decking. It was hoped that project would be completed in 2006 as well. Word at the time of this writing is that the first bundle of new decking has arrived at the boat.

The *Batfish* Memorial Foundation was created in May 2003 to help support the restoration of the submarine and to raise money for projects such as those mentioned above. Donations to the foundation are tax-deductible.

The foundation has also adopted as a project getting the submarine listed on the National Register of Historic Places.

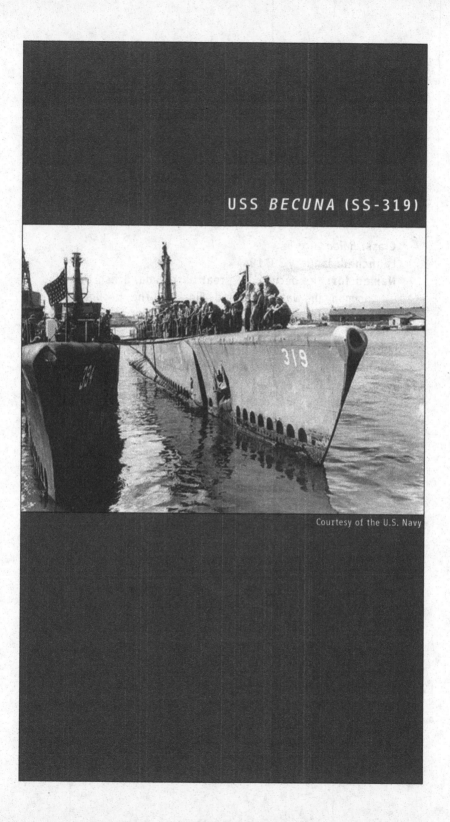

USS *BECUNA* (SS-319)

Courtesy of the U.S. Navy

USS *BECUNA* (SS-319)

Class: *Balao*
Launched: January 30, 1944
Named for: the becuna, or great barracuda, a fish that is common in waters around Florida. The becuna has earned a reputation as a ferocious hunter, is willing to attack and able to subdue much larger fish.
Where: Electric Boat Company, Groton, Connecticut
Sponsor: Mrs. G. C. Crawford, wife of Navy Commander George C. "Turkey Neck" Crawford, a former sub skipper, head of the submarine school at Groton, Connecticut, and squadron commander at Pearl Harbor
Commissioned: May 27, 1944

Where is she today?
Independence Seaport Museum
211 South Columbus Blvd. and Walnut Street
Philadelphia, Pennsylvania 19106-3199
(215) 925-5439
www.phillyseaport.org

Claim to fame: Known affectionately as "Becky," the *Becuna* had twenty-five years of service, including five World War II patrols and stints in the Korean and Vietnam wars, as well as service during the Cold War.

Lieutenant Commander Henry Dixon Sturr and his new submarine, the USS *Becuna*, were perfect examples of how submersible warships were often penalized in their scorekeeping simply because they operated so stealthily. Often patrolling alone in remote waters, attacking enemy vessels that were, themselves, on top secret missions, they usually only had their own reports to back up claims of ships sunk. Admittedly, some skippers, in an effort to impress their bosses or to earn decorations or promotions, did embellish their reports. That's why the official scorekeepers relied on other evidence to confirm tonnage sunk. But some of that evidence was questionable as well. After the war, Japanese records were spotty, often not placing key vessels where they actually were when they met their end.

Even when Henry Sturr, Annapolis class of '33, was dead-to-rights certain that he had sunk a ship, he would later learn he had only inflicted damage, that the vessel had survived. That happened on her very first war patrol.

Operating in the Celebes Sea south of the Philippines, the *Becuna* spotted a Japanese tanker carrying precious oil to an enemy outpost somewhere in the South Pacific. That was exactly the kind of target American submarines were having spectacular success in intercepting and sinking, denying the Japanese the valuable petroleum they needed to maintain the war effort.

"Battle stations, submerge!" Sturr ordered, and the dive klaxon sounded throughout the boat.

The crew quickly lined up for an attack and sent four torpedoes hissing off toward the big target. Two of them hit, the explosions close enough to rattle the newly minted submarine hard. They would not be able to stick around to watch the vessel sink, though. One of the tanker's escorts was heading their way in one big hurry. After outlasting a thunderous hailstorm of forty depth charges, Sturr recorded in his deck log and subsequent patrol report that they had definitely sunk one Japanese tanker.

After the war, the "kill" was erased from the *Becuna*'s tally. The seven-thousand-ton *Kimikawa Maru* was heavily damaged by Sturr's torpedoes but she survived.

Two weeks later, in October 1944, Sturr and his submarine had another frustrating experience. Patrolling with her sister boats the USS *Baya* (SS-318) and the USS *Hawkbill* (SS-366) south of Formosa, the wolf pack happened upon a twelve-ship enemy convoy full of highly desirable targets. After being chased for several hours, the enemy ships suddenly changed course and headed straight for the *Becuna*. Even though they had been submerged for quite a while already and were running low on both battery power and fresh air, Captain Sturr knew this would be his best opportunity to strike a blow.

He kept them submerged and quickly angled for an attack. He watched through the periscope as the ships moved into prime shooting range, then selected one large and one smaller tanker as his first targets. From the forward tubes, he fired two torpedoes each at the two vessels.

Still peering through the scope, he saw both torpedoes strike the larger tanker, the vicious blasts clearly visible at two points along the ship's side. Then he whooped loudly when two detonations wracked the smaller vessel as well.

"All four fish hit their targets!" he shouted, and the men around him in the cramped conning tower cheered. "The smaller one is going down. Can't tell on the other one. There's too much smoke for me to see."

But there was no time to wait for the smoke to clear so they could count their kills. There were more fish in this barrel.

Sturr quickly angled to shoot at a small freighter and what appeared to be a troop transport. He was so close to the second ship that he could see Japanese soldiers in their khaki uniforms, leaning over the stern railing, watching the destruction that had been set off behind them when the *Becuna*'s torpedoes struck the other ships in the convoy.

The skipper was surprised that none of the escorts had made a move to pursue their attackers, and no one on the deck of the transport seemed to be looking their way. They were certainly close enough that their periscope would be visible, and the trail of their four torpedoes led right back to where it poked out of the sea. He could only assume the water was so full of debris and oil from the damaged vessels that they were lost in the mess.

No matter, he had a good, clear shot and promptly sent three torpedoes toward the troop ship. Then he dispatched one more toward the freighter. He stuck around long enough to see two fish hit the transport and, as they went deeper and scurried away, heard the lone torpedo explode as it blasted the freighter.

Seven torpedoes, four Japanese ships sent to the bottom! The news preceded them into port. They were bona fide heroes when they pulled into Fremantle, Australia, to end the spectacularly successful patrol eight days later.

But again, as good as the attack had been, it was not quite as successful as Sturr and his *Becuna* crew thought. The first ship they hit, the larger tanker *San Luis Maru*, was moderately damaged but was still able to steam on to port for repairs. Unbeknownst to Sturr at the time, the *Hawkbill* later encountered the smaller wounded tanker, which had not sunk and was trying to make it back to port, and finished it off with four torpedoes. Since it was impossible to tell whose attack had been the fatal one, the two submarines each received half credit for the kill.

Postwar sources were never able to confirm the damage to the troop transport, nor even its presence in that part of the world at the time of the attack. Thus, no credit was given for that sinking at all.

The final vessel hit, the freighter, was considered damaged but not destroyed.

So, when the dust settled, instead of five ships sunk in two brilliant attacks while out on her very first war patrol, the *Becuna* was instead credited with one-half kill and five ships damaged.

There was a disheartening sighting, a frustrating near miss, on her second patrol, too. Like several of her sisters before her, she encountered the legendary super-battleship *Yamato* in the South China Sea. The massive warship and her sister, the *Musashi*, were the largest battleships ever built, coming in at over seventy thousand tons fully loaded. A year before, the *Yamato* had been torpedoed and heavily damaged by the USS *Skate* (SS-305).

(It is interesting to note that there was supposed to have been a third super-battleship sister, the *Shinano*. The Japanese learned valuable lessons from major defeats, however, and realized the need for a super-aircraft carrier instead. During the *Shinano*'s construction, she morphed into a carrier as a replacement for a battleship. But on the gigantic vessel's maiden voyage, shortly after emerging from Tokyo Bay, the supposedly unsinkable warship was torpedoed and sent to the bottom by the submarine USS *Archerfish* (SS-311) and her skipper, Joe Enright. The *Archerfish* was on her fifth war run at the time and, with that one sinking, tallied the most successful submarine patrol by tonnage of World War II. The Japanese navy kept the sinking of the *Shinano* a secret until after the war was over, due to the blow it would have dealt to morale.)

Now, after repairs to the damage from the *Skate*'s attack, the *Yamato* was once again on the move. During the stint in the Yokosuka navy yard, she also received new antiaircraft guns. Since her encounter with the *Skate*, she had most recently taken part in the Battle of the Philippine Sea in June 1944 and the Battle of Leyte Gulf in October of that year.

Her legend continued to grow. She seemed unstoppable. Every submariner wanted a piece of her.

Several U.S. submarines had run upon the monster since the *Skate*'s near kill, but the mammoth vessel's speed and maneuverability had been too much for them to overcome. Also, the very best escort vessels crewed with the IJN's best sailors always accompanied her, so taking her down would not be easy, and even trying would possibly prove to be suicidal.

Now, here was a relative newcomer, the *Becuna*, out on her second war patrol. With uncommon good luck, it appeared the behemoth was going to sail right over the top of them!

Captain Sturr quickly went to battle stations and made ready to fire at the *Yamato* every torpedo he had aboard. But just as he began singing out the range and coordinates of the beast, getting the data entered into the torpedo tubes, she made a sudden, unexpected U-turn.

The *Yamato* and her escorts showed the *Becuna* their sterns and were out of sight over the horizon in only a few minutes.

No need to give chase. Unless the flotilla decided to cooperate and stop or turn back their way, there was not a chance of ever catching them. It was a lost cause. The *Becuna* had joined the long list of boats that had gotten tantalizingly close to one of the war's major kills. Several other submarines had similar close encounters with the legendary vessel, but few were even able to fire a torpedo.

Commander Hank Sturr could not help but notice how quiet his crew was for the next several hours. There was none of the usual banter or horseplay. Their disappointment at not even getting off a shot at the massive target was all over their faces. It dominated their demeanor as they went quietly about their jobs.

They were not the first, nor would they be the last, but that was small consolation.

It ultimately took a barrage of naval carrier–based aircraft to send the *Yamato* to the bottom of the ocean. That came the next spring, in April 1945, two hundred miles north of Okinawa. A similar air attack had claimed her sister, the *Musashi*, the previous fall. But glad as they were that the big sisters were dispatched to the deep, it still galled most submariners that the flyboys had done them in, not their torpedoes.

The *Becuna* got her only confirmed torpedo kill on her third patrol. It was a tanker in very shallow waters off Cape Pandaran in the South China

Sea. For her trouble, she also got a seventy-depth-charge attack that rattled everyone's dental fillings and stunned their hearing for hours afterward. Despite the thunder, she eventually managed to slip back out into deeper water before any serious damage was done.

Despite the lack of credit, the *Becuna* crew knew what they had accomplished out there. Official kills or not, they had done their part to hasten the end of the costliest war in history. They did receive recognition—two combat insignias for the first and third patrols and a Presidential Unit Citation. Also, the crew members were awarded a Silver Star, two Bronze Stars, and several letters of commendation with ribbons.

She was another plunging boat who did what she was supposed to do.

After the war, the *Becuna* became a "guppy." She went back to her birthplace at Electric Boat Company in Connecticut to get the unique GUPPY (Greater Underwater Propulsion Project) modification. Diesel-powered submarines could not operate their big engines while submerged. They required air to run and vent out smoke. They were also noisy, which made it easy for an enemy vessel on the surface to locate them. While beneath the surface of the ocean, they had to rely solely on battery power, which was limited, to send juice to the electric motors that turned the screws and made them go.

The GUPPY system was simply a snorkel that allowed the boat to go just beneath the surface. From there, a pipe was extended above the water far enough to vent smoke and take in air for the engines. It was a rudimentary solution to a complicated problem, but it did work. There were drawbacks, though. Sometimes, if the boat slipped just deep enough for the top of the snorkel to go underwater and close, the engines could suck so hard seeking air on which to run that sailors throughout the boat would suffer from painful popped ears. It took only moments for the sub to fill with thick, choking diesel smoke.

The *Becuna* got other modifications while she was at Electric Boat that greatly altered her appearance when compared with the other fleet boats. She became clearly more streamlined and the area around her periscope and shears was enclosed, giving her more speed as she cut through the water while submerged. With the makeover complete and using two of her diesel engines while underwater, thanks to the GUPPY system, the *Becuna* could now achieve much more swiftness than was ever possible on battery power alone.

For the rest of her long, active life, she served mostly as an antisubmarine warfare vessel, working with the British, Canadian, and U.S. navies out of Mediterranean, northern European, and Canadian ports. She also served a rather chilly term working in Arctic ice pack exercises in the Cabot Strait. There she was assisting many of the same people who had pioneered under-ice submarine operations aboard the first nuclear-powered vessel, the USS *Nautilus* (SSN-571), only a few years before. The Cold War had gotten even colder by that time, and the ability of American vessels to operate in the Soviet Union's backyard, moving beneath and through the polar ice pack, was crucial in maintaining superiority in the stare-down.

"Becky" finally retired after twenty-five years of almost continuous duty, going to the reserve fleet in November 1969. She was officially struck from the naval register in August 1973.

Shortly after being discharged from the service, the *Becuna* was turned over to the Olympia Association. She was slated to join as a museum boat the historic cruiser USS *Olympia* (C-6) in Philadelphia, which was already floating in the Delaware River there. The *Olympia* is the oldest steel-hulled warship still afloat and a true hero of the Spanish-American War and World War I. She served as Admiral George Dewey's flagship during the Battle of Manila Bay in May 1898, an engagement that secured the Philippines for the United States and helped not only to assure the outcome of the Spanish-American War but also to establish the United States as a major Pacific naval power. Her last mission was the return of the body of the unknown soldier of World War I for burial in Arlington National Cemetery.

Both the *Olympia* and the *Becuna* are now part of the Independence Seaport Museum at Penn's Landing in Philadelphia, Pennsylvania. Other exhibits include an interactive display of shipbuilding and "Diver of the Deep," which explores man's fascination with diving beneath the surface of the sea.

The National Parks Service acknowledges that the submarine is in decent shape for something of her age. "USS *Becuna* is in good condition and aside from the addition of the snorkel and exterior changes, retains much of her World War II integrity," the Parks Service's Web site states.

The USS *Becuna* is a National Historic Landmark and is on the National Register of Historic Places.

USS *CLAMAGORE* (SS-343)

Courtesy of the U.S. Navy

USS *CLAMAGORE* (SS-343)

Class: *Balao*
Launched: February 25, 1945
Named for: a blue parrot fish found in the West Indies and
  Chesapeake Bay
Where: Electric Boat Company, Groton, Connecticut
Sponsor: Miss Mary Jane Jacobs
Commissioned: June 28, 1945

Where is she today?
  Patriots Point Naval & Maritime Museum
  40 Patriots Point Road
  Mount Pleasant, South Carolina 29464
  (843) 884-2727
  www.state.sc.us/patpt/

Claim to fame: Born too late to actively participate in
World War II, she was later modified radically to serve
the expanded needs of the modern submarine force and
had a long and valuable tenure during the Cold War.
At one point, she was sawed in half to prepare for
special—and highly secret—duty.

The *Balao*-class U.S. Navy submarine was considered to be an engineering marvel for its time. With its deep-diving capability and dual means of propulsion, it was a truly powerful warship, perfectly matched to its stealthy role in the war as it was being fought in the Pacific.

The USS *Clamagore* became an even more amazing vessel after VJ Day, one of a limited number of World War II survivors to undergo a profound makeover to make her even more useful in her second life than she had an opportunity to be in her first.

Like several of her sister boats, the *Clamagore* had high hopes during her construction and shakedown. She and her crew felt the urgency, even if the tide of the war had already turned. They knew the dangers of facing a caged, desperate enemy and were ready to go do their part to contribute to victory against Japan.

They simply arrived at the war too late to do any good.

Commissioned in June 1945, just a bit over a month before the atomic bomb was dropped on Hiroshima, she was on her way to do her duty when word of peace was radioed to all the submarines at sea. The *Clamagore* had made her way as far as Panama and was conducting get-ready exercises there when the order to cease hostilities went out to all units. No one aboard the new vessel was disappointed.

She headed back to Key West, which became an important submarine base in the early days of the Cold War. The deep, clear waters of the Caribbean and Gulf of Mexico were perfect for the kinds of exercises necessary to prepare for the next kind of naval warfare we would most likely face.

The *Clamagore* was designated flagship of Submarine Squadron Four based at the far southern tip of the United States. She carried the flag for fourteen years.

Then word came that there was a need for a new type of submarine to assist in other types of training and operations. The navy already had a number of nuclear-powered submarines in its fleet by the end of the 1950s. Still, we needed some of the old diesel boats—after modification—for specialized duty, much of which was highly classified. The *Clamagore* was chosen to be one of nine boats to have the most radical of the new cosmetic surgery.

First she went up the East Coast to the Philadelphia Navy Yard for conversion to GUPPY. Her modification was designated GUPPY II, similar to that described in the chapter on the USS *Becuna*. After that modification, she became flagship for the commander of the Task Fleet and the commander of Submarine Force, Atlantic. All the time, she was out of port, making trips all over the Caribbean, as well as longer voyages to England, Argentina, Newfoundland, and other exotic locales.

In 1960, she served as part of the U.S. Sixth Fleet in the Mediterranean and participated in Operation Springboard in the Caribbean with a number of vessels from South American navies. During that little adventure, the *Clamagore* steamed around Cape Horn, the southern tip of South America.

Then in May 1962, the *Clamagore* checked into the Charleston Naval Shipyard for her second major makeover. This one was a doozy! As part of becoming a GUPPY III conversion, the submarine was literally sawed in half, received a transplant, and was welded back together again.

One of the problems with using the 312-foot-long World War II diesel boats was the limited amount of space available for sophisticated new electronic equipment that was coming online in the late '50s and early '60s. They were well equipped in so many other ways, but they simply did not have the room for all they needed to carry.

The navy took a long, hard look at the boats that had already undergone the GUPPY II conversion. In the process, they considered the general condition of the vessel and then selected a few they figured could survive the next major modification the maritime engineers had in mind for them.

The *Clamagore* was one of the boats chosen.

The first job was to literally cut the submarine in half in the general area forward of the control room. A new fifteen-foot section of hull, weighing fifty-five tons, was added at that spot to make room for more sonar equipment, berthing space, and storerooms. Next the conning tower was modified, adding five feet of tower to accommodate the new fire-control system ("fire control" pertains to firing torpedoes, not controlling a fire aboard the boat) and other gear. The sail itself was changed to what was termed the "northern sail," putting the bridge much higher above the water, allowing it to be manned in rough weather.

The changes erased once and for all the distinctive sail of the older diesel boats. The *Clamagore* now resembled the new nuclear submarines far more than her World War II sisters. Of the nine boats so modified, the *Clamagore* is the only one that is on public display today.

On July 2, 1962, the newly rebuilt submarine had her second christening. The navy decided to do an entire ceremony, carrying out the rebirth theme of the GUPPY III conversion boats. This time a sixteen-year-old named Ann Beshany broke the champagne bottle against her bow and sent her on her way. The young lady was the daughter of Captain P. A. Beshany, Commander, Submarine Squadron Four.

As planned, the changes to the old boat extended her term of duty considerably. At a time when many of her contemporaries were being struck from the register of active vessels and sent off to the scrap heap, the *Clamagore* was playing a vital role in naval exercises around the world. She and her former World War II GUPPY mates made up much of the navy's submarine force through the mid-1960s, when the newly built nuclear boats assumed, once and for all, most of the responsibility for submerged patrols of the world's oceans.

And that is when the *Clamagore*'s usefulness finally ended. She may not have had the chance to strike a blow against the Japanese in World War II, but for three decades she did all she was asked to do in defense of her country.

After thirty years of service, the *Clamagore* was retired in June 1975. Her fate was not in doubt for long. She was acquired by Patriots Point Maritime Museum in Charleston, South Carolina, not far from where she underwent her radical redesign, and went on display there shortly afterward.

Other vessels in the park include the aircraft carrier USS *Yorktown* (CV-10), known as "the Fighting Lady" and one of the best-known ships of World War II; the destroyer USS *Laffey* (DD-724); and the Coast Guard cutter *Ingham* (WHEC-35). The park also features a Congressional Medal of Honor museum and a relatively new memorial to Cold War submarines. That memorial is dedicated to submariners, their families, and the men and women—both civilian and military—who supported the sub force during that period of America's history. Many of those people were based at Charleston.

The city's connection with submarine history is not limited to the *Clamagore* and Patriots Point. The historic Confederate submarine CSS *Hunley*, the first sub to sink an enemy vessel, is also located in Charleston. The submarine was recovered from the nearby Atlantic Ocean in August 2000 through the efforts and fund-raising of several groups along with best-selling author Clive Cussler. Archaeologists are currently examining the vessel in an attempt to learn more about her design, her eight-man crew, and exactly what caused her to sink just a short time after her successful attack on a Union ship in Charleston Harbor in February 1864.

Weekend tours of the recovery lab, including views of the *Hunley*, are offered at the Warren Lasch Conservation Center at 1250 Supply Street at the former Charleston Naval Base.

USS *PAMPANITO* (SS-383)

Courtesy of Rob Mackie and www.steelnavy.com

USS *PAMPANITO* (SS-383)

Class: *Balao*
Launched: July 12, 1943
Named for: one of the family of butterfishes found in the Gulf of California and Mexican coastal waters
Where: Portsmouth Naval Shipyard, New Hampshire
Sponsor: Mrs. James Wolfender
Commissioned: November 6, 1943

Where is she today?
USS *Pampanito* Maritime Park Association
Pier 45 at Fisherman's Wharf
San Francisco, California 94147-0310
(415) 561-7006
www.maritime.org/pamphome.htm

Claim to fame: She helped rescue six dozen British and Australian prisoners of war after the submarine unknowingly stalked the Japanese troop carrier on which they were being transported and sank another vessel loaded with POWs. She has also had an interesting—and controversial—history since coming to San Francisco, including a starring role in a major motion picture.

As you tour the USS *Pampanito* at Fisherman's Wharf in San Francisco, do not be surprised if you hear the distant, ghostly whistling of "The Colonel Bogey March," the oddly happy theme from the heartrending war movie *The Bridge on the River Kwai*. The submarine and her World War II crew are forever and tragically linked with the men who lived the events that are so graphically depicted in that motion picture.

The *Pampanito*'s route from birth to her first war patrol was a relatively quick one. Exactly one year to the day after her keel was laid down at the new building basin at Portsmouth Naval Shipyard in New Hampshire, she departed Pearl Harbor on her first of six World War II patrols.

On the first run, skipper Paul Summers and his crew had to deal with mechanical problems and almost lost the boat in a four-day stalking of an enemy convoy. During that engagement, they were certain they had dealt a mortal blow to a huge tanker but ultimately did not receive credit for the sinking.

What they did get for their trouble was a series of massive depth chargings that almost sent them to the bottom before they had even gotten started in this war. The first thunderous attacks, which came even before the *Pampanito* had fired her first torpedo, did moderate damage to the new boat. Summers and his crew managed to get their boat to the surface as soon as their attackers gave up, did some temporary repairs, and then went to flank speed in order to resume the chase.

On April 10, 1944, just after launching the two torpedoes that hit the tanker, one of the enemy escort vessels chased the *Pampanito* deep with another vicious series of depth charges. This sort of thing was getting old quick!

Later, Captain Summers wrote in his deck log a rather blasé account of what had to have been high drama beneath the surface of the sea:

2201: Pattern of 3 depth charges, fairly close. At about 300 feet, commenced taking in water through the main air induction piping. #9 torpedo tube indicating sea pressure. Evidently outer door is leaking from last depth charging.

2202: Pattern of 3 depth charges, fairly close.

2205: Had to close the hull induction drains in engine rooms and maneuvering room as water is coming in too fast. Boat is getting very heavy. One of the poppet valves in the forward torpedo tubes stuck open on firing causing flooding of the forward torpedo room bilges.

2207: Intermittent depth charges. None very close. A total of about 25 were dropped. Am having to use between 90 and 100 shaft turns with a 12–15 degree rise bubble to keep the boat from going any deeper . . .

2315: Both sound head training motors grounded out due to bilge water running over the forward torpedo room deck with a 15 degree rise bubble. Tried using a bubble in safety tank twice to hold my depth, and each time it brought the DD's over again. Excessive noise being caused by the pressure forcing water into main induction piping. . . .

The roar of water rushing into the *Pampanito*'s superstructure was drawing the Japanese destroyers like honey draws flies. Though the boat was still nominally under control, they were in real danger of sinking if they could not get the flooding under control. If the destroyer escorts stayed above them, dropping TNT on their heads, and if they were not able to check the inrushing water, they would have only two choices, neither of which was a good one.

They could surface in the middle of the enemy warships and likely be blown out of the water.

Or they could remain submerged and keep trying to control the wounded boat, running the risk of being crushed to death if they failed and the *Pampanito* plunged to the distant sea bottom.

A half hour after the captain's last notation, Sound reported that the destroyer screws appeared to be growing more distant. It had been almost fifteen minutes since the last nerve-shattering explosion of a nearby depth charge.

Finally, another tense half hour after the report that the enemy was leaving, Summers swallowed hard and gave the order to come to periscope depth. The dive officer brought the boat up high enough that the tip of the scope poked into dry air. The skipper took a look around, saw nobody, and came to the surface to inspect the damage. He also ordered his radio operator to get on the air and see if anyone else in the area could resume the chase of the convoy they had missed.

Even then, damaged from the depth-charge attack, the *Pampanito* did not break off the patrol. Staying on the surface as much as they dared, the crew pumped out the flooded induction piping and drained the seawater out of number-nine torpedo tube and made repairs that allowed them to continue the rest of the run with only a slight limp.

There were more close calls on the *Pampanito*'s second war patrol. After days of bad weather, they finally surfaced near Bungo Suido for a look-see. It was a clear night, several hours before dawn, and the crew was pleased to find calm seas. As the officer of the deck and navigator stood on the bridge, enjoying the clean sea air, one of them suddenly shouted, "Torpedo wake! Dead ahead!"

Sure enough, there was the unmistakable trail of gas from a steam-turbine-driven torpedo, like the ones the Japanese submariners favored. It was headed directly for where they would be in a few seconds.

"Left full rudder! Flank speed!" the OOD shouted into the intercom microphone. The boat heeled over immediately, the engines and rudder responding to his order and the actions of the men in the control and maneuvering rooms. They had dodged the first one and were going to do all they could to dodge any other fish that might be headed their way.

Sure enough, another trail marked the progress of a second torpedo, running right up the starboard side of the *Pampanito*, shadowing them for a moment. Had they not spotted the first one and made the evasive maneuver, this torpedo would likely have struck them broadside. Neither man on the bridge wanted to think what the result of that explosion would have been.

No one on the bridge saw a submarine on the surface in any direction, so whoever was shooting at them had to be submerged. They quickly cleared the shears and bridge and went down to periscope depth. From the relative safety there, they tried to detect the sound of an enemy sub's screws or any other noise that might indicate where the attacker was lurking.

Nothing. Except for the chirping of shrimp, the night sea was quiet. There was only the sound of a half dozen men's breathing in the conning tower.

Three weeks later, an eerily similar incident gave the crew pause once again. Early in the morning of July 16, a couple of hours prior to sunrise, lookouts spied a torpedo wake moving directly toward their boat's port beam. The submarine immediately made a sharp move to parallel the path of the approaching torpedo, giving it their smallest profile, and it missed her by less than five yards, according to the men who were on the bridge that night.

Later, Admiral Charles Lockwood, commander of the Submarine Force, Pacific Fleet, guessed that the two torpedo attacks on the *Pam-*

panito came from IJN mini-subs. That was the reason Summers and his crew detected none of the distinctive sounds of a full-sized submarine after the incidents. During the patrol, the *Pampanito* had also reported detecting enemy onshore radar, with a strength that was more than enough to give the enemy a radar-blip picture of any vessel that might be on the surface in the area. That was valuable information, as well as an explanation for how the enemy may have known of the *Pampanito*'s presence in their coastal waters on those dark, predawn nights.

War patrol number three took Summers, his crew, and the *Pampanito* to an area north of the Philippines that had been dubbed "Convoy College" because of the large amount of Japanese shipping that converged in the waters there, making their way to the Home Islands. The sub was operating in a wolf pack with the USS *Growler* (SS-215) and the USS *Sealion* (SS-315), a group dubbed "Ben's Busters" after Ben Oakley, the skipper of the *Growler*. American submarines had begun operating more and more in wolf packs for two reasons: the enemy convoys were becoming better organized and usually featured a number of destructive escort vessels, and it made it easier to avoid accidentally shooting at each other if they were working together. The skippers congregating in a pack could rendezvous, exchange notes, use lights or megaphones to communicate, and do it all without using the radio. If need be, they could also use the new VHF radio systems, too, with their limited range and less likelihood of detection.

It should be noted that there was one other advantage to being a part of a wolf pack. The boats used those get-togethers on the high seas as an opportunity to swap movies for the crews. That was about the only entertainment they had during the long patrols and it was always a good thing to get some new titles to screen in the crew's mess.

Of course, many of the American sub skippers detested the name "wolf pack." It was the semantics of the thing. Since World War I, the German U-boat captains had operated in predatory groups they called wolf packs.

Even if they had adopted the methods of the Germans, they still saw no need to take their name for them, too.

Captain Paul Summers turned thirty-one while at sea, on September 6, 1944. That same day, a Japanese convoy sailed out of Singapore, loaded with rubber, oil, and other natural resources desperately needed for the war effort. Also in that same convoy were ships that carried an unusual and interesting cargo: more than two thousand British and Australian prisoners of war.

Those POWs had already been through hell. They were survivors of the infamous "Railway of Death," the railroad built by captured soldiers and Asian civilians who were brutally used as slave labor. It is estimated that well over 100,000 people died during the construction of the railroad, mostly from starvation, dysentery, tropical diseases, abuse, overwork, and just plain cruelty.

The Japanese recognized the strategic need for the project. The railway was needed to link existing Thai and Burmese rail lines so they would create a route from Bangkok, Thailand, to Rangoon, Burma. Such a railroad was needed in order to support the Japanese occupation of the region. One of the key segments of the route involved building a bridge over the Kwae River in Thailand. The construction of that bridge and its ultimate demolition was fictionally depicted in a novel (and its name misspelled) by Pierre Boulle. In 1957, it became an Academy Award–winning motion picture starring William Holden and Alec Guinness.

In 1944, with the railway project completed, the Japanese decided to take the healthiest of the POWs—and those were obvious since they were the ones who had managed to survive the hellish ordeal—and ship them to Japan. There they were destined to work in the copper mines and in other areas where labor was in short supply.

The prisoners were well aware that they were going to pass through waters that were heavily patrolled by U.S. submarines. They also knew that the Japanese had a habit of not marking noncombatant vessels with crosses or other indicators. It was also true that in many cases and for their own reasons the Japanese did not bother to request safe passage for such ships, as they had every right to do under the rules of the Geneva Convention.

Some of the prisoners formed "rescue" teams and gave each other assignments of what to do in case they came under attack and were sunk. They hoarded rations and prepared primitive survival kits, just in case they found themselves in the water for a long period of time. They openly talked about which fate would be worse, having the ship shot from beneath them or being forced to do slave labor in the Japanese copper mines for the remainder of the war, or until they perished like so many of their comrades had done.

On September 9, the *Pampanito* and her sisters were instructed to rendezvous and prepare to locate and engage an approaching convoy. A message intercepted and decoded by intelligence spoke of a large group of vessels carrying raw materials that was quickly approaching their portion of the sea. Another wolf pack was ordered to the area to act as backup.

When all three submarines in Ben's Busters arrived late the night of the eleventh, they exchanged recognition signals and pulled closer to each other to discuss tactics for inflicting the most damage on the enemy ships. Then, with the sky overcast, the sea calm, and rain squalls on the distant horizon, they sat and waited to see if the intelligence proved to be accurate.

At one thirty the next morning, the first blips appeared on the *Pampanito*'s circling radar screen.

"Range fifteen miles," the radar tech reported, the calculated calm masking the excitement in his voice.

As planned, the *Pampanito* went to flank speed and quickly maneuvered to where the convoy was headed, ready to attack. The *Growler*, with Captain Oakley on the bridge, came at the group of ships from the west, firing on them with his deck guns. That sent the escort vessels fanning out in all directions, assuming an attack was coming at them from several different directions.

One of the destroyers spotted the *Growler* on radar and steered hard in her direction. Normal procedure would have been for Oakley to immediately take his boat deep, to run, to hide until he could sneak back into range for an attack. But the skipper stayed topside, facing bow-to-bow with the oncoming warship. At a range of just over a thousand yards—near point-blank but staring head-on into the warship's bow—the *Growler* unleashed three torpedoes at the oncoming destroyer. The first one hit, setting off a violent explosion, a concussion those on the bridge of the attacking submarine easily felt. And when the burning vessel limped past the sub, Oakley could feel the heat of the flames. The destroyer sank quickly, less than two hundred yards from where her killer bounced on the rolling waves.

Oakley's daring and unorthodox down-the-throat attack quickly became legend in the submarine service, even as others criticized the unecessary danger in which he had placed his boat and crew. Regardless, with that successful move, the *Growler* was still in the hunt, and one destroyer escort was scratched from the battle. Oakley and his boat were not slinking off somewhere to wait and try to launch an attack later. She was on the surface still, ready to fight. She went on to quickly damage two other ships before she had to withdraw from the fray long enough to reload her tubes.

Meanwhile, the *Pampanito* moved to the dark side of the convoy, trying to avoid becoming an easy-to-spot silhouette against the illumination of a newly risen full moon. In the process, the Japanese ships, already scattered in response to the *Growler*'s brazen attack, ran away, out of their torpedo range. The backup submarines were still eighty miles north, so far unaware of the battle that had begun. Summers and his pack mate worked to catch up and gain a good shooting angle, trying to keep the bulk of the convoy within radar range if not within sight from the bridge. They ran on the surface so they would have some hope of catching the fleeing targets, using the darkness to hide them as much as the moonlight would allow.

The *Pampanito* and the *Sealion* tracked the convoy for the balance of the night.

Then, just before the first rays of the morning sun appeared on the horizon, Summers and his hardworking crew found themselves in the perfect position to launch torpedoes at the zigzagging ships.

Suddenly the submarine was shaken hard by a terrible explosion. Then there was another, even closer and more stunning.

At first, everyone aboard the *Pampanito* thought they were under attack, either from aircraft bombs or shells from one of the convoy's escorts. Or they had gotten themselves into a minefield. Neither one would be a good thing.

It took a quick, instinctive swing of the periscope in the direction of the sea-rending blast to determine that the *Sealion* had already fired two salvos of torpedoes at the convoy. The first hit a tanker, and that target was already riding low in the water from the weight of her full load of oil. The brilliant flames made the sea around the doomed tanker brighter than daylight, clearly illuminating a second vessel that had been struck by the second spray of the *Sealion*'s torpedoes.

The explosions that had rocked the *Pampanito* were those blasts, the *Sealion*'s direct hits, so close, so powerful, that Summers and his crew thought they were shells striking their own boat.

That second target the *Sealion* had blasted was a freighter-transport named the *Rakuyo Maru*. Its cargo was raw rubber. Raw rubber and thirteen hundred surviving prisoners of war, the men who survived building the Railway of Death and were now bound for the copper mines in Japan.

Two of the *Sealion*'s three-torpedo salvo hit the vessel, one at the bow, the other about the midpoint of the ship. She was mortally wounded, doomed.

From his periscope, Captain Paul Summers could see men jumping from the burning, sinking vessel. Others were desperately lowering the ship's lifeboats, all escaping to the sea in the hopes that the escort craft would be able to pick them up.

Of course, Paul Summers had no way of knowing that the men jumping overboard were the Japanese guards, the men who were supposed to be overseeing the prisoners. They also took most of the lifeboats as they fled the dying transport.

The *Sealion* had already gone deep to get away from the inevitable depth charging. It did not take long before the explosives were going off all around her and she pointed her nose deeper, as far down as she dared go.

The *Pampanito* and the *Growler* had no reason to stand by and watch the two stricken ships sink. Nor did they have any reason to try to pluck enemy survivors out of the water. Of course, they still had no idea there were POWs among them.

The sub skippers had a job to do. Without hesitation, they turned their sterns to the mess their sister boat had made and were off in chase of what remained of the fleeing convoy. There were other targets to eliminate.

The *Growler* quickly caught one of the escort ships and sent it to the bottom, the explosions of her torpedoes causing concussive ripples across the expanse of the sea as the rising sun painted the scene an eerie orange.

The *Pampanito* plowed on, looking for something for her own torpedomen to shoot at.

Meanwhile, back aboard the heavily listing *Rakuyo Maru*, with no guards watching over them, the POWs who had survived the explosions and fire went desperately rummaging about, looking for anything they could lash together to make rafts, gathering up food and water, getting ready for what could be a long time in the water after their ship inevitably sank beneath them.

It would take the transport almost twelve hours to finally go under.

Other POWs were already in the water. Some were thrown overboard by the explosions, others had jumped at the first opportunity to escape the withering fires. All were clinging to anything they could find that would help keep them afloat. Tragically, many of them would die from the shock waves from the vicious nearby depth charges, the continuing attack on the *Sealion*. Others would be killed by the blasts from the escort warship that had been hit by the *Growler*.

Still unaware of the POWs and their awful predicament, the *Pampanito* tracked the bulk of the remaining ships in the convoy. As soon as darkness offered its cover once again, Summers and his crew launched a surprise attack.

"Hot run in number four!" came the sharp cry from the forward torpedo room.

"Aye, hot run in number four," acknowledged the torpedo officer, with as much calm as he could muster.

A torpedo had become stuck in the tube, its nose hard against the jammed door. That kept it from swimming away, even as the torpedo's engine ran at full speed, butting its nose against the impediment. It wouldn't be armed yet. It took several hundred feet of run in the open sea to get it to the point that it would be ready to explode upon contact with something solid. Still, these particular fish were known to be extremely temperamental. It was highly possible that the hot run could explode right there in the number-four tube.

The truth was, though, that there was little they could do at the moment about the balky weapon. And there were plenty of targets still swimming around out there. Swinging around to draw a bead on several of the vessels, trying not to think about the explosive power that was hemmed up in number four like a ticking time bomb, the sub released a total of nine torpedoes over the next few minutes—all she had to fire.

Nine torpedoes swimming away toward their quarry. All but two of them struck targets.

In all, three vessels were damaged. Two of them were clearly done for. A third was claimed as a kill but was later disallowed.

One of the dying targets was a big transport with an unusual history. It was a ship originally built in the United States as the *Wolverine State*, a passenger ship. She had been carrying passengers off the China coast when she was captured by the Japanese and renamed the *Kachidoki Maru*. She was used as a troop transport and cargo vessel, primarily carrying raw materials and soldiers between various points of the Pacific Rim and Japan.

On this voyage, the ship also carried nine hundred British and Australian prisoners of war.

Cheers rang out up and down the length of the *Pampanito* as the skipper reported the solid hits against the enemy. The thunderous explosions and sounds of vessels breaking up as seawater rushed into their holds confirmed his update.

They then decided not to launch any more torpedoes, even when a couple of smaller vessels appeared and began picking up survivors from the teeming sea. Summers backed away from all the destruction he and his gang had set loose and finally gave attention to the lethal weapon that was still stubbornly lodged in the tube up front. They were finally able to eject the sticky torpedo and reload all tubes, just in case something else interesting came swimming by. Flushed by the success of this attack, they were ready to do more damage.

The crew did get a quick shot at a destroyer later in the day, but the quicker surface ship avoided their torpedoes and steamed on. Then the fun was over. It was time to go meet up with the rest of the wolf pack and compare notes on their wonderfully successful assault.

The next day, the *Pampanito* returned to the general area where the attacks on the convoy had taken place, hoping to run into a straggler or two and finish them off. On the afternoon of September 14, after diving deep to avoid contact with an enemy aircraft that did not seem to want to go away, Summers finally brought his boat to the surface in the midst of a nasty batch of debris and thick sludge oil. Wreckage floated all about them, the remnants of the mayhem their wolf pack had unleashed.

The skipper later noted in his log what else they found there:

1605: A bridge lookout sighted some men on a raft, so stood by small arms, and closed to investigate.

1634: The men were covered with oil and filth and we could not make them out. . . . They were shouting but we couldn't understand what they were saying, except made out words "Pick us up please." Called rescue party on deck and took them off the raft. There were about fifteen (15) British and Australian Prisoner of War survivors on this raft from a ship sunk the night of 11–12 September 1944. We learned they were enroute from Singapore to Formosa and that there were over thirteen hundred on the sunken ship.

They were survivors of the *Sealion*'s attack on the *Rakuyo Maru*. They were a ragged bunch. After four days floating on the lashed-together makeshift raft, the men were hungry, thirsty, weak from exposure, and covered from head to foot with thick oil.

As soon as he got the story from the survivors, Captain Summers radioed the *Sealion* and told them what they had found. Both subs immediately began lifesaving measures, trying to pick up as many of the men as they could find while keeping a wary eye out for trouble.

Summers later recorded:

1634: As men were received on board, we stripped them and removed most of the heavy coating of oil and muck. We cleared the after torpedo room and passed them below as quickly as possible. Gave all men a piece of cloth moistened with water to suck on. All of them were exhausted after four days on the raft and three years imprisonment. Many had lashed themselves to their makeshift rafts, which were slick with grease; and had nothing but lifebelts with them. All showed signs of pellagra, beri-beri, immersion, salt water sores, ringworm, malaria etc. All were very thin and showed the results of undernour-ishment. Some were in very bad shape. . . . A pitiful sight none of us will ever forget. All hands turned to with a will and the men were cared for as rapidly as possible.

1701: Sent message asking Sealion for help.

1712: Picked up a second raft with about nine men aboard. . . .

1721: Picked up another six men.

1730: Rescued another six men.

1753: Picked up about eleven men. . . .

1824: . . . about six men.

1832: . . . about five men . . .

1957: Light fading rapidly as we picked up a single sur-vivor.

2005: Completely dark as we took aboard the last group of about ten men. Had made a thorough search of our vicinity with high periscope and kept true bearings of all rafts sighted. Felt we had everyone in sight and knew we had all we could care for if not more. When finally we obtained an exact count the number of survivors on board was 73. These together with 79 members of our crew plus 10 officers make us "a little cramped for living space."

2015: Made final search and finding no one else set course for Saipan at four engine speed.

Much of the rescue effort was recorded on movie film, using the boat's 16-millimeter camera. That footage has survived. In those pictures, we can see volunteer teams of crewmen pulling the oil-covered men aboard, even as lookouts kept an eye on the sky and radar scanned for incoming aircraft. Word would have been passed to the Japanese headquarters about the attack on the convoy and aircraft were almost a certainty.

Still the crewmen from the submarines did all they could do, throwing lines to drifting rafts, pulling them close enough to the submarine to help the men aboard. Some of the sub sailors jumped into the water to get to victims, knowing that if the sub had to suddenly duck under the surface to avoid aircraft or patrol vessels, they would be stranded there. Stranded along with the men they were attempting to rescue. A submarine on the surface in daylight is a luscious target to enemy aircraft, so the skipper would have no choice but to dive.

Any of the men working on deck would have been left behind, too, if the need to dive occurred. It took less than a minute from the order to dive and the sounding of the klaxon for the boat to be under. Anyone not in the shears or on the bridge when the order came had no hope of getting belowdecks before the hatch was closed.

No matter. The submariners knew they had to do whatever they could to rescue as many of the POWs as possible. They ignored the risk and did their jobs and tried not to think about what might happen if an aircraft suddenly popped up on the boat's radar screen.

Captain Summers sent a radio message requesting that any other vessels in the area be sent as quickly as possible to continue the rescue. Several submarines broke off pursuit of another enemy convoy to rush to the area to help. Several dozen more men were plucked from the sea before a typhoon blew in, ending the effort and sealing the fate of the other POWs who had somehow survived the sinkings until that point.

In all and according to the best count available, over twenty-two hundred POWs were aboard the two transports that were sunk by the *Sealion* and the *Pampanito*. Those two boats and two of their sisters, the *Queenfish* (SS-393) and the *Barb* (SS-220), pulled about 160 men out of the oily waters. After the war, IJN records indicated that the Japanese rescued about 140 POWs for a total of about 300 of them who were saved. The Japanese were much more successful in getting to the survivors of the ship that was sunk by Summers and the *Pampanito*. Of the 900 men on that ship, about 660 were pulled aboard Japanese vessels and taken on to work camps, as originally intended. After the war, over 500 of them— all who survived the work camps—were liberated by American troops.

The nearest safe harbor to the *Pampanito*'s position was the island of Saipan, five days away, provided they could get a decent amount of time to run on the surface. Men were sleeping everywhere on the submarine, even on the empty torpedo skids. Food supplies were limited, too, but they somehow made do, including the submariners, who, for once, silenced their usual good-natured grousing.

Clearly many of the survivors required medical attention. No sub carried a doctor, so the task of caring for the variety of ailments fell to the pharmacist's mate, Maurice Demers. Others pitched in to help as they could, feeding the men who were too weak to hold a spoon and donating clothing and toilet articles.

Despite the young PM's best efforts, one of the POWs, a Brit, died. He was buried at sea in a somber funeral ceremony.

En route to Saipan, the sub met up with the destroyer USS *Case* (DD-370), who sent over a doctor, another pharmacist's mate to assist Demers, food, and a good stock of medical supplies.

When they docked in Tanapag Harbor on Saipan on September 20, men bringing fresh fruit and ice cream met them. The process of getting the rescued POWs ashore and to medical facilities began at once.

Captain Summers was awarded the Navy Cross for his leadership in the attack on the Japanese patrol as well as for the rescue of the prisoners. The crewmen of the *Pampanito*, who so bravely dove into the water to swim out and assist survivors, received the Navy and Marine Corps Medal. So did Pharmacist's Mate Demers for his efforts to ease the suffering of the men they plucked from the oily sea.

After the third war patrol for the *Pampanito*, Commander Paul Summers was sent home for some well-deserved rest. With his three patrols at the helm of the *Pampanito* and seven more before that on the USS *Stingray*, he welcomed the break, but would return to take command of the *Pampanito*'s fifth and sixth runs.

So, when the 383 boat pulled away from Pearl Harbor for her fourth war patrol, she was under the command of Captain Frank Wesley "Mike" Fenno, a sub sailor with a unique war record. He had most recently been the skipper of the USS *Runner* (SS-275), but before that command he was on the bridge of the USS *Trout* (SS-202), one of the boats on patrol in the Pacific near the Hawaiian Islands on the day of the attack on Pearl Harbor.

Shortly thereafter, he and his boat were ordered to deliver a large cache of ammunition to Corregidor, the island that acted as a citadel at the entrance to Manila Harbor in the Philippines. After off-loading the ammo, the *Trout* picked up maybe the most interesting ballast of the war—over twenty tons of gold and silver.

It is true that Fenno requested additional ballast to make his submarine more stable on the return run, but, as luck would have it, sandbags were especially hard to come by at that time on the heavily fortified island. The military command suggested he might take on a far more interesting cargo, something that ironically had less value at the moment than the sandbags. By doing so, they could serve two purposes, getting him the ballast he needed and hauling precious cargo back for safekeeping.

The precious metal was taken from the banks in Manila ahead of the inevitable Japanese invasion and was bound for Hawaii for safekeeping. In all, almost six hundred gold bars and bulging canvas bags holding eighteen tons of silver were carefully loaded into the bilges of the *Trout*, all under the watchful eye of serious-faced soldiers. Fenno signed a receipt for the treasure but made a note that he could not personally verify the exact count since neither he nor his crew had the time or inclination to do a detailed tally.

Despite the unusual ballast in her bilges, Fenno and his crew still managed to sink two enemy vessels while making the money run back to Pearl Harbor.

Captain Fenno eventually left the *Trout* after four war patrols to assume command of the *Runner* and, eventually, the *Pampanito*. His first boat met an untimely end after his departure. On her eleventh patrol, in February 1944, the *Trout* was lost with all hands in a ferocious depth-charge attack off the Marianas.

Eighty-one sailors were dispatched on eternal patrol when Mike Fenno's former boat went down.

The *Pampanito* went to the "mothball fleet" at Mare Island, in San Francisco Bay, shortly after the end of the war. Like several other boats, she came out of retirement to serve as a training vessel, in her case as part of Naval Reserve Submarine Division 11–12.

In 1971, she was stricken from the naval registry and, unfortunately, suffered from some stripping of her equipment to supply parts to other long-in-the-tooth sister boats that were still being used in a reserve capacity. Once all her equipment was gone, a boat was little more than a steel hull, and that meant being cut apart for scrap. Thankfully, the *Pampanito* had a brighter future once she overcame a few unique hurdles.

In 1976, the boat was turned over to the Maritime Park Association, a group with designs on placing the historic vessel alongside Fisherman's Wharf in San Francisco as a tourist attraction, memorial, and museum vessel.

The effort came at an unfortunate time in our country's history, on the heels of the Vietnam War, and there was opposition to the plan from some members of the San Francisco Port Commission. They wanted no part of a warship, a symbol of the military and the horrors of war, being parked anywhere in their city. Several members talked of such a display glorifying the horrors of war at a time when the nation was better off saluting peace and pacifism.

The Maritime Park Association had no choice. They floated the sub down to a private shipyard in Stockton for storage. There she stayed, out of sight, out of mind, for over six long years, until the mood (as well as the makeup) of the Port Commission changed.

The *Pampanito* finally found a berth at the San Francisco Maritime Museum at Pier 45 in the middle of Fisherman's Wharf, where she immediately became a popular spot for tourists to visit and for sub vets to gather. She now hosts over 100,000 visitors a year as well as more than 15,000 overnight campers annually. This makes her maybe the most visited of all the museum submarines as well as one of the most popular naval exhibits in the country.

The old boat has even had a part in a major Hollywood movie—she played the part of the beleaguered submarine USS *Stingray* in *Down Periscope*, a 1996 comedy starring Kelsey Grammer, Rob Schneider, Rip Torn, William H. Macy, Bruce Dern, and Lauren Holly. During the filming of the feature, the boat was actually moved away from the dock and towed out of the bay, beneath the Golden Gate Bridge and back, making what could be called her final patrol for the benefit of the Hollywood movie cameras. It had been fifty years since her last trip beneath the Golden Gate.

The *Pampanito* is still in the process of being restored to how she was in late summer 1945. Because of the items that were stripped from her during her years of being mothballed, it has taken a great deal of effort to acquire the gear needed to reequip her. The Maritime Park Association and volunteer groups have been replacing missing equipment and spare parts that were taken from the boat during the 1970s. Almost all of the missing items have now been replaced, and much of the equipment on board the vessel has been restored to operational condition.

Quite a bit of the gear actually works, just as it did when Captain Summers steered the boat through the South China Sea. In 1999, she underwent extensive dry-dock repairs and restoration after being towed back across the bay to Alameda.

Those doing the renovations to the submarine have always tried to make reversible any of the changes necessary to do the job. Much of the work done to make the vessel more accessible to visitors can be easily undone so she can be returned with minimal effort to how she looked during World War II. For example, the torpedo loading hatches that were removed to allow for building stairs into the boat's interior are now in storage for safekeeping and could be easily returned to their original positions if desired.

The USS *Pampanito* has been declared a National Historic Landmark.

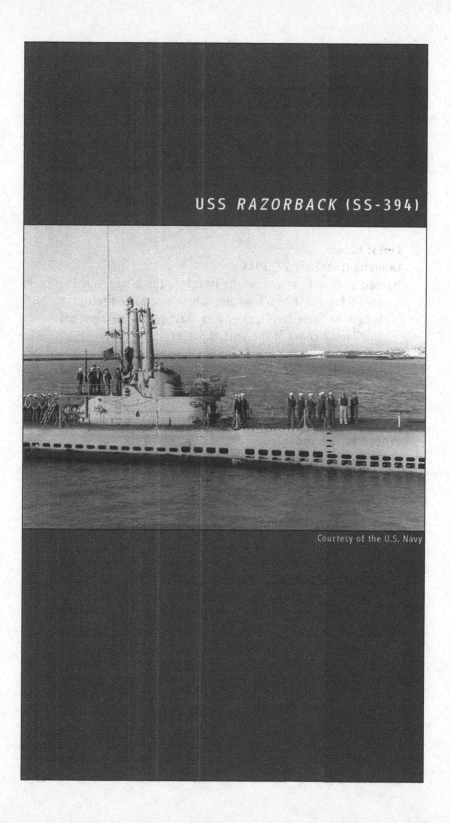

USS *RAZORBACK* (SS-394)

Courtesy of the U.S. Navy

USS *RAZORBACK* (SS-394)

Class: *Balao*
Launched: January 27, 1944
Named for: not, as you might imagine, for a hog, but instead for the finback whale, which normally reaches a length of forty-five feet and is most commonly seen off the Pacific coast of the United States
Where: Portsmouth Naval Shipyard, New Hampshire
Sponsor: Mrs. H.F.D. Davis, the wife of the manager of the Industrial Department at Portsmouth Navy Yard
Commissioned: April 3, 1944

Where is she today?
Arkansas Inland Maritime Museum
100 Riverfront Road
North Little Rock, Arkansas 72119
(501) 371-8320
www.northlr.org/maritime-museum/default.asp

Claim to fame: Despite her five World War II patrols, for which she earned five battle stars, her presence in Tokyo Bay for the Japanese surrender ceremony, the four battle stars awarded for her work during the Vietnam War, and her twenty-six years of service in the U.S. Navy, the *Razorback*'s real claim to fame might well be her amazing voyage home after being retired from the Turkish navy after decades more of faithful duty. She was the last operational World War II submarine and is the longest-serving submarine in naval history.

The submarines that were being slid down the skids at the various shipyards around the country during World War II were built to last. The same people who made engines for locomotives built their diesel power plants. The hulls and superstructures were of the strongest steel available. All systems were cobbled together to withstand the roughest seas, the deepest possible dives, the nearby vicious explosions of TNT-powered depth charges. Despite how well these boats were constructed, regular and proper upkeep was still paramount to keep them effective. Even at a time when every possible boat was needed to fight the war, they still came off patrol and went directly to a maintenance facility. There they remained idle while anything broken was fixed, regular preservation work was done, and the vessels received the latest and greatest upgraded equipment.

Still, it is doubtful that any of the men and women who designed, built, and maintained those warships would have ever guessed that one of their creations would still be active almost six decades later. That was the case with the USS *Razorback*, the longest-serving submarine in history.

She was launched at Portsmouth Navy Yard in January 1944, just a bit over two years after the "day of infamy" of Pearl Harbor. She would not be retired until the Turkish navy ultimately decommissioned her in 2001.

But even then, her oceangoing days were not over. Not by a long shot!

With a commissioning crew of sixty men, the *Razorback* followed her predecessors down the Atlantic Coast, through the Caribbean Sea, through the locks of the Panama Canal, and on across the Pacific Ocean to Pearl Harbor. Before that, though, she had had something of an inauspicious beginning to her service. While conducting sea trials, her commissioning skipper and his executive officer managed to run her aground at New London. Both officers were promptly relieved of their positions.

Commander Roy Benson, a former skipper of the USS *Trigger* (SS-237), just happened to be in New London at the time serving a tour of duty at the submarine school there. He heard the news about the unfortunate debut of her previous captain, asked for the boat, and got her.

Such a move was typical of Roy Benson. He had a reputation for being a bold and aggressive captain. As it turned out, though, he did not have much to shoot at when he got his new submarine into the war. Pickings were slim on the *Razorback*'s first run. Through no fault of Benson's or his crew's, they simply had nothing to attack.

Benson was promoted off the boat after that run and replaced by Lieutenant Commander Charles Brown. With the new skipper, their luck turned better and they were credited with sinking two enemy vessels on the second run. Then, on her third patrol, they got four more enemy ships during some exciting surface gun attacks and collected three Japanese prisoners.

Brown and the *Razorback* also had a near-tragic occurrence. Patrolling in the East China Sea, they saw through the periscopes what they believed to be an enemy transport. There was something curious about the ship, though. The vessel was not zigzagging and did not have an escort of any kind anywhere in sight. But Brown and his crew were having problems with the scopes fogging up and visibility was not the best anyway. Still, it appeared to be a worthy target at a time when targets were hard to come by.

Brown sent the crew to battle stations and ordered five torpedoes fired in a wide spread.

Only an instant after the last fish was out of its tube, the captain spotted a large red cross on the ship's hull. It was a hospital ship. Sub commanders were under strict orders to allow such vessels safe passage, no matter what.

For the first time in his career, the young skipper held his breath and prayed that the torpedoes he had just launched would miss their intended target.

Somebody must have been listening. His prayers were answered. Somehow, in setting up for the attack, the range had been miscalculated and all five weapons swept harmlessly past the hospital ship.

Later, a clerk charged with tallying the results of submarine patrols noted, in a great understatement: "It is fortunate the attack was not successful."

Brown led the *Razorback* on a total of four war patrols, but it was her fifth and final one that was easily the most noteworthy. It was not because of any heroic attack she launched or a crucial target destroyed, but for a few simple messages copied and distributed over a period of several days by the radio operator.

Five weeks into the run, they received word of the bombs dropped on Hiroshima and Nagasaki. The news that the war had ended followed shortly.

It was an odd time for the crews of Allied submarines and other naval vessels in the war zone. The boats had to stay on alert because there had been more than one incident of Japanese airplanes and warships continuing to attack American ships, even if hostilities were supposed to have ceased. But it was a time of euphoria, too.

The war was over at last. They would be going home soon.

When the official word of the war's end came, many of the submarine captains gave the order to break out the medicinal alcohol they all had aboard. A ration was given to each of the men who was not on watch. It was not much of a party, but it was the best celebration they could manage until they got ashore to do it properly.

Still, everyone kept an eye on the sky and the radarscopes, just in case.

Then, at the end of August 1945, the *Razorback* was ordered to proceed, along with eleven other submarines, into the mouth of Tokyo Bay. She was to stand by there next to the sub tender *Proteus* (AS-19) while the surrender ceremonies took place aboard the battleship USS *Missouri*.

There was some concern about this particular honor. Sailors speculated that the whole thing might be a trap. Once the *Missouri*, the submarines, and the rest of the contingent were inside Tokyo Bay, the Japanese might spring a surprise attack. They were known to be fanatical. Some had refused to lay down their arms and were fighting still. Deck guns were manned and the torpedo tubes were all loaded as the *Razorback* steamed into enemy territory.

Of course, there was no surprise attack, but some of the officers who went ashore reported the ominous sights they had seen. Hundreds of mini-submarines were in various stages of construction, ready to launch in the case of an Allied invasion.

The crew of the *Razorback* was berthed too far away to see or hear the actual surrender ceremony when it took place, but they soon read General Douglas MacArthur's brief message to those assembled on the *Missouri*'s main deck.

Just after the surrender documents were signed, he read the simple dismissing words from a slip of paper:

"Let us pray that peace be now restored to the world, and that God will preserve it always. These proceedings are closed."

As did most of her sister submarines, the *Razorback* returned to the United States immediately after the war, docking in San Diego. She received five battle stars for her service in the Pacific. For the first time, the crew was able to talk with family and friends about what they had been doing in the Pacific. In the glut of news about the atomic bombs dropped on Japan and the quick end of the war, the submarine service's contributions were, unfortunately, not fully recounted.

Once again, the silent service's stealth, the hidden way the submarines went about their business, were not conducive to newsreels or newspaper front-page photos.

JANAC (Joint Army-Navy Assessment Committee) also cut into the record of the sub sailors. The submarine command tallied about four enemy vessels sunk for about ten million tons. Relying heavily on Japanese war records, JANAC cut the total to about thirteen hundred ships and five million tons—one-third the claimed vessels and one-half the total tonnage.

Some figures were indisputable, though. Fifty-two submarines were lost during the war. Over thirty-five hundred submariners died out of the sixteen thousand who served. That was a casualty rate of nearly 22 percent, the greatest for any branch of the service in World War II.

Even using the conservative JANAC figures, less than 2 percent of the U.S. Navy had accounted for more than 55 percent of Japan's maritime losses in the war. It is impossible to count the other contributions—the warships lost to service even if they were not destroyed, the oil tankers and freighters loaded with raw materials that never reached the Home Islands with their vital cargo, the time and effort used by the enemy vessels to avoid the submarine fleet, the crucial observations of the sub crews that helped prepare for attack and follow convoy activity, the many downed pilots rescued by subs on lifeguard duty.

Even if the war was over, the *Razorback* still had plenty of fight left in her. She went back to Pearl Harbor and operated throughout the Pacific until 1949. Then, in 1952, she received the GUPPY II conversion. Soon, she was back in Pacific waters as part of the Seventh Fleet. She even took part in some of the early nuclear blast tests in the South Pacific. Later, she played a role in the Vietnam War, for which she and her crew received four battle stars and a Vietnam Service Medal. Most of that activity remains classified, even today.

The end of her service to her native country came in November 1970, and it was not immediately clear where the *Razorback* would end up.

Many of her sister diesel boats had long since met ignoble fates. Some of them were scrapped—"cut up and made into razor blades," as the old sub sailors like to describe their inglorious fate.

Many more were parked at docks around the country, placed into "reserve fleet" status, just in case they might be needed for some other kind of duty. There, many of them had their equipment stripped for use on other vessels as they simply rusted away.

Others were used for target practice, simulating enemy submersibles so that young trainees could hone their antisubmarine warfare skills. Though this was a valuable sacrifice, the navy was still sending gallant historical artifacts to the bottom of the sea each time they sank one of the diesel submarines.

A few boats were retained as training vessels. No longer rigged or seaworthy enough to steam out of port, they were parked at piers around the country, where reserve sailors could come aboard and learn to operate their systems and get other important training.

A few others, as we have seen, were saved from the scrap heap and set up as memorials to those who made the ultimate sacrifice for their country.

That did not seem to be an option for the *Razorback*.

A precious few of the diesel subs were destined to continue their service. They were allowed to switch their loyalty to the navy of a new country. Some ended up in South America. Others went to Europe and Asia.

That was the *Razorback*'s destiny. Just after being stricken from the list of active vessels in late 1970, simultaneously with her decommissioning, she was transferred to the Turkish navy. She steamed away to the far side of the world one more time, this time to ply the ancient Mediterranean, Aegean, and Black seas, most likely until the end of her days.

"North Little Rock now has a navy." Those were the words of North Little Rock, Arkansas, mayor Patrick Hays just after returning from a trip to Turkey in September 2002. His declaration came as part of the news conference at which the mayor announced the official acquisition by his city of an old diesel boat that had once been named the *Razorback*. It was their intent to bring her back home after her stint with the Turkish navy, steaming back to Arkansas across the Atlantic and up the Mississippi and Arkansas rivers.

But the story begins a year before that, and all the way across the North American continent from Arkansas, with the casual comments of a salesman to one of his customers.

It was November 2001. Bob Opple, a former sub sailor, was in his office at a heavy-equipment company near Seattle, Washington. On that day, he was talking with a visiting salesman named Len Schutt. Schutt also happened to be a former sub sailor, having served on the USS *Ronquil* (SS-396).

As they swapped sea stories, Schutt kept looking at some photos on Opple's office wall.

"That's the *Razorback*, right?" Schutt asked, eyeing the "394" visible on the submarine's sail in one of the photos.

"Sure is. I went to sea on her when I was nineteen years old," Opple confirmed. "She was a great boat."

"Well, you may not believe this, but I was aboard her a while back," the salesman declared. "Only she's called the *Murat Reis* now. Too bad, but they've probably scrapped her by now, though."

Opple couldn't believe what he was hearing. His old boat was still around. Or at least she had been when Schutt saw her several months before. Opple had assumed that she had been scrapped or sunk long before, just like many of the other boats.

He quickly got on the horn to some of his sub veteran buddies, Maurice Barksdale, a real estate consultant in Texas, and Max Bassett, who had remained in the navy until he retired to Florida. They, too, were amazed that the *Razorback* was still in existence. They discussed the idea of climbing on an airplane and visiting the submarine before it was too late. If it wasn't too late already, of course.

But along the way, someone proposed—half kidding—the idea of trying to buy the boat and bring her back to the States. The more they talked about it, though, the more it intrigued the sub vets. What at first seemed like a wild and crazy idea blossomed into a full-blown plan when they discovered that the boat had indeed been decommissioned by the Turks, but at last report she was still afloat and in decent condition.

"We're just a bunch of old submarine vets who have found ourselves a toy," Opple told a newspaper reporter.

But the sub sailors were smart enough to know they needed help with a project of this magnitude, even if their mission was a worthy one. And they also knew, from the experiences of other groups who had attempted such a task, that they would need money. Lots of money.

Then someone made a natural connection. Razorback? Arkansas!

The razorback hog is the mascot of the University of Arkansas athletic teams. Maybe someone in that great state would be interested in helping bring a true fighting razorback home.

Contacts with sub vet groups in Arkansas led to conversations with Patrick Hays, the mayor of North Little Rock. Hays already had big plans to capitalize on recent development that was planned along the Arkansas River waterfront of his town and that of Little Rock, the neighboring city across the river to the south. President Bill Clinton's library was already under construction and there had been talk of some kind of veterans' memorial park or maritime museum in the vicinity.

Thus it was that the mayor was more than willing to listen to what the sub veterans had to say. He bought into the plan immediately when he heard the details and, with the help of the Arkansas sub vet group, and especially Greg Zonner, who handled much of the considerable paperwork, they set a course to get themselves a diesel submarine to park on the river at North Little Rock.

Soon the U.S. State Department and the Turkish government were involved in serious talks. Over a roller-coaster nine months, a plan was hatched and myriad paper trails were hiked. Then, in September, Mayor Hays led a delegation to Ankara, Turkey, to see what it would take to finally secure the boat for his city.

Hays got surprising news when he and his group arrived.

Instead of having the Americans reimburse Turkey for what it had cost them to store the old submarine since negotiations had begun, or asking them to come up with money for some kind of exaggerated purchase price, the Turkish government said they would be most happy to simply give the aging vessel to the mayor and his group, gratis.

Well, that was a bargain!

Of course, the rest of the plan would not be so easy to carry out. Who was going to pay to prepare the vessel for a transoceanic transit? She was in no shape for such a trip. Could they plan on steaming across the Atlantic under the *Razorback*'s own power or would they have to settle for a tow? Her engines worked, but could they last for such a long journey? Could they actually get her floated up the Mississippi and Arkansas rivers without running aground?

There were more questions than answers, now that they had the sub, but it seemed that there was one solution to most of the anticipated difficulties. That was money.

A few weeks after the mayor's visit, Opple and some of his fellow sub sailors went to Turkey for a look-see. They were pleased with the boat's condition, considering the miles on her odometer. But there were still a lot of things that would have to be done to get her ready and secured for such a long voyage. Each of those things carried a price tag.

The first estimate to make her seaworthy and ready to propel herself home was $1.5 million. Even if they did not need her to be capable of making a dive along the way, it would take about a fifth that much money, $300,000.

The sub vets scratched their heads and thought about it for a while. It would have been fun to make a flank-speed run across the open sea, taking the occasional dive just for old times' sake, but that seemed out of the question when the bids started to come in.

There were other expenses to consider, too, as time went on. The Turks originally agreed to sell her to the city of North Little Rock for a nominal sum of one dollar, but government red tape inevitably muddied that beautiful deal. The city and vet groups would eventually have to pony up nearly $40,000 in salvage reimbursement money before they could take the boat home. They still considered it a fine bargain, but that was $40,000 they had not anticipated needing.

Somehow they found it. Most of the money came from local businesses that saw the value in the publicity and tourist dollars the submarine would bring to their city. Other contributions gathered up by the submarine veterans paid for the long tow through the Mediterranean Sea and across the Atlantic.

On May 5, 2004, the *Razorback* began her eight-thousand-mile journey from the Gulf of Izmit, with plans to arrive in Little Rock in mid- to late July. Max Bassett, Bob Opple, Greg Zonner, and Mayor Patrick Hays rode along for portions of the trip, either in the tug that was pulling the boat or aboard the old girl herself. A couple of retired Turkish sub sailors were along for the ride, too, excited about seeing the boat saved.

There were no Japanese dive-bombers, no enemy destroyers, no depth-charge attacks along the way. They made good progress despite some minor mechanical and weather glitches, easing down through the Dardanelles. There were some thoughts of taking the boat down for a dive in the vicinity of an old World War II German gunboat, sunk by the Allies in World War II, but the weather did not cooperate.

Next was the Aegean Sea and a short stopover in Greece to drop off some passengers. The Mediterranean was rough and several of the men on board got seasick. Sub sailors do get seasick, but back in the day the boat simply submerged, looking for a smoother ride. The *Razorback* had no such option on this trip. They could have dived, but it would have been a risky procedure in those rough seas.

British sailors at Gibraltar warmly greeted the submarine and her crew before she left the Mediterranean. The sub vets who were traveling along with their boat gave the Brits extensive tours and answered their many questions about the old vessel. And the hosts reciprocated with a party for one and all. A reporter from *Stars and Stripes* was there for an interview, and so were several television crews, documenting their progress.

Seas calmed considerably once they left Gibraltar and entered the Atlantic Ocean. There was one somber observation along the way. The boat paused near the spot south of the Azores where the USS *Scorpion* (SSN-589), a nuclear submarine, was lost under mysterious circumstances in May 1968. A brief memorial service was held there for the ninety-nine crewmen who perished in that incident. Max Bassett, one of the sub vets riding the boat, tossed overboard a special plaque that had been given to them by the Scorpion Association.

For most of the ride, the sub sailors were aboard the *Rhea*, the sea tug that was towing the *Razorback*. But every three or four days they would climb aboard their submarine and take a tour, making sure everything was okay, that she was not taking on water. They also stayed busy returning e-mail messages from people all over the world who were following the old boat's progress across the Atlantic.

The *Razorback* got a warm reception when she arrived in Key West, Florida, the former home port for many of her sister boats. There had been a great deal of coverage in the news media about the boat and her journey. Word had been passed along among submarine veteran groups on the Internet, via e-mail, and through their newsletters. A large contingent of sub vets was in the welcoming crowd at Key West, eager to go aboard and take a closer look at the *Razorback*. The crew managed to accommodate many tours during the stopover, taking an estimated five hundred visitors down her ladders and through her narrow passageways.

A couple of former *Razorback* sailors came aboard for the next leg of the trip.

After a trip across the Gulf of Mexico, the boat pulled into New Orleans on June 19, greeted by a city fireboat, spraying water high into the air in salute. The submarine was about to leave salt water forever, and that called for a formal welcome ceremony. Many of those who had worked so hard to get the boat this far were there to welcome her, including a large contingent of vets from USSVI, the United States Submarine Veterans organization.

Jim Barnes, commander of the Razorback Base of the USSVI, recalls, "We had people standing in line for hours in the hot sun with no shade or water, all just to take a tour."

He estimated that between fifteen hundred and two thousand people went through the boat while she was tied up at the Julia Street Wharf in New Orleans. There were plenty more television and newspaper representatives there, too.

Next came the really tricky part of the journey. Before reaching New Orleans, the crew had already had to lash the sub to the hip of the tugboat and use the sub's ancient engines to fight the current of the Mississippi. Now they had to buck the flow all the way up from New Orleans, past Baton Rouge, to north of Greenville, Mississippi, where they would enter the Arkansas at Rosedale. At one point on the Arkansas River, two barges, heavily ballasted on their outsides, were strapped to the *Razorback*'s flanks in order to lift her higher and get her through shallow water.

She made it, but with little room to spare.

On August 3, 2004, the *Razorback* arrived at the Little Rock Harbor Services facility so she could rest awhile and be prepared for her debut to the citizens of her new hometown. Mayor Hays and a group of representatives put on work clothes and gave the old girl a new coat of paint so she would look her best.

On August 29, she was officially tied up at North Little Rock and a ceremony welcomed her. As many as 150 submarine veterans were there to greet her. Even though she had had a long trip and many years of abuse, even though she had some rust streaks along her sides that were showing through the hurried paint job, and even though most of the signs inside the boat were written in indecipherable Turkish, the old sub sailors vowed to anyone who would listen that she was about the most beautiful thing they had ever seen.

Jim Barnes may have summed it up best when he was quoted as saying, "If the [school] children can go aboard and see the engineering, the cramped living space, learn of the fifty-two submarines and the thirty-five hundred men that were lost in World War Two to maintain our freedom, then this has all been worthwhile."

No one disagreed.

The *Razorback* is officially an exhibit in the Arkansas Inland Maritime Museum at North Little Rock. The museum has also made moves to acquire the USS *Hoga* (YT-146), a tugboat that valiantly helped fight fires during the attack on Pearl Harbor. Construction continues on the museum building, and the submarine is occasionally moved to a different location on the river to accommodate modifications to her berthing point along the riverbank. She does, however, remain open to visitors during the construction phase.

USS *TORSK* (SS-423)

Courtesy of the U.S. Navy

USS *TORSK* (SS-423)

Class: *Tench*
Launched: September 6, 1944
Named for: the Norwegian name of a fish, related to the codfish, that is found in the North Atlantic
Where: Portsmouth Naval Shipyard, New Hampshire
Sponsor: Mrs. Allen B. Reed, the wife of the captain of the USS *New Orleans* (CA-32), a heavy cruiser
Commissioned: December 16, 1944

Where is she today?
Baltimore Maritime Museum
802 South Caroline Street
Baltimore, Maryland 21231
(410) 396-3453
www.baltomaritimemuseum.org
www.usstorsk.org

Claim to fame: She fired the last torpedo and sank the last combatant ship of World War II, set the all-time career record for number of dives by a submarine . . . and, of course, the record for the number of times surfacing from a dive.

It was difficult for Bafford Lewellen to believe the war was so near to being over. Standing there on the bridge of the submarine he commanded, the USS *Torsk*, he surveyed the Sea of Japan with an odd mix of feelings. He and the men with whom he had sailed so far during this war had carried out the good fight.

With his previous boat, the USS *Pollack* (SS-180), he and his crew guided the old boat to a series of spectacular sinkings. Now, with this relatively new boat, he had been on the bridge for a total of two war patrols. Though targets were much harder to find by the summer of 1945, he and the crew had done what had to be done when they encountered enemy vessels.

Now something so spectacularly awesome that it was hard to even contemplate had happened. And because of that, the end of this awful conflict was suddenly imminent.

"What are you thinking, Skip?" his exec asked, noting the contemplative look on his captain's face.

"Just wondering how those boys on the other side feel now," he answered, dropping the binoculars from his eyes. "They know it's over. Are they going to lay down or will they fight on as long as they can?"

It was a true concern. The Japanese were known to be fanatical in their pursuit of the war. What other nation had ever had suicide pilots and mini-submarine drivers willing to drive their craft into anything flying the Stars and Stripes?

But only three days before, the *Torsk* had pulled seven Japanese seamen from the drink, survivors of a ship sent to the bottom by an American airplane. Granted, they weren't combatants, but they seemed more thankful than defiant when the *Torsk* showed up to pull them out of their lifeboat.

Then the next day they fired two torpedoes at a freighter. She was damaged, no doubt about it, but they were unable to determine if she went down or not. The very next day, they sent the cargo vessel *Kaiho Maru* to the bottom. They continued to keep a sharp eye from the shears and bridge and to man the radarscopes, looking for targets and approaching threats, just as they had done since leaving Portsmouth. It was no time to get lackadaisical.

"Radar contact, zero-seven-zero, twelve thousand yards!" came the sudden strident call up the hatch from the radar operator, interrupting the conversation between the skipper and his executive officer.

It was August 14, 1945. Everything about this war had changed eight days before. Yet, oddly, for a *Tench*-class submarine named the *Torsk*, now riding gently on the surface of the Sea of Japan, nothing had changed.

"Battle stations," Lewellen ordered. "Clear the bridge!"

On August 6, an astounding new weapon called the atomic bomb was loaded aboard a B-29. The bomber carried the nickname *Enola Gay*. With Colonel Paul Tibbets in the pilot's seat, the plane left the island of Tinian in the Marianas at 2:45 in the morning, bound for the Japanese Home Islands. Less than six hours later, the bomb bay doors were opened and the atomic weapon was let loose over the city of Hiroshima, a communications center and staging area for Japanese troops. It was also a location in which it had been determined that there were no prisoner of war camps.

As it was designed to do, the bomb detonated at an elevation of two thousand feet. An estimated seventy-two thousand people died. Another sixty-eight thousand were wounded. The Japanese would later estimate total casualties from that single blast at more than a quarter million. Tibbets and the *Enola Gay* were back on Tinian by mid-afternoon, their mission a success.

President Harry Truman announced the use of the atomic bomb at Hiroshima, calling the city a "military base" in his speech. He told the world that it would be the last time such a weapon would be used, providing the Japanese would immediately begin negotiating a peace settlement.

"If they [the Japanese] do not now accept our terms, they may expect a rain of ruin from the air the likes of which has never been seen on this earth," the president warned.

At the same time, Russia, a country that had remained neutral in the war with Japan (primarily because they were involved on the European front with Germany), declared war and began marching into Manchuria and northern Korea.

Still there was no hint of surrender from Japan.

Three days later, in a B-29 named *Bock's Car*, Major Charles Sweeney led his crew toward a second designated target, the city of Kokura. The target was covered with thick clouds that morning. The poor weather spared Kokura.

Major Sweeney, running low on fuel, turned away and went to his secondary objective, the port city of Nagasaki. At a few minutes before 11 a.m. on August 9, the second atomic bomb fell from the B-29's belly. As many as 100,000 eventually died as a result.

The argument rages to this day as to whether such mass destruction and loss of life were necessary. Some say the Japanese were already preparing for surrender and the end of the war was inevitable. Others argue that there were plenty of indications that they would have fought on as long as they could, that a costly invasion would have been necessary to end the war. That segment maintains that the two atomic blasts actually saved hundreds of thousands of lives on both sides of the conflict, not to mention those thousands of people who were wasting away in POW and work camps around the Pacific.

Either way, the second bomb did what it was intended to do. It ultimately brought the Pacific Ocean part of World War II to an abrupt end.

The day following the Nagasaki conflagration, Emperor Hirohito, the Japanese leader, told his cabinet to accept the unconditional surrender terms that the Allies were demanding.

Nothing had changed for the submarines patrolling the waters all around the Japanese islands. They received the radio reports of the two bombings. Many reacted with disbelief. How was such a weapon possible? And if their own country had been able to develop such an awful bomb, could others now do the same?

With no peace treaty yet signed, and with a frightening number of the planes and warships of the Imperial Japanese Navy continuing to shoot in anger, Admiral Charles Lockwood, the Pacific submarine commander, ordered his boats to continue as they had been doing, to sink any vessel flying a rising sun flag.

That was all Bafford Lewellen and the crew of the *Torsk* had on their minds as they prepared to engage whatever new targets were now dimpling their radarscopes. It did not take them long to determine that these latest interlopers were small coastal defense frigates, about eight hundred tons each. They were warships and did pose something of a threat—if not to the *Torsk*, then to other Allied vessels.

The submarine and her crew did exactly what the boat was designed to do and what the men had trained for, and what Admiral Lockwood had told them to do. They attacked and promptly sank both of the Japanese ships.

Interestingly, the final torpedo fired by the *Torsk* was one of the new acoustic Mark 27 weapons. The sub did not have to be on or near the surface to shoot those weapons. The torpedo was designed to seek the sound of a ship's screws and chase it down. Both the conventional torpedo that was fired initially and the new acoustic fish, fired from a depth of about four hundred feet, hit their targets and sent the frigates for which they were intended to the bottom. The crew of the *Torsk* clearly heard both explosions on impact and the sweet sound of a vessel breaking up from the pressure of inrushing water.

"Good job, men," Lewellen said over the boat's communicator. "Let's stay alert and ready."

But first they had to keep their heads down. Enemy planes and patrol craft from the nearby Japanese mainland kept them under for over seven hours after their successful attack.

Of course the skipper had no idea that he and his torpedomen had just launched the last torpedoes of World War II. Or that they had just sunk the last Japanese combatant vessels of the conflict.

Simply by aggressively doing their duty, they had made history.

Late on the night of August 14, 1945, Admiral Chester Nimitz, the naval commander of the Pacific theater, sent the simple, straightforward message to all of his units:

CEASE OFFENSIVE OPERATIONS AGAINST JAPANESE FORCES. CONTINUE SEARCH AND PATROLS. MAINTAIN DEFENSIVE AND INTERNAL SECURITY MEASURES AT HIGHEST LEVEL AND BE- WARE OF TREACHERY OR LAST MOMENT ATTACKS BY ENEMY FORCES OR INDIVIDUALS.

Admiral Lockwood reiterated the message to his submarine commanders. Be careful. Keep up your guard. Keep the tubes loaded. But the war with Japan was apparently over, three months short of the fourth anniversary of its fiery beginning at Pearl Harbor.

As with most other commanders, Bafford Lewellen on the *Torsk* was more than willing to allow those not on watch a celebratory ration of medicinal brandy. As his men up and down the length of the submarine whooped and hollered and sang bawdy songs, the skipper could not help but think back on where he had been over the last couple of years.

He had inherited a good crew on both boats. The *Pollack* was an old

Perch-class submarine, built before the war, and she had been stationed at Pearl Harbor at the end of 1941. She was on the way back to Pearl from refitting at Mare Island, California, on December 7, 1941. By the end of December, she was swimming in Japanese waters and shooting at anything she could find.

Lewellen had a couple of close calls when he took over the boat. One night off Honshu, he led a surface attack on a group of freighters. They were about to dive deeper and drive away from the scene when, suddenly, the boat was shaken hard by an awful blast nearby. The explosion almost buckled her hull, brutally thrusting her out of the water like a toy. Then there was an eerie glow of fire all around the *Pollack*, as if they had accidentally surfaced in the midst of the fire and brimstone of Hades. Men were knocked to the deck up and down the length of the boat by the detonation, but there were only bumps and scrapes. No one seemed seriously hurt and the damage to the sub's systems was quickly repaired so they could be on their way.

The only thing the crew could figure might account for the near-fatal explosion was that one of the torpedoes they dispatched had failed to run. Instead it dropped straight down when it emerged from the tube and detonated. Had it happened a moment sooner, before they had moved away a few feet, the old boat would have been lost for certain.

A few nights later, Lewellen and the *Pollack* were surprised mid-attack by a destroyer that had somehow sneaked up on them. Suddenly the boat was bathed in the warship's searchlight beam. The skipper, figuring they were goners either way, sent two torpedoes spinning away, right down the throat of the destroyer. Then, seemingly in the same move, he and his men tried to take the boat deep, to run and hide.

But suddenly the submarine cocked downward at a shockingly deep angle, almost standing on her nose as she plunged toward the bottom of the ocean, thousands of feet below them. The bow dive planes, the "wings" that help control the angle of dives and surfacing, had failed.

They were out of control!

Of course they would never reach the bottom in one piece. As they plummeted past three hundred feet in depth, everyone heard the old boat begin creaking and groaning under the strain of the pressure. Lewellen yelled the orders to put the engines in full emergency reverse and to blow all the ballast tanks, emptying them of water so they would be more buoyant.

All the time he prayed quietly. So did most men aboard, even as they did what they were trained to do in such an emergency.

Later, in his patrol report, Lewellen wrote:

> No one could stand anywhere aboard the *Pollack* without support. Men were hanging on to hatches, tables, controls . . . the noise was terrific. A submarine's equipment is stored for a reasonable down angle, but this angle was utterly beyond the bounds of reason. All over the boat a roar like summer thunder sounded as equipment fell or dropped or poured out of storage spaces.

Ultimately, when the depth gauges read more than 450 feet—200 feet deeper than the boat's hull was built to withstand—they were able to stop the nosedive, but the actions taken to accomplish that sent them streaking right back toward the surface in exactly the same kind of wild ride, only up this time.

To the surprise of the sailors on the deck of the IJN destroyer, the *Pollack* shot out of the sea, almost from beneath their ship. Somehow Lewellen and his crew were able to gain control, though, and take her back down before the enemy vessel could come after her.

His time on the *Torsk* had not been nearly so exciting. Soon, though, her skipper and crew would learn of their place in the history books. He and his boat would receive credit for sinking over twenty-four hundred tons of shipping in her second and final war patrol. She and the crew were able to accomplish that even though the run was cut short by the most awful weapon in military history, the atomic bombs that were dropped on Hiroshima and Nagasaki.

* * *

The *Torsk* had another spot reserved for her in the annals of submarine lore. By the end of September 1945, she was through the Panama Canal again, this time headed eastward once more for New England. She had a job to do at the navy's submarine school at New London, Connecticut. For the next ten years, she was part of Submarine Squadron Eight, serving as a "school boat" for young would-be submariners. For most of that decade, she went out into Long Island Sound and the Atlantic waters, even spending time in the Caribbean and Mediterranean seas, and in the process of teaching sailors how it was done she dutifully performed dive after dive, almost every day of her service. Since the submersions were all logged and since they could be added to those dives already recorded in the accounts of her war patrols, someone was ultimately able to calculate and compare and make a final declaration.

Before she was even a teenager, the *Torsk* became the "divingest" submarine in naval history. And her service was only half complete. By her final decommissioning, she had made over 10,600 dives, easily more than five times as many as the average boat. And, as submariners love to point out, she also surfaced an equal number of times.

There were other milestones in her long career. She underwent her snorkel conversion in 1952. In 1959, she made a rare excursion for a submarine when she took part in the ceremonies marking the opening of the St. Lawrence Seaway. From there, she steamed down the St. Lawrence into the Great Lakes and made much-heralded stops at Milwaukee, Chicago, and Buffalo. Thousands came down to the piers to visit and tour the historic boat, most of them getting their first look at a real, live submarine.

In 1960, she received the Presidential Unit Citation for her role during the Lebanon crisis. She helped enforce the blockade of Cuba in 1962 during and after the missile crisis, for which she received the Navy Commendation Medal. During that service, crew members actually stopped and boarded Russian ships, inspecting them, looking for missiles and parts during the most intense standoff since World War II.

After more time as a training vessel at the Washington Navy Yard in Washington, D.C., the *Torsk* was finally forced into retirement. By that time, she had accumulated almost twelve thousand dives, a record that will surely stand since today's modern nuclear submarines typically dive and stay submerged for weeks at a time.

Fortunately, in 1972, the state of Maryland recognized the historical significance of the old girl and sought her for a submarine memorial to be built at the Inner Harbor in Baltimore. In addition to her other significant accomplishment, the *Torsk* is also one of only two surviving *Tench*-class boats. The other is the USS *Requin* (SS-481), now at the Carnegie Science Center in Pittsburgh, Pennsylvania.

The *Tench* boats are very similar in size and design to the *Gato* and *Balao* submarines. The only difference is that they had stronger hulls and a better interior design for the ballast tanks and machinery.

Only ten *Tench*-class boats saw action in World War II. Construction stopped on two boats that were being built when the war ended. Four others were completed as GUPPY II conversions. Of the eighty boats of this design that were planned, a total of twenty-five were finished and commissioned. Several of those were eventually sold to foreign navies, including Turkey, Taiwan, Canada, Brazil, Pakistan, and Greece.

When the war ended, the United States suddenly had more submarines than it needed. She was able to hold a rather interesting garage sale.

In addition to the *Torsk*, the Maritime Museum at Baltimore also features the U.S. Coast Guard cutter USCGC *Taney* (WHEC-37), the last warship active at Pearl Harbor in December 1941 that is still afloat. Also nearby is the lightship *Chesapeake* (LV-116), along with the National Aquarium and other Inner Harbor attractions. The USS *Constellation*, the last all-sail warship, and its museum are located only steps away as well. With her tall masts and array of sails, she is quite a sight to be-hold.

The *Torsk* is blessed with a very active volunteer group. Several regu-lar volunteers can often be found aboard on weekends, giving special presentations on the submarine specifically and silent service history in general.

Volunteer "Work Weekends" are held regularly, usually once in the spring and again in the fall, and volunteers come in from all over the country to work aboard the submarine.

As with some of the other museum boats around the country, the *Torsk* has an active amateur radio club aboard that at times operates out of the boat's original radio room. Many of the submarine ham radio groups hold an operating event each spring in which stations on the museum boats are manned and on the air during the weekend, communicat-ing with each other. At the same time, other amateur radio enthusiasts around the country and the world are able to talk with the submarine sta-tions. This event is designed to raise awareness among the thousands of amateur radio enthusiasts of the museum boats while giving visitors to the submarines on those weekends a look at the radio hobby.

USS *REQUIN* (SS-481)

Courtesy of the U.S. Navy

USS *REQUIN* (SS-481)

Class: *Tench*
Launched: January 1, 1945
Named for: the requin, a sand shark
Where: Portsmouth Naval Shipyard, New Hampshire
Sponsor: Mrs. Slade D. Cutter, wife of one of World War II's most storied submarine commanders—and the first skipper of the USS *Requin*
Commissioned: April 28, 1945

Where is she today?

Carnegie Science Center
1 Allegheny Avenue
Pittsburgh, Pennsylvania 15212
(412) 237-1550
www.csc.clpgh.org/

Claim to fame: Though she never got to use her weaponry in combat, the USS *Requin* did begin her service under the command of perhaps the most decorated commander in submarine history, Slade Cutter. She also went on to become one of the navy's first radar picket boats, a first line of defense against nuclear attack.

Admiral Charles Lockwood once said, "Slade Cutter could find Japanese ships in Pearl Harbor!" He was talking about the submarine skipper who seemed to have an uncanny ability to locate enemy vessels, no matter where he was patrolling at the time. And, to make it a complete package, Cutter also had coolness under pressure and a knack for knowing exactly the best course to steer to line up for an attack on those ships once he spotted them.

For that reason, it was something of a surprise when the submarine ace suddenly got orders during a monthlong leave back in the States to proceed to Portsmouth for a new-construction command. And to top it off, the new boat was to be sponsored by none other than his wife, Frances.

That submarine was the USS *Requin*.

The plan all along was for Cutter to return to the boat he was in prior to the R&R leave to the mainland, the USS *Seahorse* (SS-304). He was to resume his command for that vessel's sixth war patrol. It was aboard the *Seahorse* that he and his crew sank an amazing twenty-one ships for better than 142,000 tons destroyed, and all that in only four war patrols (after the war, that total was cut to nineteen ships, 72,000 tons, by JANAC, but the tally still placed Cutter in a tie for second for the number of vessels sunk). Even the captain who took the helm of the *Seahorse* while Cutter was resting, Charles Wilkins, promised not to change a thing aboard the boat while he was gone.

As Wilkins said, "I'm just borrowing the boat for one run."

The navy had other plans for Cutter, and her name was the *Requin*.

The son of a corn farmer from Illinois, Slade Cutter became an all-American tackle and field goal kicker for the U.S. Naval Academy at

Annapolis. He was a pretty good football player and was eventually elected to the College Football Hall of Fame. It was his field goal that gave Navy a 3–0 win over Army in 1934, their first victory over their hated rivals in thirteen years.

True to his colorful reputation, Cutter listed his vices in the academy yearbook as chewing tobacco, swearing, and playing the flute (he was an accomplished musician and had scholarship offers out of high school to study music in college). He also passed on chances to take up professional boxing. It was his fondest dream to attend, play football at, and graduate from the U.S. Naval Academy.

Cutter got his first boat, the *Seahorse*, after he, as her executive officer, criticized his skipper. The young XO was frustrated by his captain's conservative attack tactics. In a letter to his wife, Cutter said the boat's captain was letting enemy vessels "go past us like trolley cars." He was not bashful about telling his superiors back in Pearl Harbor the same thing.

In another time and place, such denouncement of one's commanding officer might have been professional suicide. Not in Slade Cutter's case. His bold actions impressed Admiral Lockwood and the others in command of the Pacific submarine fleet. They relieved the *Seahorse* captain and put Slade Cutter at the helm of the 304 boat. It was well-placed confidence. At the helm of the *Seahorse*, he would shortly earn four Navy Crosses, the highest award for valor short of the Congressional Medal of Honor, and two Silver Stars.

Cutter took the change-of-plans assignment to the *Requin* in stride. The time he would spend getting the boat through her sea trials would give him more time at home with his family, including his newborn daughter, Anne. Besides, he sensed the war was drawing to a close, and that there was a good chance it would be over before he got back out there.

After his wife, Frances Cutter, broke the bottle of champagne against the bow of the *Requin* on New Year's Day 1945, Commander Cutter took the new submarine through her paces, getting her ready just in case she was needed halfway around the world. But things were changing rapidly out there. And at home, too.

In April, President Franklin Roosevelt died of a brain hemorrhage at his retreat in Warm Springs, Georgia. The vice president, Harry Truman, was hastily sworn in.

In Europe, Allied troops had continued their sweep across the continent toward Berlin since D-day, which had occurred the previous June. Bombers routinely pounded targets in Germany. The European war would officially end only nine days after the *Requin* was commissioned in April.

But the Japanese continued to fight on. As soon as she was seaworthy and officially commissioned, Cutter and his crew steered their new *Tench*-class boat south out of New England waters, through the Panama Canal, and on to Pearl Harbor. Using the power of his reputation, their ace skipper had been able to equip his new submarine just a bit differently from the other boats of its time. In addition to the two five-inch 25-caliber deck guns that were standard on her sisters, the *Requin* also carried two 40-millimeter raid fire cannons, which were mounted forward and aft of the bridge near the more standard guns. She also was blessed with a couple of twenty-four-tube five-inch rocket launchers, designed to send a bombardment into Japan in the event the invasion of the Home Islands was ordered.

They never had a chance to use any of that armament except for training and practice. After spending more time training off Panama, she arrived in Hawaii at the end of July 1945 and began preparations for her initial war patrol. She was still in port when news came of the atomic bomb blasts at Hiroshima and Nagasaki, and of the decision by the Japanese emperor to accept surrender terms. Three days before she was to begin her run, the *Requin* and her crew stood by as the war officially came to an end with the surrender ceremony in Tokyo Bay, not far from where they were soon supposed to be operating.

A short time later, they retraced their route, bound for the Naval Frontier Base, Staten Island, New York, to work with new sonar operators. Their job was to give the trainees there a real, live submarine to detect as they learned to operate their listening gear.

Commander Cutter was accustomed to far more weighty missions. He had little patience for being the bunny in a glorified rabbit hunt. He called it a "dull and boring assignment." It was not long before the submarine ace was reassigned once again, even though there was no longer a war to send him to. He later served as athletics director at the U.S. Naval Academy, then as head of the Naval Historical Display Center in Washington, D.C.

Cutter died in June 2005 in a retirement home near Annapolis. He was ninety-three years old.

The crew of the *Requin* never fired a shot in combat under his command but they did get a chance to serve with a true war hero, submarine icon, and legendary figure. Cutter was famous for calling together members of his previous crew after every attack for an in-depth postmortem. They recounted in detail everything that had happened, what went wrong, what went right. The object was not to place blame but to help them perform as well as possible on the next occasion.

Cutter had a reputation as a sailor's skipper, always on the side of his crew members. That only added to his strong reputation throughout the silent service.

The *Requin*, only a year old and hardly broken in yet, soon headed south again, this time to Key West and Submarine Squadron Four. Later in the year, she was back in Portsmouth to undergo an interesting transformation. There, she became the first submarine to be converted for a new type of usage: the radar picket submarine configuration.

Under her new skipper, Commander George Street, the boat began a job that would occupy her for the next dozen years, and one that was marked by both secrecy and controversy.

Street, like Commander Cutter, was a bona fide war hero. He received the Congressional Medal of Honor for a series of bold World

War II attacks while at the helm of the USS *Tirante* (SS-420). One of those involved taking his submarine all the way into the mouth of a harbor, in only sixty feet of water—not enough to effectively dive if she had needed to—and blasting a transport. In the process of backing away from all the destruction he had caused in the harbor, Street paused long enough to fire three more torpedoes at a couple of frigates near the transport, blowing them to smithereens, too.

Now, in the fall of 1946, the navy decided to experiment with installing the latest surface radar equipment on some of the relatively new and suddenly plentiful submarines. The boats would then be deployed into areas to serve as pickets, or forward observers, using the radar to detect aircraft or warships that might be approaching our military ship convoys or the North American continent in time to determine if their intent was good or bad. The mission took on even more importance in the early fifties with the increasing threat of the Soviet Union and the possibility of bomber-launched nuclear weapons. The United States needed forward radar observation worse than ever.

There were problems from the start. Despite the deactivation of her four stern torpedo tubes and the removal of the deck guns, the new radar gear left the boat crowded, and the equipment mounted on the stern would frequently be flooded and damaged by seawater.

She did serve some time north of the Arctic Circle, trying to make the experiment work. It was, so to speak, tough sledding.

The *Requin* headed in for more radical surgery. Her stern tubes were removed and that compartment was converted into a full-blown combat information center and berthing space for more sailors. Two tubes in the forward torpedo room were removed to make room for lockers for additional crew members. More radar gear was installed and the boat got a snorkel as well, so she could go beneath the surface to periscope depth and still keep her big Fairbanks Morse diesel engines running. The radar antennas that had been installed before were raised higher on their masts in order to improve their range.

This conversion was part of the unfortunately named MIGRAINE II Program. Crew members considered the acronym especially appropriate since there continued to be plenty of problems with the equipment. Also, because of the nature of her duty, the boat was required to stay at sea much longer than her sister boats that were performing more traditional chores.

In order to keep morale up on those long runs, crew members had to create unique ways to pass the time. One of the *Requin*'s skippers during this period in her life was fond of holding barbecues on deck. He had a fifty-five-gallon drum cut in half and used it for a charcoal grill. Steaks were broken out of the boat's freezer and marinated in the captain's secret recipe, then cooked on the makeshift grill.

The *Requin* remained a radar picket until 1959. By that time, sophisticated aircraft using transistorized radar had been developed. The submarine was no longer the best platform for this type of duty. Technology had passed her by.

She went to Charleston Naval Shipyard for yet another conversion as a GUPPY III. This changed the look of the boat completely as the sail was made more aerodynamic, resembling that of the nuclear submarine. All the picket radar equipment came out, too. She was now considered an "attack submarine."

As did many of her sisters, the *Requin* stayed close to home for the most part—home being the Atlantic Coast—but still ventured to the Mediterranean, Caribbean, and South America for special exercises.

One of her last jobs was to take part in the massive search for the missing nuclear submarine USS *Scorpion* (SSN-589). The boat was not located until later and, at the time, she was declared lost in the Atlantic Ocean with all hands aboard, a crew of ninety-nine men. The navy maintained the boat and her crew were lost due to mechanical malfunction, even though the *Scorpion* was on a mission to check on a mysterious Soviet task group that was operating in the vicinity of the Canary Islands. The U.S. Navy's official position came from spokesman Commander Frank Thorp: "While the precise cause of the loss remains undetermined, there is no information to support the theory that the submarine's loss resulted from hostile action or any involvement by a Soviet ship or submarine."

The *Requin*'s story from there on is a familiar one. After decommissioning in 1969, she went to St. Petersburg, Florida, where she served as a naval reserve training vessel. That meant she stayed at the pier most of the time. Many of the other boats went directly to the scrap heap, but, for a while, it appeared the 481 boat had only delayed the inevitable. When, in June of 1971, she was finally struck from the registry of active vessels—usually the kiss of death—a group in Tampa petitioned to have her towed across Tampa Bay and set up as a tourist attraction.

And there she sat, welcoming a considerable number of visitors for the next twelve years. But then the organization responsible for her upkeep went broke. She was open sporadically for another few years, but eventually the old boat was abandoned at her berth in the Hillsborough River.

She floated there at the pier for the next four years. The bridge where the legendary Slade Cutter stood was rusting away. The controls manned by hundreds of brave men through the forty years of her history were deteriorating and disappearing at the hands of vandals. The historic old vessel would soon become a boating hazard, parked for a spell in the middle of the river.

Then, in May of 1990, she was finally towed to the Tampa Shipyard to get her out of the way and to prepare her for another life. The old girl had attracted some new suitors. They included some people with enough political clout to get the job done if they ultimately determined that she was up to the trip.

A long, strange trip that would go down as an amazing first for one historic old submarine.

On February 21, 1990, Senator John Heinz from the state of Pennsylvania introduced a bill in the United States Congress—Senate Bill

S.2151. That piece of legislation, once passed and signed, allowed for the transfer of a particular submarine, the USS *Requin*, from Tampa, Florida, to the city of Pittsburgh, Pennsylvania. There it would be berthed on the north shore of the Ohio River and become an exhibit for the Carnegie Science Center.

It was an excellent idea, but a quick glance at a map of the United States tells anyone that there is no ocean anywhere near Pittsburgh in which to float a submarine to its new home. Other museum boats were located in or near the sea. The *Drum* at Mobile is on Mobile Bay, which spills into the Gulf of Mexico. The *Pampanito* is in the cold waters of San Francisco Bay. Even the *Silversides* and the *Cobia* are located in slips on Lake Michigan.

Granted, the *Batfish* made a similar journey upriver and to an inland berth at Muskogee, Oklahoma. The Carnegie Museum is located on the Ohio River in Pittsburgh, and the Mississippi and Ohio Rivers offered a marginally wider path for this similar-sized submarine. So there was only one obvious way to get her to Pittsburgh.

On August 7, 1990, the *Requin* was hooked to a tug and towed out into the waters of the Gulf of Mexico. She was carefully rigged and prepared beforehand. Nobody wanted a wave to wash over her, maybe founder her, and send her on her last dive before she had the opportunity to complete her final patrol.

The tow continued past New Orleans on the Mississippi and all the way to Baton Rouge, Louisiana. There she was lifted onto four barges and the really tricky part of the journey began, up the Mississippi to just south of Cape Girardeau, Missouri, then a right turn into the Ohio River. There were tight squeezes through the locks on either side of Paducah, through the Cannelton Lock and Dam, and through others along the way, but she made it.

On September 4, the *Requin* arrived in her new, oceanless hometown. For the next month, preparations were made for visitors. On October 20, she was formally dedicated as a memorial and museum exhibit and the public were welcomed to come aboard and have a look around. Since then, thousands have taken the museum up on its offer.

As part of the submarine's sixtieth birthday, the Carnegie Science Center completed a major renovation of the *Requin* in 2005. Some of the interior compartments were re-created to attempt to bring them to a state very similar to how they were in 1945. A complete external makeover was also accomplished with the help of volunteers and various businesses.

Oral histories have been recorded by a number of former crew members, including some from World War II crews. Their recollections aided in the accurate re-creation of the various compartments in the boat.

The museum has taken care to emphasize how the crew members lived aboard these submarines and what they did in their everyday lives. Exhibits show visitors what the submariners ate, how they breathed, how they generated electricity and desalinized seawater, and more. The object is to give visitors a good feel for life aboard a World War II submarine.

GERMAN *U-505*

Courtesy of the U.S. Navy

GERMAN *U-505*

Class: IX-C German submarine
Launched: May 24, 1941
Named for: The Germans used a simple numbering system for their submarines, beginning with the letter *U*, which stood for "underwater."
Where: Deutsche Werft, Hamburg, Germany
Sponsor: None
Commissioned: August 26, 1941

Where is she today?
Museum of Science and Industry
5700 Lake Shore Drive
Chicago, Illinois 60637-2093
(773) 684-1414
www.msichicago.org/exhibit/U505/index.html

Claim to fame: She was the most heavily damaged U-boat to ever go back to Germany for repairs and then return to the war. She became the first enemy ship boarded and captured on the high seas by U.S. forces since the War of 1812. That capture included some real prizes in addition to the U-boat—two German M4 Enigma code machines and codebooks. Allied intelligence was able to use those to crack the Third Reich's wartime code and begin to listen in on and make sense of top secret German communications.

Wars—and especially one of the magnitude of World War II—are really a series of events, of battles large and small, of victories that make the newsreels and front pages of newspapers, and of those much less conspicuous successes that are either never fully appreciated or require later analysis before they get their due credit. Sometimes it is years before the importance of an event is completely realized.

The capture of the German submarine *U-505* falls into the category of lesser-known conquests, and one that was only fully appreciated after the conflict was over. Still, today, many visitors who crawl through her hull at the Museum of Science and Industry in Chicago do not totally comprehend what the effect of her seizure was on the outcome of the war. One of the reasons the capture was not so well known is obvious. The Americans made sure nobody knew anything about it—especially the Germans—until the war was over. Because of a couple of top secret devices that were ensnared with the *U-505*, it was essential that the enemy be allowed to assume the submarine was lost with all hands, and all equipment. They could never even be allowed to suspect that she had passed intact into American hands.

It was a complicated dance, and one that would keep the spectacular capture a secret until peace was assured. At the time of the capture, the Allies were employing more than five thousand people in the effort to break the Japanese and German war codes. Oswald Jacoby, the famous expert in the card game of bridge, was even called in to help in the effort. Code breakers worked around the clock, trying to decipher intercepted messages.

The endeavor was paying big dividends. Unbeknownst to the enemy, the Allies were having more and more success in cracking the top secret transmissions as they were picked up. If the Germans knew the *U-505* and her code machine had been seized, however, the communication codes would have been changed immediately. The effort to understand those transmissions would have had to begin from scratch once more.

The German U-boats' success was legendary, the exploits of their captains almost mythical. They exacted a terrible toll on shipping—warships and noncombatants alike. The *U-505* alone claimed over forty-seven thousand tons of Allied shipping before her capture. That included at least three American ships. Their real effect on the war effort, though, was the U-boats' ability to intercept vital supplies and munitions on vessels crossing the Atlantic, bound for Europe, just as the American subs had disrupted supply routes to Japan.

The tide of the fight against the U-boats had begun to turn by 1943 with the progress of Allied antisubmarine warfare. There were also improvements in intelligence, tracking, and the use of aircraft in finding and destroying the German subs. The Americans had also devised a special collection of vessels, specially chosen to seek out and destroy the elusive submersibles. These were termed "hunter-killer task groups," and their effect on the U-boat menace was immediate. They certainly lived up to their name.

Still, though, shipping losses continued to pile up, even if most Americans were unaware of it. That information was not given to the media, primarily for morale reasons. It appeared it would be a long time yet before Allied shipping could move in the Atlantic Ocean without fear of attack from the U-boats.

One of the groups, hunter-killer Task Group 22.3, consisted of a small aircraft carrier, the USS *Guadalcanal* (CVE-60), which carried a contingent of fighter planes and torpedo bombers, and five light destroyer escort vessels. Pilots could leave the decks of the carrier and search vast areas of the ocean for submarines, using their own eyes or radar. They also had a relatively new device called a sonobuoy that could be dropped into the sea, then used to listen for the subtle sounds of U-boats that might be submerged, out of sight of human eyes or radar equipment.

When an enemy submarine was located, the pilots marked the spot and allowed the trailing warships to move in and launch depth charges. Those light destroyers were faster and more maneuverable than their larger destroyer sisters. They were faster than the U-boats, too. They were also equipped with sensitive radar and sound gear, and they carried a special arsenal, some only recently developed, including guns and torpedoes for attacking surfaced boats, little "hedgehog" bombs that only exploded upon contact with submerged vessels, and deadly depth charges that could be set to explode when they reached a predetermined distance downward.

It is appropriate that the only captured enemy U-boat is now in Chicago, because the commander of Task Group 22.3, the group that took the *U-505*, was a native Chicagoan. Captain Daniel Gallery was a Naval Academy graduate who had previously served as a pilot and flight instructor, then as head of a seaplane base in Iceland. There, his job was to seek out and destroy U-boats and other threats to the Atlantic trade routes. His pilots sank six German subs. He was awarded the Bronze Star for the work he did there.

In 1944, Gallery left solid ground for a seagoing command. He took the helm of the *Guadalcanal* and, simultaneously, command of hunter-killer Task Force 22.3. His success continued. He led the task group as they sank three more U-boats.

While proud of what he and his crews had accomplished, Daniel Gallery harbored a bold idea that he could not shake. His job was to destroy enemy submarines and he was good at it. But what if he could capture one of them? What if he could hook a line to one of the U-boats and tow it to someplace safe and secluded? It had become an obsession for the no-nonsense, by-the-book commander.

There was no doubt that it would be worth the risk and effort. The Allies would finally have access to secret German submarine technology, a chance to study exactly how the boats worked so well. But they would also have—if they pulled off the capture correctly—details on the tactics used by the Germans, and, maybe most important, the top secret communication codes the U-boats used.

That would be a treasure of mammoth proportions and, Gallery suspected, it could even be a major turning point in the war.

When he and his task group returned from patrol in the spring of 1944, he went right to work preparing a detailed plan for how such a bold capture could be carried out. For the most part, he and his officers were guessing on the fine details.

Such a high-seas capture of an enemy submarine not only had never happened, it had never been attempted. No manual on how to do such a thing existed.

They knew it wouldn't be easy. The reason the U-boats had been so successful was that they were so swift and elusive, their commanders and crews so adept. They were accustomed to cruising on the surface, scanning the horizon for smoke that indicated a ship was passing, and boldly making their move. Even in the twentieth century, the best way to spot a ship at a distance was the trail of smoke from her stacks. Once a victim was sighted, the U-boat dove and stalked its prey, using the periscope. When in range, and once the firing parameters had been plotted, torpedoes were launched. The Germans were uncannily accurate and seldom missed. For the first three years of the war, they usually swam away safely, ready to attack again.

The German boats and their crews were feared and respected, both for the design and efficiency of their equipment and for the skill with which they used it. Although the U.S. Navy approved Dan Gallery's capture plan and gave the green light to begin training his crews for a capture attempt, they did not have high hopes that anyone could actually pull it off. Still, Gallery's commanders reasoned, the prize was well worth the risks involved.

As the assault crews trained in methods of boarding a U-boat, and as others practiced how to tow such a vessel without accidentally sinking it, Commander Gallery ran up to Washington from Norfolk for a special briefing. He was allowed admittance to the Tenth Fleet, which, in reality, was no real fleet of ships at all. It was the code name for the U.S. Navy's antisubmarine command. Even deeper inside the Tenth Fleet was F-21, the highly secret room where German boats were constantly being tracked.

Gallery learned that F-21 had been keeping an eye on one particular U-boat for the past month. They followed her as she left the coast of occupied France and swam southward toward Africa. There was no way to tell specifically which submarine it was, but they knew enough to guess that it was one of the older German boats, and that it would most likely be out on patrol for about three months.

It was, of course, the *U-505*.

The Nazi submarine had had an up-and-down life so far. She had been quite successful on her first two war patrols, operating off the coast of West Africa and in the Caribbean Sea. On her third run, her luck ran out. A British aircraft attacked her near Trinidad. Three bombs struck the submarine. One was a direct hit, striking just behind the conning tower, inflicting near-mortal damage. Somehow her crew was able to make emergency repairs and she managed to limp all the way home for maintenance and a complete overhaul.

After the incident, the *U-505* was declared the most heavily damaged submarine ever to make it home for repairs and then survive to fight again. But somehow she seemed jinxed from that point forward. Her next three patrols were fruitless, each cut short by vicious depth-charge attacks. After the final one, and even though they were able to elude their pursuers without any more heavy damage, the captain of the boat calmly left the control room, went to his stateroom, and committed suicide.

As Dan Gallery watched the plots of the mysterious submarine on the maps in F-21, he had no idea of the adventures that this lone U-boat had gone through. He silently vowed that this boat, this unnamed enemy submersible, would be the one he and his crew would bag and tow off to a harbor somewhere for study.

He had identified a quarry. He had approval to try to capture it. He had a crew, trained as well as they could be trained, ready to go out there and take it.

Now, it was time to begin the stalk.

It was May 15, 1944, when the task group sailed from Norfolk, Virginia, bound for a patrol area in the North Atlantic, not far from the Canary Islands. That was also the vicinity in which they expected the U-boat to be operating. When the ships arrived in the area, they received regular updates from F-21 about the probable location and course of the U-boat they had identified.

As he stood on the bridge of his light carrier, Dan Gallery tried not to think about all the things that could go wrong with the plan. First, they were trying to find one minnow in a very big lake. As they looked for that fish, other boats were probably out there too, eagerly looking for targets just like the *Guadalcanal* and her accompanying destroyers. And the minnow they sought had mighty big teeth, along with the capability of using them.

Even if they could somehow get the submarine to the surface and subdued, they knew that the Germans would do all they could to keep their boat from falling into American hands. They would certainly open valves to the sea so the sub would quickly take on water and sink to the far, distant bottom. They would get the crew off the sub and into lifeboats, but the boat would be well on her way to sinking by then.

It would be a reasonable assumption, too, that explosive scuttle charges would be set and armed, just to make sure the boat went to the bottom before the Americans could get a line on her—charges that may or may not go off before a boarding party climbed up on her decks and went down her ladders.

As he scanned the horizon, peering intently for any sign of a periscope poking above the waves, Gallery ran through the checklists in his head. He hoped his men were prepared for whatever they might encounter if they actually got this fighting fish on the hook. In the distance, he could see several of his Wildcat fighter planes getting smaller and smaller as they went off to hunt. He knew his sonar operators were listening intently to the returned signals from the sonobuoys, too. They hoped to get an inkling of noise from the submerged U-boat to let them know F-21 was right, that the thing was down there.

Two weeks had passed on the patrol already. The tedious search had everyone's nerves on edge. Now, they were short on fuel. They desperately needed to steer toward Casablanca for refueling at the American base located there before continuing the search.

But the odds would be hopelessly stacked against them by then. The hunted boat could have gone off in any direction by the time they returned to their assigned patrol box. Even if F-21 could somehow reacquire the target, it might be too far away for Gallery's group to make a run at her.

Finally, reluctantly, Gallery knew they were at the end of their rope. They would soon be running on fumes, and this was no place to have ships dead in the water. He sent out the message to retrieve the planes. They would turn and head east toward the African coast, temporarily abandoning the search. The commander tried to keep the disappointment from his voice as he gave the order to let the U-boat go for now.

It had been a long shot at best, he told himself. If it were easy to latch on to a U-boat, somebody would have done it already.

Then, not ten minutes later, as he turned to go belowdecks to try to get some rest, Dan Gallery received an urgent message from one of his escort destroyers, the USS *Chatelain* (DE-149).

"Possible contact. Sounds like a U-boat!"

The commander glanced at the clock on the bridge and made an entry in his ever-present notebook: 11:09 a.m., June 4, 1944.

Quickly he gave the order to maneuver the *Guadalcanal* in order to put distance between the carrier and where the suspected U-boat appeared to be, beneath the surface of the ocean. Though only a small aircraft carrier, she was still a luscious target for an enemy submarine. It was not his nature to run, but he needed the carrier to stay afloat. So did the aircraft that circled in the distance. Besides, he had other vessels better designed than his to approach and attack the U-boat.

The USS *Pillsbury* (DE-133) and USS *Jenks* (DE-665) joined the *Chatelain* as she pointed her bow toward where the sonar thought they had heard the German boat. Then, without hesitation, the attack began the instant there was confirmation that a submarine most definitely lurked beneath them.

The *Chatelain* was on top of the enemy vessel much too quickly. Depth charges dropped there would fall harmlessly behind the U-boat by the time they drifted down to where they suspected she was running. Instead, the destroyer launched a barrage of twenty-four hedgehogs, scattering them out in the direction where they calculated the sub would be headed. Crew members watched the surface of the sea, looking for the hull of a surfacing submarine, or for the flotsam and oil that would indicate they had damaged something down there below them.

There was nothing.

The *Chatelain* maneuvered quickly to run out ahead of the U-boat. There she would be able to drop depth charges that would intercept the sub a couple of hundred feet below.

From above, two fighter planes circled, and then fired a barrage into a spot in the ocean where they believed they could see something hovering in the depths. The *Chatelain* circled again and, as she approached a position ahead of the spot marked by the planes' bullets, began jettisoning depth charges from the launchers on her decks. The detonators on each package were set for a relatively shallow explosion.

These big barrels were much more powerful than those used earlier in the war. Filled with thirty-five pounds of a new explosive called

Torpex, they were more than half again as intense as TNT. They were designed to explode at a depth that was determined before they were shot overboard. That setting was determined by the reports from the circling pilots who had visual contact with what still appeared to be a U-boat.

"You struck oil!" one of the fighter pilots yelled.

Just under seven minutes after the first geyser of water from the initial depth charge erupted from the sea, there was evidence they had created some havoc. Sure enough, a sizable oil slick was forming in the area that was neatly surrounded by the depth-charge blasts. They had done damage. Now they were eager to see how much.

Back on the *Guadalcanal*, Dan Gallery watched and monitored the activity from a distance, waiting for reports. He could see the eruption of the depth-charge explosions and hear their muffled *whooomp!* as each one detonated. He had already given his boarding parties on the destroyers the command to get ready to launch their boats. The report of the oil slick was promising, even if it did cause some mixed emotions. Even if they were not able to capture the sub, which was their first and fondest wish, they may well have sent the deadly enemy vessel to the muddy, cold Atlantic bottom.

Would the German skipper ever consider bringing his boat to the surface if he knew she was mortally wounded? Or, if the depth charges had not destroyed his sub already, would he decide to plunge it and his crew to their deaths rather than surrender to the Americans?

Gallery had to wonder what decision he would make were he in the same situation. Those were the kinds of instantaneous life-and-death decisions commanders were required to make in wartime.

Before he had time to ponder the situation, though, the call came. The U-boat was surfacing! The vicious, pinpoint depth-charge attack had done its job. The Germans had been forced up!

Now, Gallery thought, the fun really begins.

Soon, through his binoculars, he could see the broached German submarine, first her shears, then her sail, then the tops of her decks emerging from the foamy water. She appeared to be awfully close to the *Chatelain*, only seven hundred yards or so away from her. If someone on the sub's decks managed to get to her guns, there could be a point-blank battle out there.

Then, just as planned and before the Germans had time to shoot back, the *Chatelain* opened fire on the submarine's decks. So did the crewmen aboard the *Jenks* and the *Pillsbury*, raking the boat with a vicious barrage. Even the two Wildcat fighter planes came in on screaming dives, guns rattling.

Meanwhile, aboard the enemy sub, Lieutenant Harald Lange, the commander of the *U-505*, had ordered the setting of the timers on the scuttling charges and the opening of valves in the boat. As soon as he realized the boat was heavily damaged and uncontrollable, he knew he had no choice but to surface. He told his crew to open all hatches and abandon ship as soon as the hatch covers were above water, then to try to get the lifeboats into the water. Otherwise they would all be dragged down with the *U-505* when the scuttle charges blew.

With the damaged rudder stuck hard to starboard, the sub circling drunkenly, and with the flooding already under way, Lange knew they only had minutes to get up the ladders, out the hatches, and into the sea.

When he opened the hatch to the bridge and popped through, the German skipper was struck almost at once by a bullet from the hail of gunfire that was pinging off his boat's hull. He was slightly wounded. Lange yelled to his crew to stop whatever they were doing and get out of the submarine immediately.

The men did as ordered, leaving their stations so quickly that the engines were left running. Their attempts at scuttling the boat were unfinished, too. Still taking on gunfire, the crew members scrambled out the hatches, across the deck, and into the roiling sea. Better to take their chances with a hailstorm of bullets and the ocean waves than to stay aboard and go down with their doomed submarine.

Back on the *Chatelain*, her skipper, Lieutenant Commander Dudley Knox, watched the submarine circling. There was immediate concern that some crew members remained aboard the sub and that the looping route they were running might mean they were lining up for a desperate torpedo attack on his ship. Knox ordered the firing of a single torpedo, but it ran ahead of the *U-505*, missing her by only a few yards.

Commander Gallery ordered that the destroyers and planes cease firing and sent the first boarding party away from the *Pillsbury*. He told the other ships to begin pulling survivors from the sea, to have their weapons ready, and to take them all alive if possible.

Now, facing the dangerous but very likely possibility that the captured submarine had been rigged to explode right in their faces, Gallery could only hope the boarding party could get the next step accomplished. Things had gone according to plan so far. But they would have to hurry or they would almost certainly lose the U-boat.

Even if she was not a ticking time bomb, she was obviously taking on water and already rode alarmingly low in the water.

With the *Chatelain* and the *Jenks* busily plucking the German submariners from the water at gunpoint, a motor whaleboat crossed the distance from the the *Pillsbury* to the now-empty-but-still-steaming submarine. Aboard that boat were nine sailors under the leadership of a young lieutenant junior grade named Albert David.

There was no way for them to know what awaited them below the decks of the submarine. There could certainly still be Germans aboard, ready to kill anyone who came down the hatches. The Americans would have to be ready to fight—hand to hand if necessary—in order to commandeer the boat.

She was clearly sinking. They had to find out where the flooding was and stop it. And the whole thing could blow up at any time, too.

Just catching the sub was a task unto itself. She was still running in a broad circle, moving at about seven or eight knots, her big diesel engines rumbling dutifully along.

Albert David and his men were finally able to catch her, tie up to her flank, and climb onto the U-boat's deck. They fought to hold their balance in the rough seas and with the circling motion of the sub. Then they tried to concentrate on what they had learned in their training back in Norfolk. From here on, they would need to follow their instructions to the letter. But they also needed to be ready to improvise, depending on what they might find in the dark interior of the wounded enemy boat.

By this time, the stern of the *U-505* was covered with water and the sea reached almost to the top of the conning tower. They had to get below and they had to do it quickly so they could close the valves. If they couldn't find all the main sources of flooding, the boat would be lost for sure and they could go down with her.

David and his men knew, too, that the Germans had almost certainly set the timers on the scuttle charges, and that they could be located anywhere on the boat. As their feet touched the top rungs of the ladders, they had no way of knowing that the fleeing crew had only had time to set one charge, that the switch on that charge was corroded and failed to close. David and the others took heart in the fact that there had not been an explosion already. The Germans would have wanted the charge to go off before any boarding party got aboard to minimize the chance it could be disarmed first.

The object was not to try to blow up the assault party; it was to destroy the submarine before anyone else could get aboard.

As they climbed to the top of the conning tower, the Americans stepped around one dead German sailor. His body lay on the deck, obviously a victim of the gun attack. Quickly they dropped down the open hatches and fanned out in different directions, again performing the way they had been trained to do back in Norfolk.

Machinist's Mate First Class Zenon Lukosius was the first to locate the source of so much of the flooding. The Germans had opened a big pipe, called a sea strainer, and the seawater was coursing through in torrents, spreading through open doorways into all compartments. Lukosius quickly tracked down the strainer cover and secured the opening, shutting off the worst of the inrushing seawater.

Meanwhile, the other members of the boarding party had located the armed scuttle charge and tore away the wires, disarming it. There was no way to be certain that was the only one. A nerve-racking, systematic search of all the sub's compartments began, working from the control room forward and aft. Others in the crew hurriedly gathered up every chart, codebook, and scrap of paper they could find, including two M4 Enigma code machines. They took it all topside to be carried back to one of the ships. This was valuable material to liberate. The assault would now be a success, even if the submarine were still lost.

The *Pillsbury* pulled alongside the moving sub to try to put over towlines, ignoring the continued risk of an explosion or of the submarine foundering and going down. As she jostled against the sub, the German boat's bow plane rammed through the destroyer's side, opening a gash, flooding several compartments. The *Pillsbury* had to pull away to take care of her own wounds.

There was another struggle going on by that time, and it had nothing to do with the Germans, their submarine, or the boarding party. It originated back in Norfolk. When Captain Gallery reported back to U.S. naval headquarters the news of the successful seizure of the U-boat, there was the expected round of hearty congratulations. But then, almost immediately, a terse message was sent to Gallery, ordering him in no uncertain terms to abandon his plans to tow the U-boat to Africa, even though it was the closest and most logical friendly beach. Ports there were reportedly crawling with German spies. Instead he was to pull the dead-in-the-water vessel all the way to Bermuda, a journey of close to twenty-five hundred miles. The trip would have to be accomplished on a short fuel supply, too.

Gallery questioned the wisdom of that plan, but he was told to do as ordered and not question the decision. He was also instructed to refrain from any further mention of the event on the radio. His men were to be told in no uncertain terms not to tell anyone—anyone!—what they had accomplished that day. Each sailor in the task group was ordered to sign an oath of secrecy before the day was over, verifying he understood what would happen to him if word of the sub's capture got out. If anyone specifically were charged with revealing the taking of the *U-505*, it would result in the death penalty for treason. A similar order went to all three thousand members of the various hunter-killer task groups in the Atlantic.

No one was to learn of the capture of the *U-505*, least of all the German high command.

The news of the submarine's capture had sent a certain admiral back in Norfolk into a rage. Admiral Ernest King, commander of the Atlantic Fleet, was too angry for the moment to appreciate the skill and bravery of his sailors and what they had accomplished out there. He knew if the Germans found out one of their U-boats and its codebook and Enigma machines had been captured, then the hard-won translation of that code that they had done already would become worthless. So would the codebooks and Enigma machines that Gallery and his boys had captured. The enemy would immediately change to another set of ciphers, and it might take years to break those, even if they could ever be figured out.

It had happened before. In 1943, guerrillas broke into the Japanese embassy in Portugal. Assuming their diplomatic codes had been compromised, the Japanese changed them. Of course, the Allies had broken the code sometime before that, but that hard-won accomplishment was useless the instant the Japanese learned of the break-in half a world away. The new version of the Japanese code would still not be broken by the time the war ended.

Now, there was a chance of that same thing happening with the Germans and their submarine codes. That possibility was what set Admiral King off on a tirade. Some in the Tenth Fleet reported that the admiral was mad enough to demand that Captain Gallery be court-martialed the instant he returned to Norfolk. That never happened. Gallery had permission from his superiors to attempt the capture.

For the time being, Daniel Gallery had no inkling of the hot water his glorious mission had gotten him into.

Besides, the commander had his hands full, trying not to lose the sub now that he had her. There was still a good chance the boat was going to sink, and her rudder was still jammed hard to the starboard. That would make it difficult to control her enough to tow her to land.

Water was still getting into the submarine from somewhere, likely due to the damage caused by the *Chatelain*'s depth-charge attack. Another whaleboat had made its way from the *Guadalcanal* to the *U-505* by then, and those men were assisting the first bunch in looking for any more scuttle charges, still-open sea cocks, and any damage that might be contributing to the flooding.

The *Guadalcanal* had finally succeeded in securing towlines to the submarine and salvage operations began in earnest, even as the stern of the sub disappeared completely and waves rolled threateningly over most of the boat's decking.

Commander Earl Trosino crawled around in the flooded bilges, treading filthy, oily water beneath the vessel's diesel engines, tracing pipes and closing valves leading to damaged piping.

Later, in an August 1945 article for the *Saturday Evening Post*, Daniel Gallery described how Trosino "risked his life many times . . . squirming into inaccessible corners . . . where he wouldn't have a chance to escape in the case the sub started to sink." He credited Trosino and "his total disregard of his own safety" for their success in saving the *U-505*.

Radioman John Fisher was among the early crew members to board the submarine. He was sent over because he knew what the Enigma machines looked like, and which papers were the most important to get off the boat. He remembers a captured sailor from the *U-505* who was

Polish. One of the American sailors was of Polish descent and they quickly discovered that they were distant relatives.

The U-boat sailor volunteered to go back aboard the damaged submarine and show the Americans how to disconnect the rudder so it would no longer be an impediment. In return, the sailor wanted asylum in the United States. His deal was approved and he kept his end of the bargain. The U-boat sailor was later seen aboard an airplane taking off from the *Guadalcanal*, headed for the United States. Fisher never knew if he received his asylum or whether he went to a POW camp like the rest of his shipmates.

The surviving German sub's crew members were all pulled from the sea and from their lifeboats and taken to the *Guadalcanal*. In all, fifty-eight submarine sailors were rescued. Only one German was killed, the one the boarding party saw on deck when they climbed aboard. In addition to the captain, his executive officer and one enlisted man were wounded. Those men were taken back to Bermuda along with their boat. From there they went to a POW camp in Ruston, Louisiana.

There they were treated very well, as was typical of prisoners of war captured by the United States. They were isolated from other prisoners, however, and the United States was absolutely and unashamedly guilty of one major breach of Geneva Convention rules: the Germans were not allowed to write letters to their families back home to let them know they were okay. Later that year, the German navy informed the *U-505*'s family members that their men and the U-boat they were aboard were long overdue, that they were missing and presumed dead.

Admiral King directly ordered the departure from the dictates of the Geneva Convention. It was essential that no one knew the *U-505* was in American hands.

The prisoners made several efforts to let their government know what had happened. They tried some slick tricks to try to get word of their capture back to their families, too. At one point, they fashioned some balloons and filled them with home-brewed helium, made from cleaning supplies they found at the camp. Messages were attached to the balloons and they were released into the Louisiana night. They apparently never made it to anyone who could relay those messages to Berlin.

After the war, the prisoners were allowed to return home to their surprised and grateful families.

Despite the difficulties, Gallery and his task force, with some help, were able to begin the tow of their prize to Port Royal Bay, Bermuda. Salvage crew members disconnected the boat's diesel engines from her electric motors and allowed her propellers to turn as she was being towed. This actually worked to charge the batteries enough that the submarine's pumps could be used to remove water from her compartments. After three days, with the submarine riding high in the water and no longer in any danger of sinking, the task force was met by a sea tug. It hooked up and continued the tow. They also met a tanker, bringing much-needed fuel for the thirsty warships.

Once in Bermuda, the *U-505* was the object of attention from a whole group of navy engineers, intelligence agents, and others. She was a virtual treasure trove of information. Her codebooks gave instant access to the communications between Berlin and her U-boats that were still operating in the Atlantic. That information gave the Allies a powerful new ability to find and destroy the elusive U-boats. An especially surprising discovery was that the Germans had recently begun using a new type of acoustic torpedo. Now they had an actual working model to study.

While there are numerous turning points in any conflict, the capture of the *U-505* in June of 1944 was certainly a major one in World War II. Also, the skill and bravery of the men who risked their lives in commandeering the submarine were part of an inspirational story that could not be told in its entirety until well after the war had ended.

The *U-505* was the first man-of-war captured on the high seas by the U.S. Navy since the War of 1812, over 130 years previously. For his death-defying actions that day leading the initial boarding party, Lieutenant Albert David was awarded the Congressional Medal of Honor. The other members of the party received the Navy Cross.

In awarding the task group the Presidential Unit Citation, Admiral Royal Ingersoll, Commander in Chief, U.S. Atlantic Fleet, said, "Undeterred by the apparent sinking condition of the U-boat, the danger of explosions of demolition and scuttling charges, and the probability of enemy gunfire, the small boarding party plunged through the conning tower hatch, did everything in its power to keep the submarine afloat and removed valuable papers and documents. Succeeding, and more fully equipped, salvage parties, faced with dangers similar to those which confronted the first group to enter the submarine, performed seemingly impossible tasks in keeping the U-boat afloat until it could be taken in tow. After three days of ceaseless labor the captured U-boat was able to withstand, with constant care, the rigors of a twenty-four-hundred-mile tow to its destination."

Ingersoll did not stop there. He concluded by adding, "The Task Group's brilliant achievement in disabling, capturing, and towing to a United States base a modern enemy man-of-war taken in combat on the high seas is a feat unprecedented in individual and group bravery, execution, and accomplishment in the Naval History of the United States."

Those awards came after the war was over and the capture of the *U-505* no longer had to be kept secret.

The German high command never found out that one of their U-boats had been captured or that their codebooks had fallen into Allied hands. They must have wondered why, though, from that point on, the enemy seemed to be one step ahead of their submarine operations. The effectiveness of the legendary German U-boats would not be the same the rest of the war.

Captain Daniel Gallery escaped any consequences from Admiral King's displeasure. By getting the captured vessel back to Bermuda, and by keeping the secret of its capture, he saved his career. He was awarded the Distinguished Service Medal for his efforts.

Of course, the attempt to take a U-boat had been approved by his superiors and sanctioned and supported by the commanders at Tenth Fleet and F-21, so he was completely in the right in what he did. He had accomplished exactly what he had conceived, what he set out to do. He had captured a German U-boat and all the intelligence treasures she held, and he had done it with no casualties among his crew. Then he succeeded in bringing the U-boat back so she could be dissected. That contributed to his country's victory over a crafty enemy.

Now, his quarry safely delivered, Captain Gallery could get back to work. He would not be trying to capture any other boat, though. Instead he and his task group were trying to find other German boats and send them to the bottom of the Atlantic Ocean. After the war, he eventually made the rank of rear admiral and commanded Carrier Group Six during the Korean War. He retired from the navy in 1960 and became a prolific writer on naval subjects. Gallery also kept up a continuing and spirited correspondence with many of his old adversaries who patrolled in the German U-boats.

But Dan Gallery was not quite finished with his prize.

The day would come when he would help commandeer the *U-505* one more time.

When the European portion of World War II ended, there was no point in keeping the secret of the *U-505* any longer. The navy issued a short press release in May of 1945. That was the first news the German crew members' families had that their men might still be alive.

Shortly afterward, the Nazi submarine went out on a tour of sorts. The object was to raise money for war bonds to help finance the continuing conflict against the Japanese in the Pacific. In exchange for purchasing a set amount of war bonds, visitors could climb aboard a real, live German U-boat and ramble around inside her. There they could see the very location where the *Pillsbury*'s crew members disarmed the scuttle charge. Visitors could touch the valves the boarding party had managed to close only minutes before the vessel would have sunk forever.

The *U-505* visited several cities along the eastern seaboard. It is no surprise that she proved to be a very popular attraction wherever she went.

After the navy learned all they could from the captured submarine, she went to Portsmouth, New Hampshire, for temporary storage. The plan was to eventually use her for target practice, allowing future submarine torpedomen to get a chance to launch their fish at a real German U-boat.

That's when Daniel Gallery once again steamed across the *U-505*'s path.

He got wind that his trophy was about to meet an ignoble end so he went to work, trying to find her a permanent home. He had captured her once upon a time. He could darn well do it again.

That's when the Chicago native hatched a plan. He mentioned to his brother the possibility that the U-boat would be destroyed, and what a shame it was. Father John Gallery, who lived back in the Windy City, contacted the folks at the Museum of Science and Industry over near the lake. As it happened, the museum had been considering adding a submarine to its collection. They had had little luck so far in the more than ten years since they began contemplating the addition of a plunging boat to their collection. They were immediately excited about the possibilities of acquiring such a historic and noteworthy vessel as the *U-505*.

Gallery led a contingent to the office of Under Secretary of the Navy Charles S. Thomas in Washington, D.C. He convinced the undersecretary that the *U-505* belonged on the banks of Lake Michigan, not at the bottom of the Atlantic Ocean. There was a catch, though. The navy had no interest in paying a single cent of taxpayer money to assist the museum in the move, and they would not continue to pay for her storage in Portsmouth any longer. Either she went to Chicago or to the bottom of the sea. One or the other had to happen soon.

The City of Chicago and private donors ponied up the quarter million dollars needed to pay for the move and to get the submarine prepared to receive visitors. Soon, the U-boat was making another monumental journey while under tow. This time, she was pulled out the Piscataqua River and into the Atlantic. Then she was headed northeast, around New Brunswick, Nova Scotia, and Prince Edward Island, and ultimately into the St. Lawrence River. She negotiated two dozen locks in the St. Lawrence Seaway. Then she passed through four of the five Great Lakes before arriving in Chicago in June 1954.

The original plan was to continue the journey another eight hundred feet, across Lake Shore Drive, to the main museum building. That was the most daunting part of the entire trek. Using a series of rails, the sub crossed the busy street in one night. It took them another week to move the submarine from the side of the road to the museum.

On September 25, 1954, the *U-505* was dedicated to the memory of war victims everywhere and became a permanent exhibit at the museum. She was designated a National Historic Landmark in 1989.

After the boat was exposed to Chicago weather for half a decade, the museum decided to let her make one more move—inside to a climate-controlled environment. The team used original construction drawings and old photos to restore much of the boat to her original color and condition prior to the move. All the while, the museum management was trying to figure out the best way to accomplish and pay for this enormous and daunting task.

After about two years of planning and work, and at a cost of about $35 million, the *U-505* was rolled along on massive dollies a distance of one thousand feet. Then she was lowered, using monstrous jacks, to a position that was four stories below street level. Special viewing platforms were set up so museum visitors could watch the amazing engineering feat as it played out.

Thousands of miles from the nearest ocean, the old submersible vessel had once again gone deep—into the earth of America's heartland.

The *U-505* and her exhibit at Chicago's Museum of Science and Industry have become one of the most visited submarine museum sites in the country and a very popular Chicago tourist attraction. As many as thirty million visitors have toured her compartments and examined the various equipment and artifacts that are on display nearby.

The museum features a number of other exhibits as well as an Omni-Max theater.

There were officially 1,682 submarine war patrols during World War II. A total of 465 different skippers commanded at least one of those patrols. Sixty of those who commanded a sub would eventually become rear admirals. Twelve advanced to the rank of vice admiral. Three others became full admirals. Two of them eventually served terms in the U.S. Congress.

One of those former skippers, Tom Dykers (USS *Jack*, SS-259), became a television producer, and in 1957 and 1958 developed the series *The Silent Service*, which told the true stories of many of the submarines that took part in World War II and the Korean War, including some of those covered in this book. Dykers also hosted and narrated the series.

Three former World War II submarine skippers committed suicide. Another, upon his natural death, had his final wishes honored when he was cremated and his ashes were launched from a submarine's torpedo tube off Key West, Florida.

The first submarine force casualty suffered in World War II was G. A. Myers, Seaman Second Class, who was shot through the right lung when the USS *Cachalot* (SS-170) was strafed during the attack on Pearl Harbor, December 7, 1941. The sailor survived and the *Cachalot* left on her first war patrol five days after the attack . . . without Seaman Myers.

The Imperial Japanese vessel *I-176* was the only Japanese sub to sink an American submarine during the war. The USS *Corvina* (SS-226) was lost with eighty-two men on November 16, 1943.

During 1944, Japan lost fifty-six of its submarines. Seven of those were to U.S. submarines. Of the seven, three were sunk by the USS *Batfish* (SS-310) during a period of just over three days in February 1945.

There were so many submarine attacks on the Singapore-to-Japan shipping routes in 1944 that one Japanese commander told his men, "You could walk from Singapore to Tokyo on American periscopes."

After the war, Fleet Admiral Chester Nimitz, who commanded all warships in the Pacific, acknowledged the contributions of the subs and their crews by saying, in his usual understated way, "We shall never forget that it was our submarines that held the lines against the enemy while our fleets replaced losses and repaired wounds."

Vice Admiral Charles Lockwood, who commanded the submarine fleet, was a bit more colorful in his praise: "I can assure you that they went down fighting and that their brothers who survived them took a grim toll of our savage enemy to avenge their deaths."

I am indebted to the World War II submarine veterans, as well as those who served on these wonderful old boats after the war. They were kind enough to respond to my call for help when I began researching the stories of their gallant old ladies. As I told them, I wanted to tell human stories, tales of the men who went off to war on the plunging boats.

Many of them provided details and fact verification along with far more sea stories than I could ever fit into a book such as this. As you might expect, they are proud of their service and of their submarines. Too many of them are gone—boats and sailors alike—and their stories are dying with them. These veterans are anxious, even desperate, to have their contribution documented and remembered. That is why they work so hard to save as many of the World War II vessels as they can.

I also salute those who work so hard to build the myriad Web sites devoted to these vessels. Their preservation of stories, patrol logs, photos, and the like made my research much easier than it might have been. A simple Web search by vessel name or hull number will generate a listing of many of these sites, which are often produced and maintained by volunteers.

Thanks to Jim Flanders, one of the leaders of the Submarine Veterans Amateur Radio Association, who steered me in the right direction on several occasions. And to Mac Borg, Chairman of the Board of the North Jersey Media Group, both for taking time to talk with me about the USS *Ling* and for not making a big deal of the fact that the New Jersey Naval Museum has apparently not paid his company the one dollar a year rent they agreed upon. Thanks, too, to John Fisher, who took time from dinner one evening to tell me about his view of the capture of the *U-505*, even if we did spend too much time talking about our mutual hobby of ham radio (he's K2JF and I'm N4KC).

The experiences of Kiyoshi Uehara during the sinking of the *Tsushima Maru* by the *Bowfin* and his subsequent rescue were taken from several sources, including an interview conducted in 2003 by Yuko Tamashiro that has been reproduced in many places on the Internet. Uehara had taken his admonitions to not discuss the tragedy seriously and did not talk about it for over sixty years, until that interview. Some accounts suggest he now plans to write his autobiography. I hope he does. The story deserves its own book.

A number of detailed books have been written about many of the submarines covered in this book and they were useful to me in confirming historical and anecdotal accounts of the stories I have chosen to include here. One source was a compilation of all wartime skippers put together by Jon D. Jacques titled *Submarine Skippers of World War II: A Data Study*. By far the best source of detailed and complete history of the action seen by the submarine service in World War II is the late Clay Blair Jr.'s exhaustive book, *Silent Victory: The U.S. Submarine War Against Japan*.

I also salute the NavSource Naval History project, a nonprofit organization dedicated to making photographs of naval vessels easily available to those who want them. They have pulled together over forty thousand images, many of them from official U.S. Navy sources and in the public domain, and put them into a searchable database on the Internet. That Web site can be accessed at www.navsource.org.

The Historic Naval Ships Association is a group made up of those who operate the various naval museums and memorials. They, too, are an excellent source of information about all vessels that have been set up as museums around the United States and in some foreign countries. Their Web site is www.hnsa.org. The information in the appendix that lists maritime museums and memorials was compiled in part from their Web site.

In a foreword on the site, William S. Dudley, former Director of Naval History for the U.S. Navy, says, "It is important that we support the dedicated efforts of the many volunteers whose work enables us to visit these ships. Naval veterans would want us to maintain and interpret these vessels, as a source of patriotism and inspiration for the naval service, as well as a potential source of recruitment. It is often said about naval vessels that they are more than floating structures of wood, hemp, and canvas; more than riveted iron or welded steel brought into being so that they can be fought against the enemy. They take on the spirit of the men and women who serve in them, and the ships' names become a source of motivation and strength for their sailors."

And, by the way, a source of motivation and strength for all of us who appreciate their bravery and the sacrifices they made on our behalf.

Museums/Memorials with a Naval or Maritime Theme

This is a list of naval or maritime museums and/or memorials in the United States and Canada that are members of the Historical Naval Ships Association. They are arranged by type of vessel. Some museums may be listed under more than one vessel type. Note that many museums observe seasonal hours and closings.

Aircraft Carriers

Aircraft Carrier *Hornet* Museum
P.O. Box 460
Pier 3, Alameda Point
Alameda, CA 94501
(510) 521-8448
Fax: (510) 521-8327
E-mail: info@uss-hornet.org
www.uss-hornet.org

Intrepid Sea-Air-Space Museum
Pier 86
West 46th Street & 12th Avenue
New York, NY 10036-4103
(212) 245-0072
Fax: (212) 245-7289
www.intrepidmuseum.org

Lady Lex Museum on the Bay
2914 North Shoreline Boulevard
Corpus Christi, TX 78403
(361) 888-4873

Fax: (362) 883-8361
E-mail: ladylex@intcomm.net
www.usslexington.com/

San Diego Aircraft Carrier Museum
910 North Harbor Drive
San Diego, CA 92101-3321
(619) 544-9600
Fax: (619) 544-9188
E-mail: sdacm@aol.com
www.midway.org

Patriots Point Naval & Maritime Museum
40 Patriots Point Road
Mount Pleasant, SC 29464
(843) 884-2727
Fax: (843) 881-4232
E-mail: wwhills@infoave.net
www.state.sc.us/patpt/
www.ussyorktown.com/yorktown/

Battleships

USS *Alabama* Battleship Commission
Battleship Memorial Park
2703 Battleship Parkway, P.O. Box 65
Mobile, AL 36601-0065
(800) GANGWAY/(800) 426-4929
Fax: (251) 433-2777
E-mail: ussalbb60@aol.com
www.ussalabama.com

USS *Arizona* Memorial
National Park Service
1 Arizona Memorial Place
Honolulu, HI 96818-3145
(808) 422-2771
Fax: (808) 483-8608
www.nps.gov/usar/
www.arizonamemorial.org
www.pearlharbormemorial.com

Battleship Cove
5 Water Street, P.O. Box 111
Fall River, MA 02722-0111
(508) 678-1100
Fax: (508) 674-5597
E-mail: battleship@battleshipcove.org
www.battleshipcove.org

USS *Missouri* Memorial Association
P.O. Box 879
Aiea, HI 96818-4572
(808) 423-2263
Toll-free: (888) 877-6477
Fax: (808) 423-0700
E-mail: webmaster@ussmissouri.com
www.ussmissouri.com

USS *North Carolina* Battleship Memorial
Box 480
Wilmington, NC 28402
(910) 251-5797
Fax: (910) 251-5807
E-mail: ncbb55@battleshipnc.com
www.battleshipnc.com/index.htm

Battleship *New Jersey* Museum
62 Battleship Place
Camden, NJ 08103-3302
(856) 966-1652
Fax: (856) 966-3131
E-mail: homeportalliance@aol.com
www.battleshipnewjersey.org

San Jacinto State Historical Park
3523 Highway 134
LaPorte, TX 77571
(281) 479-2431
Fax: (281) 479-4197
E-mail: barry.ward@tpwd.state.tx.us
www.usstexasbb35.com

USS *Arizona* Memorial
National Park Service
1 Arizona Memorial Place
Honolulu, HI 96818-3145
(808) 422-2771
Fax: (808) 483-8608
E-mail: wmhughes@attbi.com
www.ussutah.org

Battleship *Wisconsin*
c/o Hampton Roads Naval Museum
1 Waterside Drive, Suite 248
Norfolk, VA 23510-1607
(757) 322-2987
Fax: (757) 445-1867
E-mail: mmosier@nsn.cmar.navy.mil
www.hrnm.navy.mil

Coast Guard Vessels

USCGC *Bramble* Museum
1115 6th Street
Port Huron, MI 48060-5346
(810) 982-0891
E-mail: mtpopelka@comcast.net
www.phmuseum.org/

Baltimore Maritime Museum
802 S. Caroline St.
Baltimore, MD 21231
(410) 396-3453
Fax: (410) 396-3393
E-mail: admin@baltomaritimemuseum.org
www.baltomaritimemuseum.org

The *Glacier* Society
P.O. Box 1419
Bridgeport, CT 06601-1419
(866) ICE-PLAY (866-423-7529) toll-free, or (203) 375-6638
E-mail: info@glaciersociety.org
www.glaciersociety.org

Wisconsin Maritime Museum
75 Maritime Drive
Manitowoc, WI 54220-6843
(920) 684-0218
(866) 724-2356 toll-free
Fax: (920) 684-0219
E-mail: museum@wisconsinmaritime.org
www.wisconsinmaritime.org

Patriots Point Naval & Maritime Museum
40 Patriots Point Road
Mount Pleasant, SC 29464
(843) 884-2727
Fax: (843) 881-4232
E-mail: wwhills@infoave.net
www.state.sc.us/patpt/

Great Lakes Naval Memorial and Museum
1346 Bluff Street
Muskegon, Michigan 49441
(231) 755-1230
Fax: (231) 755-5883
E-mail: ss236sub@aol.com
www.silversides.org

The Overfalls Maritime Museum Foundation
P.O. Box 413
Lewes, DE 19958-0413
E-mail: elainesimmerman@earthlink.net
www.overfalls.org/

Lightship *Relief*
Address for visiting:
Jack London Square
Oakland, California
Address for inquiries:
U.S. Lighthouse Society
244 Kearny Street—Fifth Floor
San Francisco, CA 94108-4526

(415) 362-7255
Fax: (415) 362-7464

Vancouver Maritime Museum/St. Roch
National Historic Site
1905 Ogden Ave.
Vancouver, BC V6J 1A3
(604) 257-8300
Fax: (604) 737-2621
E-mail: genvmm@vancouvermaritimemuseum.com
www.vancouvermaritimemuseum.com/

Maritime Heritage Center
1002 Valley Street
Seattle, WA 98109-4668
(206) 447-9800
Fax: (206) 447-0598
E-mail: seaport@oz.net
www.nwseaport.org

Cruisers

Buffalo & Erie County Naval & Military Park
One Naval Park Cove
Buffalo, NY 14202
(716) 854-3200
Fax: (716) 847-6405
E-mail: info@buffalonavalpark.org
www.buffalonavalpark.org/

Independence Seaport Museum
211 South Columbus Boulevard and Walnut Street
Philadelphia, PA 19106-3199
(215) 925-5439
Fax: (215) 925-6713
E-mail: seaport@indsm.org
www.phillyseaport.org

United States Naval Shipbuilding Museum
Massachusetts Military Research Center
739 Washington Street

Quincy, MA 02169
(617) 479-7900
Fax: (617) 479-8792
E-mail: seawitchskipper@aol.com
www.uss-salem.org

Destroyers and Escorts

USS *Barry*
Address for Visiting:
USS *Barry*
707 Riverside Drive S.E.
Pier 2
Washington Navy Yard, DC 20374-5038
(202) 433-3377
Organization Address:
Officer in Charge/N36
Naval Support Activity Washington
Building 200/3
901 M Street SE
Washington Navy Yard, DC 20374-5001
(202) 433-6111
Fax: (202) 433-2382

Boston National Historical Park
Charlestown Navy Yard
Boston, MA 02129-4543
(617) 242-5601
Fax: (617) 242-5621
www.nps.gov/bost/Cassin_Young.htm

HMCS *Fraser*
233 LaHavre Street
Bridgewater, NS B4V 2T6
(902) 543-3925
Fax: (902) 624-1537
E-mail: saguenay@fox.nstn.ca

HMCS *Haida* National Historic Site
57 Guise St. E.

Hamilton, ON L8L 8K4
(905) 526-0911
E-mail: haida.info@pc.gc.ca
www.pc.gc.ca/haida

Battleship Cove
5 Water Street, P.O. Box 111
Fall River, MA 02722-0111
(508) 678-1100
Fax: (508) 674-5597
E-mail: battleship@battleshipcove.org
www.battleshipcove.org

USS *Kidd* Veterans Memorial
305 South River Road
Baton Rouge, LA 70802
(225) 342-1942
Fax: (225) 342-2039
E-mail: info@usskidd.com
www.usskidd.com

Patriots Point Naval & Maritime Museum
40 Patriots Point Road
Mount Pleasant, SC 29464
(843) 884-2727
Fax: (843) 881-4232
E-mail: wwhills@infoave.net
www.state.sc.us/patpt/

Southeast Texas War Memorial and Heritage Foundation
P.O. Box 3005
Orange, TX 77631-3005
(409) 882-9191
Fax: (409) 883-7795
E-mail: tdepwe@gt.rr.com
www.hnsa.org/ships/orleck.htm

Destroyer Escort Historical Museum
USS *Slater*
P.O. Box 1926
Albany, NY 12201-1926

(518) 431-1943
Fax: (518) 432-1123
E-mail: shipsDE766@aol.com
www.ussslater.org

Cavalla Historical Foundation
2504 Church Street
Galveston, TX 77550
(409) 744-7854
Cell: (409) 770-3196
E-mail: macm@galvestonparkboard.org
www.cavalla.org

Buffalo & Erie County Naval & Military Park
One Naval Park Cove
Buffalo, NY 14202
(716) 854-3200
Fax: (716) 847-6405
E-mail: info@buffalonavalpark.org
www.buffalonavalpark.org/
www.ussthesullivans.net/

Bremerton Historic Ships Association
300 Washington Beach Avenue
Bremerton, WA 98337-5668
(360) 792-2457
Fax: (360) 377-1020
E-mail: dd951@sinclair.net

Patrol Vessels

USS *Aries* Hydrofoil Memorial, Inc.
5479 West 24 Highway
Huntsville, MO 65259-3003
(660) 777-3300
Fax: (660) 777-3302
E-mail: esjames@cvalley.net
www.ussaries.org

Battleship Cove
5 Water Street, P.O. Box 111

Fall River, MA 02722-0111
(508) 678-1100
Fax: (508) 674-5597
E-mail: battleship@battleshipcove.org
www.battleshipcove.org

Maritime Museum of San Diego
1492 N. Harbor Drive
San Diego, CA 92101
(619) 234-9153
Fax: (619) 234-8345
E-mail: info@sdmaritime.org
www.sdmaritime.com

Admiral Nimitz State Historic Site—National Museum of the Pacific War
340 East Main Street
Fredericksburg, TX 78624
(830) 997-4379
Fax: (830) 997-8220
E-mail: nimitzm@ktc.com
www.nimitz-museum.org/

PTF 3 Restoration Project
Boy Scout Troup 544, Inc.
P.O. Box 740789
Orange City, FL 32774-0799
(800) 694-7161
E-mail: info@Scout544ptf.com
www.scout544ptf.com/

PTF-26
Address for Visiting:
16800 Highway 160
Rio Vista, CA
Address for inquiries:
Liberty Maritime Museum
2912 Janet Drive
West Sacramento, CA 95691
E-mail: Liberty-Maritime@msn.com

Submarine Memorial Association
78 River Street
Hackensack, NJ 07601-7110
(201) 342-3268
E-mail: njnavalmuseum@yahoo.com
www.njnm.com

USS *Alabama* Battleship Commission
Battleship Memorial Park
2703 Battleship Parkway, P.O. Box 65
Mobile, AL 36601-0065
(800) GANGWAY/(800) 426-4929
Fax: (251) 433-2777
E-mail: ussalbb60@aol.com
www.ussalabama.com

National Vietnam War Museum
3400 North Tanner Road
Orlando, FL 32826-3433
(407) 273-0201
Fax: (407) 273-6794
E-mail: nvwm@bellsouth.net
www.nvwm.com/

Mare Island Historic Park Foundation
328 Seawind Dr.
Vallejo, CA 94590
(707) 557-1538
E-mail: kenzad01@sbcglobal.net
www.mareislandhpf.org

The Navy Museum
805 Kidder Breese St. SE
Washington Navy Yard, DC 20374-5060
(202) 433-4882
Fax: (202) 433-8200
www.history.navy.mil

The Canadian Naval Memorial Trust
HMCS *Sackville*

P.O. Box 99000 Station Forces
Halifax, NS B3K 5X5
(902) 429-2132 (June to September)
(902) 427-0550 x2837 (October to May)
Fax: (902) 427-1346
E-mail: secretary@hmcssackville-cnmt.ns.ca
www.hmcssackville-cnmt.ns.ca

Merchant Cargo

American Victory Mariners Memorial and Museum Ship, Inc.
705 Channelside Drive
Tampa, FL 33602
(813) 228-8766
Fax: (813) 228-8769
E-mail: AMVIC@aol.com
www.americanvictory.org

The Steamship *William G. Mather* Museum
305 Old Erieside Avenue
Cleveland, Ohio 44114
(216) 574-6262
Fax: (216) 574-2536
E-mail: wgmather@aol.com
www.wgmather.nhlink.net/

National Liberty Ship Memorial, Inc.
Pier 23
The Embarcadero
San Francisco, CA 94111
(415) 544-9809
Fax: (415) 441-3712
E-mail: liberty@ssjeremiahobrien.org
www.ssjeremiahobrien.org

Project Liberty Ship, Inc.
Box 25846
Highlandtown Station
Baltimore, MD 21224-0564
Ship: (410) 558-0646; staff: (410) 661-1550
Fax: (410) 558-1737

E-mail: john.w.brown@usa.net
www.liberty-ship.com

U.S. Merchant Marine Veterans of WWII
P.O. Box 629
San Pedro, CA 90733-0629
(310) 519-9545
Fax: (310) 519-0265
E-mail: webmaster@lanevictoryship.com
www.lanevictory.org/

SS *Red Oak Victory*
Richmond Museum of History
1337 Canal Boulevard
Berth 6A
Richmond, CA 94804
(510) 237-2933
Fax: (510) 235-7259
E-mail: info@ssredoakvictory.org
www.ssredoakvictory.org

Miscellaneous

Navy Memorial Museum
6096 Route 96A
Romulus, NY 14541-9730
(315) 585-6203; off-season (800) 357-1814
E-mail: LST848@aol.com

Vicksburg National Military Park
3201 Clay Street
Vicksburg, MS 39180-3495
(601) 636-2199
Fax: (610) 638-7329
E-mail: vick_interpretation@nps.gov

Port Columbus National Civil War Naval Museum
Box 1022
Columbus, GA 31902-1022
(706) 327-9798
Fax: (706) 324-7225

E-mail: visitor@portcolumbus.org
www.portcolumbus.org

SS *City of Milwaukee* National Historic Landmark
111 Arthur Street (US-31 North)
Manistee, MI 49660
(231) 723-3587
www.carferry.com

Liberty Maritime Museum
2912 Janet Drive
West Sacramento, CA 95691
E-mail: Liberty-Maritime@msn.com

USS LST Ship Memorial, Inc.
840 LST Drive
Evansville, IN 47713
(812) 435-8678
E-mail: webskipper@lstmemorial.org
www.lstmemorial.org

The Mariners' Museum
100 Museum Drive
Newport News, VA 23606
(757) 596-2222
Fax: (757) 591-7320
E-mail: info@mariner.org
www.mariner.org

Potomac Association
540 Water Street
P.O. Box 2064
Oakland, CA 94604-2064
(510) 627-1215 (Monday–Friday)
(510) 627-1502 (24-hour info line)
Fax: (510) 839-4729
E-mail: info@usspotomac.org
www.usspotomac.org

National Mississippi River Museum & Aquarium
3rd Street and Ice Harbor

P.O. Box 266
Dubuque, Iowa 52004-0266
(563) 557-9545
Fax: (563) 583-1241
E-mail: rivermuse@mwci.net
www.mississippirivermuseum.com

Sailing Vessels

Mystic Seaport Museum
75 Greenmanville Avenue
P.O. Box 6000
Mystic, CT 06355-0990
(860) 572-0711
Fax: (860) 572-5344
E-mail: visitor.services@mysticseaport.org
www.mysticseaport.org

USS *Constellation*
Constellation Dock Pier 1
301 East Pratt Street
Baltimore, MD 21202-3134
(410) 539-1797
Fax: (410) 539-6238
E-mail: webcentral@constellation.org
www.constellation.org

USS *Constitution*
Charlestown Navy Yard
Boston, MA 02129-1797
(617) 242-5671
Fax: (617) 242-5616
www.ussconstitution.navy.mil

US Brig *Niagara*
150 Front Street, Suite 100
Erie, PA 16507
(814) 452-2744
Fax: (814) 455-6760
E-mail: sail@brigniagara.org
www.brigniagara.org

Commanding Officer, USCGC *Eagle*
U.S. Coast Guard Academy
45 Mohegan Avenue
New London, CT 06320
(860) 444-8595
Fax: (860) 444-8445
www.cga.edu/eagle/eagle.htm

National Museum of American History
Smithsonian Institution
12th Street and Constitution Ave. NW
Washington, DC 20560-0628
(202) 633-3909
Fax: (202) 357-4256

Submarines

USS *Batfish* (SS-310)
Muskogee War Memorial Park
3500 Batfish Road
P.O. Box 253
Muskogee, OK 74402
(918) 682-6294
E-mail: ussbatfish@yahoo.com
www.ussbatfish.com
www.batfish.org

Independence Seaport Museum
211 South Columbus Blvd. and Walnut Street
Philadelphia, PA 19106-3199
(215) 925-5439
Fax: (215) 925-6713
E-mail: seaport@indsm.org
www.phillyseaport.org

Oregon Museum of Science and Industry
1945 SE Water Avenue
Portland, OR 97214-3354
(503) 797-4000
Fax: (503) 797-4500

E-mail: r.g.walker@omsi.edu
www.omsi.edu/visit/submarine/

USS *Bowfin* Submarine
Museum & Park
11 Arizona Memorial Drive
Honolulu, HI 96818
(808) 423-1341
Fax: (808) 422-5201
E-mail: info@bowfin.org
www.bowfin.org

Cavalla Historical Foundation
2504 Church Street
Galveston, TX 77550
(409) 744-7854
Cell: (409) 770-3196
E-mail: macm@galvestonparkboard.org
www.cavalla.org

Patriots Point Naval & Maritime Museum
40 Patriots Point Road
Mount Pleasant, SC 29464
(843) 884-2727
Fax: (843) 881-4232
E-mail: wwhills@infoave.net
www.state.sc.us/patpt/

Wisconsin Maritime Museum
75 Maritime Drive
Manitowoc, WI 54220-6843
(920) 684-0218
(866) 724-2356 toll-free
Fax: (920) 684-0219
E-mail: museum@wisconsinmaritime.org
www.wisconsinmaritime.org

USS *Cod* Submarine Memorial
1089 East 9th Street

Cleveland, OH 44114
(216) 566-8770
E-mail: usscod@en.com
www.usscod.org

Buffalo & Erie County Naval & Military Park
One Naval Park Cove
Buffalo, NY 14202
(716) 854-3200
Fax: (716) 847-6405
E-mail: info@buffalonavalpark.org
www.buffalonavalpark.org/

USS *Alabama* Battleship Commission
Battleship Memorial Park
2703 Battleship Parkway, P.O. Box 65
Mobile, AL 36601-0065
(800) GANGWAY/(800) 426-4929
Fax: (334) 433-2777
E-mail: ussalbb60@aol.com
www.ussalabama.com

Intrepid Sea-Air-Space Museum
Pier 86
West 46th Street & 12th Avenue
New York, NY 10036-4103
(212) 245-0072
Fax: (212) 245-7289
www.wa3key.com/growler.html
www.intrepidmuseum.org

USS *Saratoga* Museum Foundation, Inc.
P.O. Box 28581
Providence, RI 2908-0581
(401) 831-8696
Fax: (401) 831-8707
E-mail: SaratogaMuseum@aol.com
www.saratogamuseum.org

Submarine Memorial Association
78 River Street

Hackensack, NJ 07601-7110
(201) 342-3268
E-mail: njnavalmuseum@yahoo.com
www.njnm.com

Battleship Cove
5 Water Street, P.O. Box 111
Fall River, MA 02722-0111
(508) 678-1100
Fax: (508) 674-5597
E-mail: battleship@battleshipcove.org
www.battleshipcove.org

Freedom Park
2497 Freedom Park Road
Omaha, NE 68110
(402) 345-1959
E-mail: freedomparkomaha@aol.com
www.freedomparkomaha.org

Historic Ship *Nautilus* & Submarine Force Museum
1 Crystal Lake Road
Groton, CT 06349-5571
(800) 343-0079
(860) 694-3558
Fax: (860) 694-4150
E-mail: nautilus@subasenlon.navy.mil
www.ussnautilus.org

USS *Pampanito*
Maritime Park Association
P.O. Box 470310
San Francisco, CA 94147-0310
(415) 775-1943
Fax: (415) 441-0365
E-mail: pampanito@maritime.org
www.maritime.org/pamphome.htm

USS *Razorback*
Address for Correspondence:

Arkansas Inland Maritime Museum
P.O. Box 5757
224 South Locust Street
North Little Rock, AR 72119
Address for Visiting:
Arkansas Inland Maritime Museum
USS *Razorback*
100 Riverfront Road
North Little Rock, AR
(501) 371-8320
www.northlr.org/maritime-museum/default.asp

USS *Requin* (SS-481)
Carnegie Science Center
1 Allegheny Avenue
Pittsburgh, PA 15212
(412) 237-1550
Fax: (412) 237-3375
www.csc.clpgh.org/

Great Lakes Naval Memorial and Museum
1346 Bluff Street
Muskegon, MI 49441
(231) 755-1230
Fax: (231) 755-5883
E-mail: ss236sub@aol.com
www.silversides.org

Baltimore Maritime Museum
802 S. Caroline St.
Baltimore, MD 21231
(410) 396-3453
Fax: (410) 396-3393
E-mail: admin@baltomaritimemuseum.org
www.baltomaritimemuseum.org
www.usstorsk.org

German U-boat *U-505*
Museum of Science and Industry
5700 Lake Shore Drive

Chicago, IL 60637-2093
(773) 684-1414
Fax: (773) 684-5580
www.msichicago.org/exhibit/U505/index.html

Albacore Park
600 Market Street
Portsmouth, NH 03801
(603) 436-3680
Fax: (603) 436-3680
E-mail: jbsergeant@aol.com
www.USSALBACORE.org

Science Museum of Virginia
2500 West Broad Street
Richmond, VA 23220
(804) 864-1477
Fax: (804) 367-9348
www.smv.org/info/aluminautex.htm

Vancouver Maritime Museum
1905 Ogden Avenue
Vancouver, BC V6J 1A3
(604) 257-8300
Fax: (604) 737-2621
E-mail: genvmm@vancouvermaritimemuseum.com
www.vancouvermaritimemuseum.com/

Naval Undersea Museum
Navy Region Northwest
1103 Hunley Road
Silverdale, WA 98315-1103
(360) 396-4148
Fax: (360) 396-7944
http://keyportmuseum.cnrnw.navy.mil

Paterson Museum
2 Market Street
Paterson, NJ 07501-1704
(973) 881-3874

Fax: (973) 881-3435
E-mail: patersonmuseum@hotmail.com

Warren G. Lasch Conservation Center
Supply Street
Old Charleston Naval Base
North Charleston, SC
(843) 743-4865
(843) 723-9797 (hotline)
Fax: (843) 744-1482
E-mail: russo@hunley.org
www.hunley.org

National Guard Militia Museum of New Jersey
P.O. Box 277
Sea Girt, NJ 08750
(732) 974-5966
Fax: (732) 974-5984

United States Naval Shipbuilding Museum
Massachusetts Military Research Center
739 Washington Street
Quincy, MA 02169
(617) 479-7900
Fax: (617) 479-8792
E-mail: jfahey@uss-salem.org

The Navy Museum
805 Kidder Breese St. SE
Washington Navy Yard, DC 20374-5060
(202) 433-4882
Fax: (202) 433-8200
www.history.navy.mil

Tugs and Minesweepers

H. Lee White Marine Museum
P.O. Box 101
West First Street Pier
Oswego, NY 13126

(315) 342-0480
Fax: (315) 343-5778
E-mail: hlwmarinemuseum@aol.com
www.hleewhitemarinemuseum.com

Coordinated Maritime Services
1551 Shelter Island Drive
San Diego, CA 92106
(619) 200-7417
E-mail: rbentley@sandiegoboating.com
www.sdmaritimeinformationcenter.org

Luna Preservation Society
P.O. Box 1866
Brookline, MA 02446
(617) 730-9776
Fax: (617) 730-9818
E-mail: tugluna@aol.com
www.tugboatluna.org

Others (including military history preservation organizations, for-profit museums, and attractions)

Note: Many of these organizations are attempting to acquire or have recently acquired historic naval vessels for their areas.

Battleship *Texas* Foundation
10575 Katy Freeway, #393
Houston, TX 77024-1012
(713) 827-9620
Fax: (713) 827-9621
Travis LaGrone, Executive Director
E-mail: tllagrone@aol.com
www.battleshiptexas.org

Bellingham International Maritime Museum
P.O. Box 28220
Bellingham, WA 98228
(360) 592-4112
Fax: (360) 592-4112
www.bimm.us

Council of American Maritime Museums
c/o Columbia River Maritime Museum
1792 Marine Drive
Astoria, OR 97103-3525
(503) 325-2323
Fax: (503) 325-2331
E-mail: ostermiller@crmm.org

Council on America's Military Past
P.O. Box 1151
Fort Myer, VA 22211-0151
(703) 912-6124
Fax: (703) 912-5666
E-mail: camphart1@aol.com

USS *Farenholt* Association
10010 East Watson Road
St. Louis, MO 63126-2306
E-mail: rgarwitz@aol.com

Marine Corps Museum of the Carolinas
626 Newbridge Street
Jacksonville, NC 28540-5433
(910) 937-0033
Fax: (910) 937-0537
SgtMajor Joseph Houle, USMC (Ret.)
E-mail: sgtmajmcnc@bizec.rr.com
www.mcmuseum.com

National Association of Fleet Tug Sailors (NAFTS)
c/o Tom Thomas
9416 Mohawk Road
Bend, OR 97702
(541) 383-9099
E-mail: snipe@nafts.com
www.nafts.com

Naval Historical Center
Washington Navy Yard
805 Kidder Breese St. SE

Washington Navy Yard, DC 20374-5060
(202) 433-2210
Fax: (202) 433-3593
Captain Peter O. Wheeler, Acting Director
www.history.navy.mil

Naval Historical Center Detachment Boston
Bldg. 24, BNHP
Charlestown Navy Yard
Boston, MA 02129-4543
(617) 242-0752
Fax: (617) 241-5232
E-mail: richwhelan@att.net

Naval Historical Foundation
1306 Dahlgren Ave. SE
Washington Navy Yard, DC 20374-5055
(202) 678-4333
Fax: (202) 889-3565
E-mail: ccreekman@navyhistory.org
Captain Charles T. Creekman, Jr., USN (Ret.), Executive Director
www.navyhistory.org

National Maritime Heritage Foundation
236 Massachusetts Avenue NE, Suite 410
Washington, DC 20002
(202) 547-1250
Fax: (202) 547-0250
www.nmhf.org

Naval Order of the United States
4833 Willet Drive
Annandale, VA 22003-3952
(703) 323-0929
Fax: (703) 323-0929
E-mail: jimbrooke@aol.com
www.navalorder.org

Naval Submarine League
P.O. Box 1146

Annandale, VA 22003
(703) 256-0891
Fax: (703) 642-5815
E-mail: subexec@starpower.net
C. Michael Garverick, Executive Director
www.navalsubleague.com

Navy MSO Association, Inc. (minesweeper crew members organization)
1807 Woodvine Circle
San Antonio, TX 78232-4978
(210) 490-5315
E-mail: nmsoa@nmsoa.org
W. W. "Mike" Warren, Cofounder & Vice President
www.nmsoa.org

Surface Navy Association
2550 Huntington Avenue, Suite 202
Alexandria, VA 22303-1400
(703) 960-6800
Fax: (703) 960-6807
E-mail: navysna@aol.com
Captain William Erickson, USN (Ret.), Executive Director
www.navysna.org

Tin Can Sailors, Inc.
P.O. Box 100
Somerset, MA 02726-0100
(800) 223-5535
E-mail: tcs@destroyers.org
Thomas J. Peltin, President
Terry L. Miller, Executive Director
www.destroyers.org

Torsk Volunteer Association, Inc.
5171 Columbia Road
Columbia, MD 21044
(410) 789-7939
Fax: (410) 789-7939
www.usstorsk.org

U.S. Naval Institute
291 Wood Road
Annapolis, MD 21402
(410) 268-6110
E-mail: twilkerson@usni.org
MajGen Thomas L. Wilkerson, USMC (Ret.)
www.usni.org

U.S. Navy Cruiser Sailors Association
21 Colonial Way
Rehoboth, MA 02769-1220
(508) 252-3524
Fax: (508) 252-3524 (call first)
E-mail: usncsa@aol.com
Edward J. August, Treasurer
www.navycruisers.org
Robert Polanowski, President
E-mail: skica130@aol.com

U.S. Navy Memorial Foundation
701 Pennsylvania Ave. NW, #123
Washington, DC 20004-2608
(202) 737-2300
Fax: (202) 737-2308
E-mail: ahoy@lonesailor.org
www.lonesailor.org

Adams Class Veterans Association
8520 West Clarendon Avenue
Phoenix, AZ 85037-2723
E-mail: Tecrosserbsausnr@aol.com
www.adamsclassddgvets.org/

American Academy of Industry
P.O. Box 293
Chicago Ridge, IL 60415
(708) 425-8443
Fax: (773) 928-4047
E-mail: dh483@aol.com
Daniel G. Hecker, President

Amphibious Forces Memorial Museum
8070 E. Mill Plain Blvd., Box #204
Vancouver, WA 98664-2002
(503) 244-4297
Fax: (503) 244-4297
E-mail: mstrchiflci713@comcast.net
www.amphibiousforces.org/

Combatant Craft of America
1400 East Ludlow Ridge Road
Port Ludlow, WA 98365-9247
(360) 437-0125
E-mail: dwithers@lot66.com
Dan L. Withers, Chairman
www.warboats.org

USS *Conolly* Museum & Memorial
3832 Manchester Circle
Plano, TX 75023
(972) 612-7061
Fax: (972) 612-7854
E-mail: rkrusinows@aol.com
Robert Krusinowski, President
www.dd979.com

Dunkirk Historical Lighthouse and Veteran's Park Museum
P.O. Box 69
1 Light House Point Drive
Dunkirk, NY 14048
(716) 366-5050
Harold R. Lawson, Executive Director
www.usssphinxarl24memorial.com

USS *Forrest Sherman* DD-931 Foundation, Inc.
720 Reedy Circle
Bel Air, MD 21014-6814
(410) 836-9260
Fax: (410) 836-9260
E-mail: kurt.wagemann@verizon.net

Kurt Wagemann, President
www.ussforrestsherman.org

Forty Eight Stars, Inc.
1220 Kirby Street
Palatka, FL 32177-5028
(386) 937-4902
Fax: (386) 328-9410
Boyd Thompson, Executive Director

Historic Ships Memorial at Pacific Square
P.O. Box 191242
San Francisco, CA 94119-1242
(415) 905-5700
E-mail: wstepone@aol.com
Edward J. Cummings, President
www.ussiowa.org
www.battleshipiowa.org

Historic Tugboat Education and Restoration Society
3020 Bridgeway, Suite 315
Sausalito, CA 94965-2839
(818) 370-2203
Fax: (818) 883-3428
E-mail: onesailorgirl@yahoo.com
Melissa J. Parker, President and Founder
www.ussnokomis.com

The Last Patrol Museum and Memorial
P.O. Box 5659
Toledo, OH 43613-0659
(419) 825-5108
E-mail: lastpatrol@aol.com
John T. Nowakowski, Commanding Officer

Maine Submarine Memorial Association
P.O. Box 563
Yarmouth, ME 04096-0563
(207) 846-6235
E-mail: qmsspilot@aol.com

Miami-Dade Historical Maritime Museum
600 Biltmore Way, #820
Coral Gables, FL 33134-7532
(305) 799-1143
Fax: (786) 268-0969
E-mail: fransboetes@attbi.com

Milwaukee—USS *Edson* Historic Naval Ship Project
P.O. Box 144
Greendale, WI 53129-0144
(414) 425-5957
E-mail: dcaswellwi@aol.com
Captain Richard F. Caswell, CEC, USNR (Ret.), President
www.ussdesmoines.org

National Submarine Science Discovery Center
421 Monmouth Street
Newport, KY 41071-1841
(859) 655-7700
Fax: (859) 655-9577
E-mail: info@NSSDC.us
www.nssdc.us

USS *Ranger* Museum Foundation
P.O. Box 566
Clackamas, OR 97015
(503) 550-5777
E-mail: bedami@juno.com
Dan Mills, Executive Director
www.ussrangercv61.org

Saginaw Valley Naval Ship Museum
3372 East Woodland Drive
Bay City, MI 48706-1670
(989) 686-3125
Fax: (989) 686-0725
E-mail: kegley@chartermi.net
www.ussedson.org

USS *Saratoga* Museum Foundation
P.O. Box 28581

Providence, RI 02908-0581
(401) 831-8696
Fax: (401) 831-8707
E-mail: savesara@aol.com
www.saratogamuseum.org

The Tamaroa Maritime Foundation
P.O. Box 28042
Richmond, VA 23228-0042
(804) 273-0247
Fax: (804) 273-0885
www.tamaroa.org

Tug *Pegasus* Preservation Project
83 Murray Street, #4
New York, NY 10007-2173
E-mail: info@tugpegasus.org
www.tugpegasus.org

USS *Williamsburg* Preservation Society, Inc.
352 Hickory Point Road
Pasadena, MD 21122
(410) 437-0652
E-mail: kimnlulu@aol.com

Jacksonville Historical Society
c/o Jerry R. Spinks
3215 Oak Street
Jacksonville, FL 32205-8621
(904) 384-4055
Fax: (904) 384-4055
E-mail: jrosss@att.net

Kenner State Naval Museum Commission
624 Williams Blvd.
Kenner, LA 70062-7675
(504) 468-7293
Fax: (504) 468-7599
E-mail: csas@kenner.la.us

USS LST-393
560 Mart Street
Muskegon, MI 49440-1044
(231) 722-4730
Fax: (231) 726-6636
E-mail: pharker393@msn.com

USS *Radford* National Naval Museum
132 West Canal Street
Newcomerstown, OH 43832-1102
(740) 498-4446
Fax: (740) 498-8803
E-mail: vane@saferinternet.org
www.ussradford446.org

Scorpion (B-427)
To Visit:
Next to *Queen Mary*
1126 Queens Highway
Long Beach, CA 90802-6331
Correspondence:
Newco Pty Ltd., LLC
36 Lake View Circle
Palm Springs, CA 92264-5508
E-mail: stanp@js-net.com
www.queenmary.com/attractions.php?page=subinfo

The 52 Lost Submarines of World War II

- December 10, 1941   *Sealion* (SS-195)   Sunk by aerial attack, 4 men lost

- January 20, 1942   *S-36* (SS-141)   Ran aground, no one was lost

- January 24, 1942   *S-26* (SS-131)   Rammed by escort, 46 men lost, 2 survivors

- February 11, 1942   *Shark I* (SS-174)   Sunk by surface craft, 58 men lost

- March 3, 1942   *Perch* (SS-176)   Sunk by surface craft, 11 men lost, all survivors

		taken prisoner, 8 died in POW camp
• June 19, 1942	*S-27* (SS-132)	Ran aground, no one was lost
• July 30, 1942	*Grunion* (SS-216)	Sank but cause remains unknown, 70 men lost
• August 16, 1942	*S-39* (SS-144)	Ran aground, no one lost
• January 9, 1943	*Argonaut* (SS-166)	Sunk by surface craft, 105 men lost
• February 16, 1943	*Amberjack* (SS-219)	Sunk by surface craft and aircraft attack, 74 men lost
• March 5, 1943	*Grampus* (SS-207)	Sunk by surface craft, 71 men lost
• March 15, 1943	*Triton* (SS-201)	Sunk by surface craft, 74 men lost
• April 3, 1943	*Pickerel* (SS-177)	Sunk by surface craft, 74 men lost
• April 22, 1943	*Grenadier* (SS-210)	Sunk by aerial attack, 4 men lost, rest of crew taken prisoner, 4 died in POW camp
• May 28, 1943	*Runner* (SS-275)	Sunk by enemy mine, 78 men lost
• June 12, 1943	*R-12* (SS-89)	Sank but cause remains unknown, 42 men lost, 3 survived
• August 29, 1943	*Pompano* (SS-181)	Sunk by enemy mine, 76 men lost
• September 9, 1943	*Grayling* (SS-209)	Sank but cause is unknown, 76 men lost
• September 28, 1943	*Cisco* (SS-290)	Sunk by surface craft and aerial attack, 76 men lost
• October 7, 1943	*S-44* (SS-155)	Sunk by surface craft, 55 men lost, 2 survivors taken prisoner
• October 11, 1943	*Wahoo* (SS-238)	Sunk by aerial attack, 80 men lost
• October 12, 1943	*Dorado* (SS-248)	Sunk in the Caribbean Sea by attack from friendly aircraft, 76 men lost

- November 16, 1943   *Corvina* (SS-226)   Sunk by enemy submarine, 82 men lost

- November 19, 1943   *Sculpin* (SS-191)   Sunk by surface craft, 63 men lost, 21 survivors taken prisoner

- November 23, 1943   *Capelin* (SS-289)   Sunk by surface craft, 78 men lost

- January 5, 1944   *Scorpion* (SS-278)   Sunk by enemy mine, 76 men lost

- February 26, 1944   *Grayback* (SS-208)   Sunk by surface craft and aerial attack, 80 men lost

- February 29, 1944   *Trout* (SS-202)   Sunk by surface craft, 81 men lost

- March 26, 1944   *Tullibee* (SS-284)   Sunk by her own torpedo, 79 men lost, 1 survivor taken prisoner

- April 7, 1944   *Gudgeon* (SS-211)   Sunk by surface craft and aerial attack, 78 men lost

- June 1, 1944   *Herring* (SS-233)   Sunk by surface craft, 84 men lost

- June 14, 1944   *Golet* (SS-361)   Sunk by surface craft, 82 men lost

- July 4, 1944   *S-28* (SS-133)   Sank but cause remains unknown, 52 men lost

- July 26, 1944   *Robalo* (SS-273)   Sunk by enemy mine, 77 men lost, 4 survivors, all of whom died in POW camp

- August 13, 1944   *Flier* (SS-250)   Sunk by enemy mine, 78 men lost, 8 survivors

- August 24, 1944   *Harder* (SS-257)   Sunk by surface craft, 79 men lost

- October 3, 1944   *Seawolf* (SS-197)   Sunk by friendly destroyer, 79 men lost along with 17 U.S. soldiers who were also aboard

- October 17, 1944   *Escolar* (SS-294)   Sunk by enemy mine, 80 men lost

- October 24, 1944   *Darter* (SS-227)   Ran aground, no one was lost

- October 24, 1944   *Shark II* (SS-314)   Sunk by surface craft, 87 men lost

- October 25, 1944   *Tang* (SS-306)   Sunk by her own torpedo, 78 men lost, 9 survivors taken prisoner

- November 7, 1944   *Albacore* (SS-218)   Sunk by enemy mine, 86 men lost

- November 8, 1944   *Growler* (SS-215)   Sank but cause is unknown, 85 men lost

- November 9, 1944   *Scamp* (SS-277)   Sunk by surface craft and aerial attack, 83 men lost

- January 12, 1945   *Swordfish* (SS-193)   Sank but cause is unknown, 85 men lost

- February 4, 1945   *Barbel* (SS-316)   Sunk by aerial attack, 81 men lost

- March 20, 1945   *Kete* (SS-369)   Sank but cause is unknown, 87 men lost

- March 26, 1945   *Trigger* (SS-237)   Sunk by surface craft and aerial attack, 89 men lost

- April 8, 1945   *Snook* (SS-279)   Sank but cause is unknown, 84 men lost

- May 3, 1945   *Lagarto* (SS-371)   Sunk by surface craft, 85 men lost

- June 18, 1945   *Bonefish* (SS-223)   Sunk by surface craft, 85 men lost

- August 6, 1945   *Bullhead* (SS-332)   Sunk by aerial attack, 84 men lost

Note: Some dates of sinking are estimates based on best information. Sometimes a boat's loss was listed as the date on which she was scheduled to return from patrol and failed to do so.

Don Keith is an award-winning author, journalist, and broadcast personality. He was twice named Personality of the Year by *Billboard* magazine. His first novel, *The Forever Season*, was named Fiction of the Year by the Alabama Library Association. *Gallant Lady*, his true story of the USS *Archerfish*, was a featured selection of the Military Book Club. Don lives in Indian Springs Village, Alabama, with his wife, Charlene. His Web site is www.donkeith.com.